Maps Contained in the Publications of the *American Bibliography,* 1639-1819:

An Index and Checklist

by
JIM WALSH

The Scarecrow Press, Inc.
Metuchen, N.J., & London
1988

This work was made possible, in part, by a University of Wyoming Faculty Research Grant-in-Aid . However, the contents do not necessarily reflect the position or policy of that institution, and no official endorsement of these materials should be inferred.

Z
1215
S48
maps
index

British Library Cataloguing-in-Publication data available

Library of Congress Cataloging-in-Publication Data

Walsh, Jim, 1951-
    Maps contained in the publications of the American bibliography, 1639-1819.

    Bibliography: p.
    1. United States--Maps--Bibliography. 2. Evans, Charles, 1850-1935. American bibliography--Indexes. 3. Shaw, Ralph Robert, 1907- . American Bibliography--Indexes. I. Title.
Z6027.U5W35 1988 [GA405]   016.912'73   88-31916
ISBN 0-8108-2193-1

To Beth,

My Love,

My Wife,

My Best Friend

TABLE OF CONTENTS

PREFACE

In October, 1983, while I was the Maps and Documents Librarian at the University of Wyoming, I helped a student use the microcard edition of the <u>American Bibliography</u>. It occurred to me then that maps were a major part of the bibliography but, it also occurred to me, that there was no direct access to the individual maps when you used the Evans and Shaw/Shoemaker bibliographies.

A major cartographic resource existed but was virtually unaccessible, due to the lack of an adequate reference source! All that was needed was a checklist of all of the maps in the two bibliographies and an index to that checklist. This is that index and checklist.

ACKNOWLEDGEMENTS

This index and checklist is the result of the work and efforts of many people, even though only one name appears on the title page. I would be remiss if I did not take this opportunity to thank all of the people whose help, support and expertise made my work so much easier and this book so much better.

First, I thank my wife, Beth, for her continued support and encouragement throughout the entire project. She was always there when I needed her.

Next, I want to thank Jean and Jon Jones who so graciously and generously let me use their computer. A special thanks goes to Jon, whose computer expertise and patience with a "computer illiterate" are two reasons why this index and checklist was completed.

Karla Christensen and Shelly Basham probably had the most difficult task of anyone associated with this book--typing the initial draft from my handwritten notes. Words cannot begin to describe such an accomplishment. Thank you Karla and Shelly.

I want to thank the University of Wyoming Research Coordination Committee who saw the research value of this index and checklist and awarded me a Faculty Research Grant-in-Aid Award in 1985. A special thanks to Carol Collier, Patti Thobro and Chris Van Burgh of Coe Library's Government Documents Department at U.W. for their support and adjusting their work schedules while I was on leave.

A word of thanks goes to the administration of Wessell Library for allowing me to work a flex-schedule during the final stages of work on the index and checklist.

I also want to thank the following individuals of the American Antiquarian Society for their assistance and hospitality: Nancy Burkett, Joanne Chaison, Marie Lamoureux, Marie-Therese Poisson and Barbara Trippel Simmons. The American Antiquarian Society houses one of the most complete research collections on early American history and without this collection and staff this index and checklist would not have been completed. I have never met a friendlier and more helpful library staff.

Finally, I want to thank the unknown individual I helped with the microprint edition of the _American Bibliography_ back in October, 1983. Your question was the first step in this entire process. Whoever you are and wherever you are, thank you so much.

INTRODUCTION

The purpose of <u>Maps Contained in the Publications of the American Bibliography, 1639-1819: An Index and Checklist</u> is twofold:

    (1) It is an index and checklist of all map separates and maps contained in books which are part of the the <u>American Bibliography</u>, 1639-1819 (i.e., the Evans Bibliography, 1639-1800 and the Shaw/Shoemaker Bibliography, 1801-1819). The index and checklist, in this respect, can be used in conjunction with the Evans and Shaw/Shoemaker bibliographies.

    (2) It is a reference source and finding aid for the identification and verification of the existence of maps, published between 1639-1819, for most geographic areas throughout the world. The index and checklist, in this respect, can be used by itself as a cartobibliography.

It is not intended to be a descriptive and annotated guide to the maps published during this 180 year period. Thus, scale, map dimensions, notes, unique characteristics, etc., are not included in the index and checklist.

Arrangement

The index and checklist is comprised of three parts:

PART I lists the maps contained in the Evans Bibliography, 1639-1800.

PART II lists the maps contained in the Shaw/Shoemaker Bibliography, 1801-1819.

PART III contains six different indexes which provide access to PARTS I and II by date and place of publication, name (author, cartographer, etc.), book and map title and geographic location.

Entries in the index and checklist are arranged by the numbers used in the Evans and Shaw/Shoemaker bibliographies. As a result, the index and checklist is a chronological listing of publications (The exceptions to this are the few entries which are included in the supplement and addenda volumes to the two bibliographies and appear at the end of PARTS I and II out of chronological order, but in numerical order following the numbering sequence of the two bibliographies).

Spelling

Spelling was not standardized during the 18th and 19th
centuries. This lack of standardization resulted in inconsistent
spellings of many words and place names. It was just that--
inconsistencies-- during this time of American publishing. Since
there were no accepted standards, various spellings were used and
these variations were not considered misspelled words. These
inconsistencies appear in this index and checklist.

The author has not corrected nor included [sic] after
spelling variations because they were not typographical or
editorial errors when the map or book was published. These
variations are distinguishing features and characteristics of
many book and map titles and are essential to the identification
of a specific bibliographic or cartographic citation.

Some examples of spelling variations are listed below:

PRESENT DAY	18TH & 19TH CENTURY
gulf	gulph
show	shew
Pittsburgh	Pittsburg
Kentucky	Kentucke, Kentuckey
Tennessee	Tennassee
Switzerland	Swisserland
Maryland	Mariland
Chile	Chili
Pennsylvania	Pennsilvania
Ocracoke	Occacock, Ocracock

This is just a sampling of the spelling variations and many
more exist throughout this index and checklist. It is mentioned
here so that the reader is aware of this fact and does not assume
that words and place names have been misspelled throughout this
index and checklist.

Format

There are two forms of entries which are found in PARTS I
and II of the index and checklist. The first is an entry for a
map separate which is a map sheet published, sold and distributed
independent of any other publication. The second form of entry
is a book citation with the map(s) contained in that book, atlas,
gazetteer, etc. following the citation. Examples of each type of
entry are shown on the next page with explanations of the various
parts of each entry.

EXAMPLE I: MAP SEPARATE CITATION

E-02318[1]
THE TOWN OF BOSTON, IN NEW ENGLAND.[2] John Bonner.[3] Boston:[4]
    Francis Dewing, for Bonner and Price,[5] 1722.[6]

   [1]Entry number from the respective bibliography. The author
   has provided the initial letter to distinguish between an
   entry from Evans (E-) or Shaw/Shoemaker (S-).

   [2]Map title. It is in CAPITAL LETTERS. When a map is
   untitled, the author has provided one and it appears in
   brackets, e.g., [MARYLAND].

   [3]Cartographer.   [4]Place of publication.

   [5]Publisher and/or printer.

   [6]Date of publication of the map.

EXAMPLE II: BOOK CITATION

S-44515[1]
Kilbourn, John.[2] The Ohio Gazatteer.[3] 5th ed.[4] Columbus:[5] John
    Kilbourn,[6] 1818.[7]

   MAP OF OHIO[8] (F).[9]

   PLAT OF THE TOWN OF COLUMBUS[8] (44).[9]

   [1]Entry number.   [2]Author.

   [3]Book title.   [4]Edition.

   [5]Place of publication.   [6]Publisher and/or printer.

   [7]Date of publication of the book, not the map.

   [8]Map title(s). If a cartographer is cited on the map, his
       name will appear after the map title and before the map
       location in the book.

   [9]Location of the map within the book. A number, arabic or
       Roman numeral, indicates that the map is located on
       that page or is adjacent to that page. A letter
       indicates one of the following: (F), the map is located
       at the beginning of the book; (B), the map is located
       at the end of the book; and (UP), the book does not
       have page numbers. In the case of unpaged versions of
       the Bible, the book where the map appears is provided
       in brackets, e.g., [In Numbers].

Anything which appears in [brackets] in PARTS I and II has been supplied by the author. Also, the uniform title, <u>Bible</u>, is used throughout PARTS I and II for all versions and editions of the Bible.

Verification

Various sources and collections were used to verify the spelling and bibliographic information in each entry and they are listed below:

American Antiquarian Society Collection. Worcester, MA: American Antiquarian Society.

Bristol, Roger P. <u>Index of Printers, Publishers and Booksellers Indicated by Charles Evans in His American Bibliography</u>. Charlottesville: Bibliographical Society of the University of Virginia, 1961.

Bristol, Roger P. <u>Supplement to Charles Evans' American Bibliography</u>. Charlottesville: published for the Bibliographical Society of America and the Bibliographical Society of Virginia by the University Press of Virginia, 1970.

<u>Early American Imprints, 1639-1800</u>. Microcard and microfiche editions, based on the Evans Bibliography. New Canaan, CT: READEX Microprint Corporation.

<u>Early American Imprints, 1801-1819</u>. Microcard edition, based on the Shaw/Shoemaker Bibliography. New Canaan, Ct: READEX Microprint Corporation.

Evans, Charles. <u>American Bibliography: A Chronological Dictionary of All Books, Pamphlets and Periodical Publications Printed in the United States of America from the Genesis of Printing in 1639 down to and Including the Year 1800</u>. 14 volumes. Chicago: Charles Evans (vol. 1-12); Worcester, MA: American Antiquarian Society (vol. 13-14), 1903-1959.

Evans, Charles. <u>American Bibliography: A Chronological Dictionary of All Books, Pamphlets and Periodical Publications Printed in the United States of America from the Genesis of Printing in 1639 down to and Including the Year 1800</u>. Reprint edition. 14 volumes. New York: Peter Smith, 1941-1967.

Shaw, Ralph R. and Shoemaker, Richard H. <u>American Bibliography; A Preliminary Checklist for 1801 [to] 1819</u>. 19 volumes. New York: Scarecrow Press, 1959-1963.

Shaw, Ralph R. and Shoemaker, Richard H. <u>American
  Bibliography; A Preliminary Checklist for 1801 to 1819:
  Addenda, List of Sources, Library Symbols</u>. New York:
  Scarecrow Press, 1965.

Shaw, Ralph R. and Shoemaker, Richard H. <u>American
  Bibliography; A Preliminary Checklist for 1801 to 1819:
  Corrections, Author Index</u>. New York: Scarecrow Press,
  1966

Shaw, Ralph R. and Shoemaker, Richard H. <u>American
  Bibliography; A Preliminary Checklist for 1801 to 1819:
  Printers, Publishers and Booksellers Index,
  Geographical Index</u>. Compiled by Frances P. Newton.
  Metuchen, NJ: Scarecrow Press, 1983.

Shipton, Clifford K. and Mooney, James E. <u>National Index of
  American Imprints Through 1800: The Short-Title Evans</u>.
  Worcester, MA: American Antiquarian Society, 1969.

--ooOoo--

PART I:

THE AMERICAN BIBLIOGRAPHY,
1639-1800:

THE EVANS BIBLIOGRAPHY

E-02318
THE TOWN OF BOSTON, IN NEW ENGLAND. John Bonner. Boston: Francis
    Dewing, for Bonner and Price, 1722.

E-02512
Colden, Cadwallader. Papers Relating to an Act of the Assembly of
    the Province of New York, for the Encouragement of the
    Indian Trades &c. New York: William Bradford, 1724.

    A MAP OF THE COUNTREY OF THE FIVE NATIONS BELONGING TO THE
        PROVINCE OF NEW YORK AND OF THE LAKES NEAR WHICH THE
        NATIONS OF FAR INDIANS LIVE WITH PART OF CANADA TAKEN
        FROM THE MAP OF THE LOUISIANE DONE BY MR. DE LISLE IN
        1718. (B).

E-02513
A MAP OF THE COUNTREY OF THE FIVE NATIONS BELONGING TO THE
    PROVINCE OF NEW YORK AND OF THE LAKES NEAR WHICH THE NATIONS
    OF FAR INDIANS LIVE WITH PART OF CANADA & RIVER ST.
    LAWRENCE. 2nd Issue. Cadwallader Colden. New York: William
    Bradford, 1724.

E-03438
A PLAN OF THE CITY OF NEW YORK FROM AN ACTUAL SURVEY. James Lyne.
    New York: William Bradford, 1731.

E-03710
Pennsylvania Province. Articles of Agreement Made and Concluded
    Upon Between the Right Honourable the Lord Proprietary of
    Maryland, and the Honourable the Proprietarys of Pensilvania
    &c. Philadelphia: Benjamin Franklin, 1733.

    [PENNSYLVANIA AND MARYLAND] (B).

E-03921
A MAP OF THE COUNTREY OF THE FIVE NATIONS OF INDIANS, BELONGING
    TO THE PROVINCE OF NEW YORK AND OF THE LAKES NEAR WHICH THE
    NATIONS OF FAR INDIANS LIVE WITH PART OF CANADA & RIVER ST.
    LAWRENCE. Cadwallader Colden. New York: William Bradford,
    1735.

E-03922
A NEW MAP OF THE HARBOUR OF NEW YORK, BY A LATE SURVEY. New York:
    William Bradford, 1735.

E-05063
South Carolina Province. The Report of the Committee of Both
    Houses of Assembly of the Province of South Carolina.
    Charleston, SC: Peter Timothy, 1742.

    A PLAN OF THE HARBOUR OF ST. AUGUSTINE AND THE ADJACENT
        PARTS IN FLORIDA REPRESENTING THE FIELD OF ACTION WITH
        THE DISPOSITION OF THE FORCES BEFORE THAT CASTLE IN THE
        EXPEDITION UNDER GENERAL OGLETHORPE IN 1740 (B).

E-05783
A PLAN OF THE CITY AND FORTRESS OF LOUISBURG; WITH A SMALL PLAN
    OF THE HARBOUR. Richard Gridley. Boston: John Smibert, 1746.

E-06021
New Jersey. A Bill in the Chancery of New Jersey, At the Suit of
    John, Earl of Stair, and Others. New York: James Parker,
    1747.

    [ATLANTIC SEA COAST]. James Turner (B).

    [NEW YORK AND NEW JERSEY COASTS]. James Turner (B).

    [STATEN ISLAND]. James Turner (B).

E-06316
A MAP OF PENNSYLVANIA, NEW JERSEY, NEW YORK, AND THREE LOWER
    COUNTIES, ON DELAWARE. Lewis Evans. New York: James Parker,
    1749.

E-07209
A PLAN OF THE CITY OF PHILADELPHIA, TAKEN BY GEORGE HEAP, FROM
    THE JERSEY SHORE, UNDER THE DIRECTION OF NICHOLAS SKULL,
    SURVEYOR GENERAL OF THE PROVINCE OF PENNSYLVANIA. George
    Heap. Philadelphia: s.n., 1754.

E-07363
Blodget, Samuel. A Prospective-Plan of the Battle Near Lake
    George, on the Eigth Day of September, 1755. Boston: Richard
    Draper, for Samuel Blodget, 1755.

    A PROSPECTIVE-PLAN OF THE BATTLE NEAR LAKE GEORGE ON THE
        EIGTH DAY OF SEPTEMBER, 1755. Samuel Blodget. (B).

E-07390
PLAN OF THE BATTLE OF LAKE GEORGE, BETWEEN THE ENGLISH AND THE FRENCH AND INDIANS. Timothy Clement. Boston: s.n., 1755.

E-07411
Evans, Lewis. Geographical, Historical, Political, Philosophical, and Mechanical Essays. Philadelphia: Franklin and Hall, 1755.

    A GENERAL MAP OF THE MIDDLE BRITISH COLONIES IN AMERICA; VIZ VIRGINIA, MARILAND, DELAWARE, PENSILVANIA, NEW JERSEY, NEW YORK, CONNECTICUT, AND RHODE ISLAND: OF AQUANISHUONIGY, THE COUNTRY OF THE CONFEDERATE INDIANS; COMPREHENDING AQUANISHUONIGY PROPER, THEIR PLACE OF RESIDENCE, OHIO AND TIIUXSOXRUNTIE THEIR DEER-HUNTING COUNTRIES, COUXSAXRAGE AND SKANIADARADE, THEIR BEAVER-HUNTING COUNTRIES; OF THE LAKES ERIE, ONTARIO AND CHAMPLAIN, AND PART OF NEW FRANCE: WHEREIN IS ALSO SHEWN THE ANTIENT AND PRESENT SEATS OF THE INDIAN NATIONS. Lewis Evans. (B).

E-07412
Evans, Lewis. Geographical, Historical, Political, Philosophical, and Mechanical Essays. 2nd ed. Philadelphia: Franklin and Hall, 1755.

    A GENERAL MAP OF THE MIDDLE BRITISH COLONIES IN AMERICA; VIZ VIRGINIA, MARILAND, DELAWARE, PENSILVANIA, NEW JERSEY, NEW YORK, CONNECTICUT, AND RHODE ISLAND: OF AQUANISHUONIGY, THE COUNTRY OF THE CONFEDERATE INDIANS; COMPREHENDING AQUANISHUONIGY PROPER, THEIR PLACE OF RESIDENCE, OHIO AND TIIUXSOXRUNTIE THEIR DEER-HUNTING COUNTRIES, COUXSAXRAGE AND SKANIADARADE, THEIR BEAVER-HUNTING COUNTRIES; OF THE LAKES ERIE, ONTARIO AND CHAMPLAIN, AND PART OF NEW FRANCE: WHEREIN IS ALSO SHEWN THE ANTIENT AND PRESENT SEATS OF THE INDIAN NATIONS. Lewis Evans. (B).

E-07413
Evans, Lewis. Geographical, Historical, Political, Philosophical, and Mechanical Essays. 2nd ed. Philadelphia: Franklin and Hall, 1755.

    A GENERAL MAP OF THE MIDDLE BRITISH COLONIES IN AMERICA; VIZ VIRGINIA, MARILAND, DELAWARE, PENSILVANIA, NEW JERSEY, NEW YORK, CONNECTICUT, AND RHODE ISLAND: OF AQUANISHUONIGY, THE COUNTRY OF THE CONFEDERATE INDIANS; COMPREHENDING AQUANISHUONIGY PROPER, THEIR PLACE OF RESIDENCE, OHIO AND TIIUXSOXRUNTIE THEIR DEER-HUNTING

COUNTRIES, COUXSAXRAGE AND SKANIADARADE, THEIR BEAVER-
HUNTING COUNTRIES; OF THE LAKES ERIE, ONTARIO AND
CHAMPLAIN, AND PART OF NEW FRANCE: WHEREIN IS ALSO
SHEWN THE ANTIENT AND PRESENT SEATS OF THE INDIAN
NATIONS. Lewis Evans. (B).

E-07657
CHART OF DELAWARE BAY FROM THE SEA COAST TO REEDY ISLAND. Joshua
Fisher. Philadelphia: John Turner, for John Davis, 1756.

E-08144
Grew, Theophilus. The New York Pocket Almanack, for the Year
1759. New York: Hugh Gaine, 1758.

AN EXACT PLAN OF THE HARBOUR OF LOUISBOURG (UP).

E-08153
Hutchins, John Nathan. Hutchins's Almanack or Ephemeris for the
Year of Christian Account, 1759. New York: Hugh Gaine, 1758.

PLAN OF LOUISBOURG (B).

E-08280
Weatherwise, Abraham. Father Abraham's Almanack (On an Entirely
New Plan) for the Year of Our Lord, 1759. Philadelphia:
William Dunlap, 1758.

[LOUISBOURG] (B).

E-08282
Weatherwise, Abraham. Father Abraham's Almanack (On an Entirely
New Plan) for the Year of Our Lord, 1759. New York: Hugh
Gaine, 1758.

[LOUISBOURG] (B).

E-08420
More, Roger. Poor Richard, 1760: The American Country Almanack,
for the Year of Christian Account, 1760. New York: Samuel
Parker, 1759.

A PLAN OF THE CITY OF QUEBEC (34).

SKETCH OF FORT DU QUESNE, NOW PITTSBURG, WITH THE ADJACENT
COUNTRY (38).

6

E-08422
More, Roger. Poor Thomas Improved: Being More's Country Almanack
    for the Year of Christian Account, 1760. New York: William
    Weyman, 1759.

    PLAN OF THE CITY OF QUEBEC (32).

E-08423
More, Roger. Poor Thomas Improved: Being More's Country Almanack
    for the Year of Christian Account, 1760. New York: William
    Weyman, 1759.

    PLAN OF THE CITY OF QUEBEC (32).

E-08489
TO THE HONOURABLE THOMAS PENN AND RICHARD PENN, THIS MAP OF THE
    IMPROVED PART OF THE PROVINCE OF PENNSYLVANIA. Nicholas
    Scull. Philadelphia: Turner and Davis, 1759.

E-08550
The Bill of Complaint in the Chancery of New Jersey, Brought by
    Thomas Clark, and Others, against James Alexander Esqr., and
    Others. New York: William Weyman, 1760.

    [ELIZABETH-TOWN AND WOODBRIDGE, NEW JERSEY] (B).

E-08619
Der Hoch-Deutsch Americanische Calendar, Auf Das Jahr Nach Der
    Gnadenreichen Geburth Unsers Herrn und Heylands Jesu Christi
    1761. Germantown, PA: Christoph Sower, 1760.

    [ORLEANS, QUEBEC] (45).

E-08672
More, Roger. De Americaanse Almanak Voor't Jaar Na Christi
    Geboorte 1761. New York: James Parker, 1760.

    A MAP OF THE COUNTRY BETWEEN CROWN-POINT AND F. EDWARD (33).

E-08673
More, Roger. Poor Roger; Or the American Country Almanack for the
    Year of Christian Account, 1761. New York: James Parker,
    1760.

    A MAP OF THE COUNTRY BETWEEN CROWN-POINT AND F. EDWARD (33).

E-08675
More, Roger. <u>Poor Thomas Improved: Being More's Country Almanack</u>
<u>for the Year of Christian Account, 1761</u>. New York: William
Weyman, 1760.

[NEW ENGLAND, NEW YORK, AND CANADA] (36).

E-08748
Tobler, John. <u>The Pennsylvania Town and Country Man's Almanack</u>
<u>for the Year of Our Lord 1761</u>. Germantown, PA: Christoph
Sower, 1760.

[QUEBEC CAMPAIGN OF 1759] (UP).

E-09267
PLAN OF THE IMPROVED PORT OF THE CITY OF PHILADELPHIA SURVEYED BY
THE LATE NICHOLAS SCULL. Nicholas Scull. Philadelphia: s.n.,
1762.

E-10167
Smith, William. <u>An Historical Account of the Expedition Against</u>
<u>the Ohio Indians, in the Year 1764</u>. Philadelphia: William
Bradford, 1765.

    A GENERAL MAP OF THE COUNTRY ON THE OHIO AND MUSKINGHAM,
    SHEWING THE SITUATION OF THE INDIAN TOWNS WITH RESPECT
    TO THE ARMY UNDER THE CONTROL OF COLONEL BOUQUET.
    Thomas Hutchins (B).

    A TOPOGRAPHICAL PLAN OF THAT PART OF THE INDIAN COUNTRY
    THROUGH WHICH THE ARMY UNDER THE COMMAND OF COLONEL
    BOUQUET MARCHED IN THE YEAR 1764. Thomas Hutchins (B).

E-11183
A NEW PLAN OF YE GREAT TOWN OF BOSTON IN NEW ENGLAND IN AMERICA,
WITH THE MANY ADDITIONAL BUILDINGS AND NEW STREETS TO THE
YEAR 1769. John Bonner. Boston: William Price, 1769.

E-11434
TO HIS EXCELLENCY SR. HENRY MOORE, BART. CAPTAIN GENERAL AND
GOVERNOR IN CHIEF, IN & OVER THE PROVINCE OF NEW YORK & THE
TERRITORIES DEPENDING THEREON IN AMERICA, CHANCELLOR & VICE
ADMIRAL OF THE SAME. THIS PLAN OF THE CITY OF NEW YORK, IS
MOST HUMBLY INSCRIBED BY HIS EXCELLENCY'S MOST OBEDIENT
SERVANT BERND. RATZER, LIEUTT. IN THE 60TH REGT. SURVEYED IN
1767. Bernard Ratzer. New York: Bernard Ratzer, 1769.

E-11850
TO THE HONORABLE THOMAS PENN AND RICHARD PENN, ESQUIRES, TRUE AND
    ABSOLUTE PROPRIETORS AND GOVERNORS OF THE PROVINCE OF
    PENNSYLVANIA AND THE TERRITORIES THEREUNTO BELONGING AND TO
    THE HONORABLE JOHN PENN, ESQUIRE, LIEUTENANT GOVERNOR OF THE
    SAME THIS MAP OF THE PROVINCE OF PENNSYLVANIA IS HUMBLY
    DEDICATED BY THEIR MOST OBEDIENT HUMBLE SERV'T. W. SCULL.
    William Scull; Henry Dawkins, sculp't. Philadelphia: James
    Nevil, for William Scull, 1770.

E-11959
American Philosophical Society. <u>Transactions</u>. Volume 1.
    Philadelphia: Bradford and Bradford, 1771.

    [PENNSYLVANIA AND MARYLAND] (292).

E-13324
Hawkesworth, John. <u>A New Voyage Round the World in the Years
    1768, 1769, 1770, and 1771</u>. 2 volumes. New York: James
    Rivington, 1774.

    [CAPT. JAMES COOK'S NAVIGATIONS]. Volume 1. Bernard Romans
        (1).

E-13629
Smith, William. <u>An Examination of the Connecticut Claim to Lands
    in Pennsylvania</u>. Philadelphia: Joseph Crukshank, 1774.

    [CONNECTICUT] (B).

E-14057
Gaine, Hugh. <u>Gaine's Universal Register</u>. New York: Hugh Gaine,
    1775.

    PLAN OF THE CITY OF NEW YORK (F).

E-14344
<u>New York and Country Almanack for the Year 1776</u>. New York: Shober
    and Loudon, 1775.

    PLAN OF BOSTON (3).

E-14440
Romans, Bernard. <u>A Concise Natural History of East and West
    Florida</u>. New York: Bernard Romans, 1775.

ENTRANCE OF TAMPA BAY (79).

PENSACOLA HARBOUR (84).

MOBILE BAR (85).

E-14441
CHART CONTAINING PART OF EAST FLORIDA, THE WHOLE COAST OF WEST
    FLORIDA WITH ALL THE SOUNDINGS &C. ALL THE MOUTHS OF THE
    MISSISSIPPI (3 sheets). Bernard Romans. New York: Bernard
    Romans, 1775.

E-14442
CHART CONTAINING THE PENINSULA OF FLORIDA, THE BAHAMA ISLANDS,
    THE NORTH SIDE OF THE ISLAND OF CUBA, THE OLD STREIGHT OF
    BAHAMA, AND ALL THE ISLANDS, KEY, ROCKS, &C IN THESE SEAS
    (6 sheets). Bernard Romans. New York: Bernard Romans, 1775.

E-14443
MAP FROM BOSTON TO WORCESTER, PROVIDENCE AND SALEM, SHEWING THE
    SEAT OF THE PRESENT UNHAPPY CIVIL WAR IN NORTH AMERICA.
    Bernard Romans. Philadelphia: Robert Aitken, 1775.

E-14444
MAP OF THE SEAT OF CIVIL WAR IN AMERICA. Bernard Romans.
    Philadelphia: Robert Aitken, 1775.

E-14475
Stevenson, Roger. Military Instructions for Officers Detached in
    the Field. Philadelphia: Robert Aitken, 1775.

    [WESTPHALIA, PRUSSIA] (90).

E-14678
Clairac, Louis. Field Engineer. Philadelphia: Robert Aitken,
    1776.

    WATERBERGH CASTLE NEAR DECKENDORF (36).

    CASTLE OF O IN BAVARIA (42).

    PILSTING IN BAVARIA (56).

    DECKENDORF, BAVARIA (66).

    RUSSENHEIM, BAVARIA (76).

RUSSENHEIM, BAVARIA (78).

RUSSENHEIM, BAVARIA (82).

SPIRE, BAVARIA (84).

BATTLE OF FONTENOY (130).

CAMP OF NORDHEIM (170).

E-14829
Low, Nathaniel. <u>An Astronomical Diary or, Almanack, for the Year of Christian Era, 1777</u>. Boston: Gill, Fleet and Fleet, 1776.

A VIEW OF THE PRESENT SEAT OF WAR, AT AND NEAR NEW YORK (3).

E-15096
Stearns, Samuel. <u>The North American's Almanack, for the Year of Our Lord, 1777</u>. Worcester, MA: Stearns and Bigelow, 1776.

[NEW YORK CITY] (F).

E-15212
Warren, Isaac. <u>The North American's Almanack, for the Year of Our Lord Christ, 1777</u>. Worcester, MA: Stearns and Bigelow, 1776.

[NEW YORK CITY] (4).

E-15303
Gaine, Hugh. <u>Gaine's Universal Register</u>. New York: Hugh Gaine, 1777.

PLAN OF THE CITY OF NEW YORK (2).

E-15553
<u>The Philadelphia Almanack for the Year 1778</u>. Philadelphia: s.n., 1777.

A PLAN OF THE CITY OF PHILADELPHIA (F).

E-15803
Gaine, Hugh. <u>Gaine's Universal Register</u>. New York: Hugh Gaine, 1778.

PLAN OF THE CITY OF NEW YORK (F).

E-16141
Proceedings of a General Court Martial...for the Trial of Major
    General St. Clair. Philadelphia: Hall and Sellers, 1778.

    [TICONDEROGA AND MOUNT INDEPENDENCE] (B).

E-17241
Murray, James. An Impartial History of the War in America,
    between Great Britain and the United States. Volume 1.
    Boston: Coverly and Hodge, 1781.

    PLAN OF THE TOWN OF BOSTON, WITH THE ATTACK ON BUNKERS HILL.
        John Norman (256).

E-17610
Murray, James. An Impartial History of the War in America,
    between Great Britain and the United States. Volume 2.
    Boston: Coverly and Hodge, 1782.

    THE TOWN OF FALMOUTH, BURNT BY CAPTAIN MOET, OCTOBER 18,
        1775 (F).

E-17998
Ledyard, John. A Journal of Capt. Cook's Last Voyage to the
    Pacific Ocean. Hartford, CT: Nathaniel Patten, 1783.

    CHART SHOWING THE TRACKS OF THE SHIPS EMPLOYED IN CAPTAIN
        COOK'S LAST VOYAGE TO THE PACIFIC OCEAN IN THE YEARS
        1776, 1777, 1778, 1779 (F).

E-18338
Bailey, Francis. Bailey's Pocket Almanac. Philadelphia: Francis
    Bailey, 1784.

    A MAP OF THE UNITED STATES OF AMERICA. Henry Pursell (F).

E-18467
Filson, John. The Discovery, Settlement and Present State of
    Kentucke. Wilmington, DE: James Adams, 1784.

    THIS MAP OF KENTUCKE, DRAWN FROM ACTUAL OBSERVATIONS IS
        INSCRIBED WITH THE MOST PERFECT RESPECT, TO THE
        HONORABLE THE CONGRESS OF THE UNITED STATES OF AMERICA;
        AND TO HIS EXCELLCY, GEORGE WASHINGTON LATE COMMANDER
        IN CHIEF OF THEIR ARMY BY THEIR HUMBLE SERVANT JOHN
        FILSON. Henry Pursell. (B).

E-18615
Morse, Jedidiah. Geography Made Easy. New Haven, CT: Meigs,
    Bowen, and Dana, 1784.

    A MAP OF THE UNITED STATES OF AMERICA (F).

    THE WORLD (F).

E-19108
Nathan Ben Salomon. An Astronomical Diary or Almanack for the
    Year of Our Lord Christ, 1786. New Haven, CT: Meigs, Bowen,
    and Dana, 1785.

    MAP OF THE UNITED STATES OF AMERICA (B).

E-19126
New Jersey. The Petitions and Memorials of the Proprietors of
    West and East Jersey to the Legislature of New Jersey. New
    York: Shepard Kollock, 1785.

    THE STATE OF NEW JERSEY (B).

E-19211
Ramsay, David. The History of the Revolution of South Carolina.
    2 volumes. Trenton: Isaac Collins, 1785.

    A SKETCH OF THE SITUATION AND STATIONS OF THE BRITISH
        VESSELS UNDER THE COMMAND OF SIR PARKER ON THE ATTACK
        UPON FORT MOULTRIE ON SULLIVAN ISLAND, JUNE 28, 1776.
        Volume 1 (140).

    SOUTH CAROLINA AND PARTS ADJACENT; SHEWING THE MOVEMENTS OF
        THE AMERICAN AND BRITISH ARMIES. Volume 2 (v).

    A SKETCH OF THE OPERATIONS BEFORE CHARLESTON, THE CAPITAL OF
        SOUTH CAROLINA. Volume 2 (45).

    A SKETCH OF CHARLESTON HARBOUR SHEWING THE DISPOSITION OF
        THE BRITISH FLEET UNDER THE COMMAND OF VICE ADML.
        MARIOT ARBUTHNOT IN THE ATTACK OF FORT MOULTRIE ON
        SULLIVAN ISLAND IN 1780. Volume 2 (51).

    A PLAN OF THE INVESTMENT OF YORK & GLOUCESTER BY THE ALLIED
        ARMIES IN SEPTR. & OCTR., 1781. Volume 2 (322).

E-19232
Sackett, Nathaniel. _A Memorial_. New York: Shepard Kollock, 1785.

[OHIO] (F).

E-19465
American Philosophical Society. _Transactions_. Volume 2.
    Philadelphia: Robert Aitken, 1786.

A CHART OF THE GULF STREAM (314).

E-19533
BUELL'S MAP OF THE UNITED STATES. Abel Buell. New London, CT:
    Timothy Green, 1786.

E-19648
FITCH'S MAP OF THE NORTH WEST PARTS OF THE UNITED STATES, FROM
    PITTSBURG TO THE MISSISSIPPI, AND FROM THE LAKE OF THE WOODS
    TO THE JUNCTION OF THE OHIO WITH THE MISSISIPPI. John Fitch.
    Philadelphia: John Fitch, 1786.

E-20424
Hutchins, Thomas. _A Topographical Description of Virginia,_
    Pennsylvania, Maryland, and North Carolina, Comprehending
    the Rivers Ohio, Kenhawa, Siota, Cherokee, Wabash, Illinois,
    Mississippi, &c. Boston: John Norman, 1787.

A PLAN OF THE SEVERAL VILLAGES IN THE ILLINOIS COUNTRY WITH
    PART OF THE RIVER MISSISSIPPI ETC. (F).

A PLAN OF THE RAPIDS IN THE RIVER OHIO (8).

E-20471
M'Culloch, John. _Introduction to the History of America_.
    Philadelphia: Young and M'Culloch, 1787.

A MAP OF THE UNITED STATES OF N. AMERICA. Engraved by Henry
    Pursell (F).

E-20476
M'MURRAY'S MAP OF THE UNITED STATES OF AMERICA, ACCORDING TO THE
    DEFINITIVE TREATY OF PEACE, SIGNED AT PARIS, SEPTEMBER 3,
    1783. William M'Murray. Philadelphia: William Spotswood,
    1787.

E-21037
Cutler, Manasseh. <u>An Explanation of the Map Which Delineates That Part of the Federal Lands</u>. Newport, RI: Peter Edes, 1788.

   A MAP OF THE FEDERAL TERRITORY, FROM THE WESTERN BOUNDARY OF PENNSYLVANIA, TO THE SCIOTA RIVER, AND EXTENDING SO FAR NORTH, AS TO COMPREHEND A PART OF LAKE ERIE, AND SHEW THE COMMUNICATION BETWEEN THE OHIO, AND GREAT WESTERN LAKES BY THE MUSKINGUM AND CAYAHOGA RIVERS. Boston: Adams and Nourse, 1788 (B).

E-21277
A MAP OF THE COUNTRY BETWEEN ALBEMARLE SOUND, AND LAKE ERIE, COMPREHENDING THE WHOLE OF VIRGINIA, MARYLAND, DELAWARE, AND PENNSYLVANIA, WITH PARTS OF SEVERAL OTHER OF THE UNITED STATES. S.J. Neele. Philadelphia: Prichard and Hall, 1788.

E-21333
Nicholson, William. <u>An Introduction to Natural Philosophy</u>. 3rd ed. 2 volumes. Philadelphia: Thomas Dobson, 1788.

   PROPORTIONAL MAGNITUDES OF THE PLANETARY ORBITS. Volume 1. (144).

   THE TELESCOPIC APPEARANCE OF THE MOON. Volume 1. (150).

   NORTHERN HEMISPHERE [CELESTIAL CHART]. Volume 1. (166).

   SOUTHERN HEMISPHERE [CELESTIAL CHART]. Volume 1. (166).

E-21412
MAP OF THE STATES OF VIRGINIA, NORTH CAROLINA, SOUTH CAROLINA, AND GEORGIA, WITH EAST AND WEST FLORIDA. Joseph Purcell. New Haven, CT: Amos Doolittle, 1788.

E-21651
American Philosophical Society. <u>Transactions</u>. 2nd ed. Volume 1. Philadelphia: Robert Aitken, 1789.

   [PENNSYLVANIA AND MARYLAND] (357).

E-21696
TOPOGRAPHICAL MAP OF VERMONT. William Blodget. New Haven, CT: s.n., 1789.

E-21738
Clark, Matthew. <u>A Complete Chart of the Coast of America, from
   Cape Breton into the Entrance of the Gulf of Mexico</u>. Boston:
   Clark and Carleton, 1789.

   CHART OF THE COAST OF AMERICA THRO THE GULPH OF FLORIDA (1).

   CHART OF THE COAST OF AMERICA THROUGH THE GULPH OF FLORIDA
      TO THE ENTRANCE OF THE GULPH OF MEXICO (2).

   CHART OF THE COAST OF AMERICA THRO THE GULPH OF FLORIDA (3).

   CHART OF THE COAST OF AMERICA FROM ST. HELLENS SOUND TO ST.
      JOHNS RIVER (4).

   CHART OF THE COAST OF AMERICA FROM THE NORTH OF ST.
      AUGUSTINE TO AYE'S INLET (5).

   CHART OF THE COAST OF AMERICA FROM CAPE FEAR TO HELENS SOUND
      (6).

   CHART OF THE COAST OF AMERICA FROM CAPE HENRY TO ALBEMARLE
      SOUND (7).

   CHART OF THE COAST OF AMERICA FROM ALBEMARLE SOUND TO CAPE
      LOOKOUT (8).

   CHART OF THE COAST OF AMERICA FROM NEW YORK HARBOUR TO CAPE
      MAY (9).

   CHART OF THE COAST OF AMERICA FROM CAPE FEAR TO CAPE LOOKOUT
      (10).

   CHART OF THE COAST OF AMERICA FROM CAPE MAY TO MACHAPUNGO
      (11).

   CHART OF THE COAST OF AMERICA FROM NEW YORK TO RHODE ISLAND
      (12).

   CHART OF THE COAST OF AMERICA FROM GEORGE'S BANK TO RHODE
      ISLAND INCLUDING NANTUCKET SHOALS (13).

   CHART OF THE COAST OF AMERICA FROM CAPE ELIZABETH TO MOUSE
      HARBOUR (14).

   CHART OF THE COAST OF AMERICA FROM CAPE COD TO CAPE
      ELIZABETH (15).

   CHART OF THE COAST OF AMERICA FROM MOUSE HARBOUR TO MAHOME
      BAY (16).

CHART OF THE COAST OF AMERICA FROM CHARLOTTE BAY TO PORT HOWE (17).

CHART OF THE COAST OF AMERICA FROM CAPE FORCHU TO LIVERPOOL HARBOUR (18).

E-21741
Colles, Christopher. <u>A Survey of the Roads of the United States of America</u>. New York: Cornelius Tiebout, for Christopher Colles, 1789. (NOTE: map numbers 34-39 were not used).

NEW YORK TO STRATFORD (1-7).

NEW YORK TO POUGHKEEPSIE (8-13).

STRATFORD TO POUGHKEEPSIE (15-20).

POUGHKEEPSIE TO ALBANY (14, 21-25).

ALBANY TO NEWBOROUGH (26-33).

NEW YORK TO ELIZABETHTOWN (40).

NEW YORK TO BRUNSWICK (41-42).

NEW YORK TO KINGSTON (43).

NEW YORK TO TRENTON (44).

NEW YORK TO BRISTOL (45).

NEW YORK TO CRANBERRY (45*).

NEW YORK TO FRANKFORT (46).

NEW YORK TO ALLENTOWN (46*).

NEW YORK TO PHILADELPHIA (47, 49-50).

NEW YORK TO BLACKHORSE (47*).

NEW YORK TO MOUNT HOLLY (48).

PHILADELPHIA TO ANNAPOLIS (51-61).

ANNAPOLIS TO BLADENSBURG (62-63).

ANNAPOLIS TO ALEXANDRIA (64-65).

ANNAPOLIS TO DUMFRIES (66).

ANNAPOLIS TO FREDERICKSBURG (67-68).

ANNAPOLIS TO TODD'S ORDINARY (69).

ANNAPOLIS TO BOWLING GREEN ORDINARY (70).

ANNAPOLIS TO HEAD LYNCH'S ORDINARY (71).

ANNAPOLIS TO HANOVER COURT-HOUSE (72).

ANNAPOLIS TO HANOVER-NEWCASTLE (73).

ANNAPOLIS TO NEW KENT COURT-HOUSE (74-75)

ANNAPOLIS TO WILLIAMSBURG (76-77).

ANNAPOLIS TO YORK (78-79).

WILLIAMSBURGH TO AYLETT'S WAREHOUSE (80-81).

WILLIAMSBURG TO SNEED'S ORDINARY (82).

WILLIAMSBURG TO PORT ROYAL (83-84).

WILLIAMSBURG TO HOOE'S FERRY (85-86).

E-21861
Gordon, William. The History of the Rise, Progress, and
    Establishment of the Independence of the United States of
    America. 3 volumes. New York: Hodge, Allen and Campbell,
    1789.

    A NEW MAP OF THE STATES OF PENNSYLVANIA NEW JERSEY NEW YORK
        CONNECTICUT RHODE ISLAND MASSACHUSETTS AND NEW
        HAMPSHIRE INCLUDING NOVA SCOTIA AND CANADA FROM THE
        LATEST AUTHORITIES (F).

E-21978
Morse, Jedidiah. The American Geography. Elizabethtown, NJ:
    Shepard Kollock, 1789.

    A MAP OF THE STATES OF VIRGINIA NORTH CAROLINA SOUTH
        CAROLINA AND GEORGIA COMPREHENDING THE SPANISH
        PROVINCES OF EAST AND WEST FLORIDA EXHIBITING THE
        BOUNDARIES AS FIXED BY THE LATE TREATY OF PEACE BETWEEN
        THE UNITED STATES AND THE SPANISH DOMINIONS. Joseph
        Purcell (xii).

A MAP OF THE NORTHERN AND MIDDLE STATES; COMPREHENDING THE
WESTERN TERRITORY AND THE BRITISH DOMINIONS IN NORTH
AMERICA (32).

E-22021
The New York Directory, and Register, for the Year 1789. New
York: Hodge, Allen and Campbell, 1789.

PLAN OF THE CITY OF NEW YORK (F).

E-22033
Norman, John. The Boston Directory. Boston: John Norman, 1789.

PLAN OF THE TOWN OF BOSTON (F).

E-22121
A COMPLEAT PLAN OF THE CITY MARIETTA AT THE CONFLUENCE OF THE
RIVERS OHIO AND MUSKINGUM. Edward Ruggles. New London:
Timothy Green, 1789.

E-22406
Churchman, John. An Explanation of the Magnetic Atlas.
Philadelphia: James and Johnson, 1790.

TO GEORGE WASHINGTON, PRESIDENT OF THE UNITED STATES OF
AMERICA, THIS MAGNETIC ATLAS OR VARIATION CHART, IS
HUMBLY INSCRIBED, BY JOHN CHURCHMAN (540).

E-22486
Encyclopaedia, or, a Dictionary of Arts, Sciences, and
Miscellaneous Literature. Volumes 1 and 2. Philadelphia:
Thomas Dobson, 1790.

A GENERAL MAP OF NORTH AMERICA FROM THE BEST AUTHORITIES.
Volume 1 (540).

SOUTH AMERICA FROM THE BEST AUTHORITIES. Volume 1 (541).

ASIA. Volume 2 (394).

THE MOTION OF SATURN JUPITER AND MARS IN RESPECT OF THE
EARTH. Volume 2 (416).

THE MOTION OF VENUS AND MERCURY IN RESPECT OF THE EARTH.
Volume 2 (420).

THE MOON IN HER MEAN LIBRATION WITH THE SPOTS ACCORDING TO RICCIOLI CASSINI &C. Volume 2 (432).

THE PRINCIPAL FIXED STARS IN THE NORTH HEMISPHERE DELINEATED ON THE PLANE OF THE EQUATOR. Volume 2 (440).

THE PRINCIPAL FIXED STARS IN THE SOUTH HEMISPHERE DELINEATED ON THE PLANE OF THE EQUATOR. Volume 2 (444).

VIEW OF THE PROPORTIONAL MAGNITUDES OF THE PLANETARY ORBITS. Volume 2 (480).

NORTHERN HEMISPHERE WITH THE FIGURES OF THE CONSTELLATIONS. Volume 2 (572).

SOUTHERN HEMISPHERE WITH THE FIGURES OF THE CONSTELLATIONS. Volume 2 (575).

E-22670
Milligan, Jacob. The Charleston Directory and Revenue System of the United States. Charleston, SC: Thomas Bowen, 1790.

PLAN OF THE CITY OF CHARLESTON, SOUTH CAROLINA (F).

E-22681
Morse, Jedidiah. Geography Made Easy. 2nd ed. Boston: Thomas and Andrews, 1790.

THE WORLD (F).

THE SOLAR SYSTEM (13).

PLATE TO SHEW THE FIGURE OF THE EARTH (15).

MAP OF THE UNITED STATES OF AMERICA (37).

SOUTH AMERICA (250).

EUROPE (262).

ASIA (300).

AFRICA (310).

E-22682
Morse, Jedidiah. The History of America. Philadelphia: Thomas Dobson, 1790.

SOUTH AMERICA (F).

A GENERAL MAP OF NORTH AMERICA (114).

E-22698
A NEW GENERAL CHART OF THE WEST INDIES, FROM THE LATEST MARINE
    JOURNALS AND SURVEYS. Osgood Carleton. Boston: John Norman,
    1790.

E-22804
A POCKET MAP OF THE STATE OF PENNSYLVANIA. Philadelphia: William
    Spotswood, 1790.

E-23091
Workman, Benjamin. Elements of Geography. 2nd ed. Philadelphia:
    John M'Culloch, 1790.

    THE WORLD (F).

    THE SOLAR SYSTEM (6).

    A MAP OF THE UNITED STATES OF N. AMERICA (56).

E-23092
Workman, Benjamin. Elements of Geography. 3rd ed. Philadelphia:
    John M'Culloch, 1790.

    WORLD (F).

    THE SOLAR SYSTEM (6).

    NORTH AMERICA (64).

    UNITED STATES OF AMERICA (66).

    SOUTH AMERICA (89).

    EUROPE (93).

    ASIA (111).

    AFRICA (115).

E-23101
An Account of the Soil, Growing Timber, and Other Productions of
    the Lands in the Countries Situate in the Back Parts of the
    States of New York and Pennsylvania. London: s.n., 1791.

A MAP OF THE GENESEE TRACT IN THE COUNTY OF ONTARIO, THE
    STATE OF NEW YORK (F).

A MAP OF THE GENESEE LANDS IN THE COUNTY OF ONTARIO AND
    STATE OF NEW YORK (F).

E-23104
A GEOGRAPHICAL AND HYDROGRAPHICAL MAP, EXHIBITING A GENERAL VIEW
    OF THE ROADS AND INLAND NAVIGATION OF PENNSYLVANIA, AND PART
    OF THE ADJACENT STATES, WHICH ARE NOW THE OBJECT OF
    IMPROVEMENT, WITH THE VIEW TO BRING TO MARKET, BY THE MOST
    EASY LAND & WATER CARRIAGE, THE TRADE OF THE SUSQUEHANNA AND
    OHIO WATERS, AND THAT EXTENSIVE TERRITORY, BOUNDING ON AND
    AND CONNECTED WITH THE GREAT LAKES. John Adlum and John
    Wallis. Philadelphia: s.n., 1791.

E-23159
Bartram, William. Travels Through North & South Carolina,
    Georgia, East & West Florida, the Cherokee Country, the
    Extensive Territories of the Muscogulges. Philadelphia:
    James and Johnson, 1791.

    A MAP OF THE COAST OF EAST FLORIDA FROM THE RIVER ST. JOHN
        SOUTHWARD NEAR TO CAPE CANAVERAL (1).

E-23160
Bartram, William. Travels Through North & South Carolina,
    Georgia, East & West Florida, the Cherokee Country, the
    Extensive Territories of the Muscogulges. Philadelphia:
    James and Johnson, 1791.

    A MAP OF THE COAST OF EAST FLORIDA FROM THE RIVER ST. JOHN
        SOUTHWARD NEAR TO CAPE CANAVERAL (1).

E-23166
Belknap, Jeremy. The History of New Hampshire. Volume 2. Boston:
    Thomas and Andrews, 1791.

    A NEW MAP OF NEW HAMPSHIRE (xvi).

E-23185
Bible. Worcester, MA: Isaiah Thomas, 1791.

    THE ANCIENT CITY OF JERUSALEM AND PLACES ADJACENT (449).

22

E-23186
Bible. 2 volumes. Worcester, MA: Isaiah Thomas, 1791.

    THE ANCIENT CITY OF JERUSALEM AND PLACES ADJACENT. Volume 2
       (484).

E-23337
Duncan, William. The New York Directory and Register for the Year
    1791. New York: Swords and Swords, 1791.

    PLAN OF THE CITY OF NEW YORK (F).

E-23453
A MAP OF THE STATE OF PENNSYLVANIA, (ONE OF THE UNITED STATES OF
    AMERICA.) INCLUDING THE TRIANGLE LATELY PURCHASED OF
    CONGRESS AND CONTINUING THE BOUNDARY LINES OF THE STATE, AS
    RUN BY THE THE RESPECTIVE COMMISSIONERS, WITH PART OF LAKE
    ERIE, AND PRESQU' ISLE. Reading Howell. Philadelphia: s.n.,
    1791.

E-23454
A MAP OF PENNSYLVANIA, AND PARTS CONNECTED THEREWITH, RELATING TO
    THE ROADS AND INLAND NAVIGATION, ESPECIALLY AS PROPOSED TO
    BE IMPROVED BY THE LATE PROCEEDINGS OF ASSEMBLY. Reading
    Howell. Philadelphia: James Trenchard, 1791.

E-23579
Morse, Jedidiah. Geography Made Easy. 3rd edition, abridged.
    Boston: Thomas and Andrews, 1791.

    THE WORLD (F).

    THE SOLAR SYSTEM (10).

    PLATE TO SHEW THE FIGURE OF THE EARTH (14).

    A MAP OF THE UNITED STATES OF AMERICA (36).

    SOUTH AMERICA (250).

    EUROPE (262).

    ASIA (300).

    AFRICA (310).

E-23637
Norman, John. _The American Pilot_. Boston: John Norman, 1791.

    A CHART OF NANTUCKET SHOALS (1).

    A CHART OF THE BANKS OF NEWFOUNDLAND (2).

    [GULPH OF ST. LAWRENCE] (3).

    [BAY OF FUNDY] (4).

    [SOUTHERN COAST OF MAINE] (5).

    [GEORGES BANK] (6).

    A CHART FROM NEW YORK TO TIMBER ISLAND, INCLUDING NANTUCKET
        SHOALS (7).

    A CHART OF THE COAST OF AMERICA FROM CAPE HATERAS TO CAPE
        ROMAN (8).

    A CHART OF SOUTH CAROLINA AND GEORGIA (9).

    A CHART FROM NEW YORK TO WHIMBLE SHOALS (10).

    A CHART OF THE SEA COAST FROM THE ISLAND OF CYENNE TO THE
        RIVER POUMARON (11).

    A NEW GENERAL CHART OF THE WEST INDIES (12).

E-24099
Bible. New York: Hodge and Campbell, 1792.

    AN ACCURATE MAP OF THE HOLY LAND, WITH ADJACENT COUNTRIES
        TAKEN FROM THE BEST AUTHORITIES [In Joshua] (UP).

E-24124
A NEW AND CORRECT MAP OF THE STATE OF CONNECTICUT ONE OF THE
    UNITED STATES OF AMERICA FROM ACTUAL SURVEY. William
    Blodget. Middletown, CT: Joel Allen, for William Blodget,
    1792.

E-24125
A NEW AND CORRECT MAP OF THE STATE OF CONNECTICUT ONE OF THE
    UNITED STATES OF AMERICA FROM ACTUAL SURVEY. William
    Blodget. Norwich, CT: William Blodget, 1792.

E-24265
A NEW AND CORRECT MAP OF NEW YORK. Simeon DeWitt. Albany: s.n.,
    1792.

E-24281
Duncan, William. The New York Directory, and Register, for the
    Year 1792. New York: Swords and Swords, 1792.

    PLAN OF THE CITY OF NEW YORK (F).

E-24296
A PLAN OF THE CITY OF WASHINGTON, IN THE TERRITORY OF COLUMBIA,
    CEDED BY THE STATES OF VIRGINIA AND MARYLAND TO THE UNITED
    STATES OF AMERICA, AND BY THEM ESTABLISHED, AS THE SEAT OF
    THEIR GOVERNMENT, AFTER THE YEAR 1800. Andrew Ellicott.
    Philadelphia: s.n., 1792.

E-24323
PLAN OF THE TOWN OF BALTIMORE AND ITS ENVIRONS. A.P. Folie.
    Philadelphia: s.n., 1792.

E-24411
A MAP OF THE STATE OF PENNSYLVANIA, WITH PART OF LAKE ERIE AND
    PRESQUE ISLE, ALSO, THE RIVERS SUSQUEHANA, OHIO, ALLEGHANY,
    MONONGAHELA, AND LESSER STREAMS, THE MOUNTAINS, ROADS,
    PORTAGES, ETC. Reading Howell. Philadelphia: s.n., 1792.

E-24412
[PENNSYLVANIA AND ENVIRONS]. Reading Howell. Philadelphia: James
    Trenchard, 1792.

E-24437
Josephus, Flavius. The Whole and Genuine Works of Flavius
    Josephus. New York: William Durell, 1792.

    CORRECT MAP OF THE COUNTRIES SURROUNDING THE GARDEN OF EDEN
        OR PARADISE WITH THE COURSE OF NOAH'S ARK DURING THE
        FLOOD (8).

    AN ACCURATE MAP OF THE HOLY LAND WITH ADJACENT COUNTRIES.
        Thomas Bowen (66).

    JERUSALEM (326).

E-25040
Williams, Jonathan. Memoir on the Use of the Thermometer in
    Navigation. Philadelphia: s.n., 1792.

    [NORTH ATLANTIC COAST] (F).

E-25103
American Philosophical Society. Transactions. Volume 3.
    Philadelphia: Robert Aitken, 1793.

    [NORTH ATLANTIC OCEAN] (88).

E-25648
Imlay, Gilbert. A Topographical Description of the Western
    Territory of North America. Volume 1. New York: Samuel
    Campbell, 1793.

    NEW MAP OF THE STATES OF GEORGIA, SOUTH AND NORTH CAROLINA,
        VIRGINIA AND MARYLAND, INCLUDING THE SPANISH PROVINCES
        OF WEST AND EAST FLORIDA FROM THE LATEST SURVEYS.
        Cornelius Tiebout (F).

    A PLAN OF THE RAPIDS OF THE OHIO (110).

    A MAP OF THE STATE OF KENTUCKY, DRAWN FROM THE BEST
        AUTHORITIES (260).

E-25847
Morse, Jedidiah. The American Universal Geography. 2 volumes.
    Boston: Thomas and Andrews, 1793.

    THE WORLD FROM THE BEST AUTHORITIES. Volume 1 (F).

    A MAP OF THE NORTHERN AND MIDDLE STATES; COMPREHENDING THE
        WESTERN TERRITORY AND THE BRITISH DOMINIONS IN NORTH
        AMERICA. Volume 1 (308).

    THE DISTRICT OF MAINE FROM THE LATEST SURVEYS. Osgood
        Carleton. Volume 1 (344).

    A MAP OF PENNSYLVANIA WITH PART OF THE ADJACENT STATES FROM
        THE LATEST SURVEYS. Osgood Carleton. Volume 1 (468).

    A MAP OF THE STATES OF VIRGINIA NORTH CAROLINA SOUTH
        CAROLINA AND GEORGIA COMPREHENDING THE SPANISH
        PROVINCES OF EAST AND WEST FLORIDA EXHIBITING THE
        BOUNDARIES BETWEEN THE UNITED STATES AND SPANISH
        DOMINIONS AS FIXED BY THE TREATY OF PEACE IN 1783.
        Joseph Purcell. Volume 1 (532).

SOUTH AMERICA. Volume 1 (642).

WEST INDIES ACCORDING TO THE BEST AUTHORITIES. Volume 1
(666).

EUROPE. Volume 2 (F).

ASIA. Volume 2 (384).

AFRICA. Volume 2 (484).

E-25925
Norman, John. The American Pilot. Boston: John Norman, 1793.

A CHART OF NANTUCKET SHOALS (1).

A NEW CHART OF THE SEA COAST FROM THE ISLAND OF CYENNE TO
THE RIVER POUMARON (2).

A NEW GENERAL CHART OF THE WEST INDIES (3).

A CHART OF SOUTH CAROLINA AND GEORGIA (4).

CHART OF THE COAST OF AMERICA FROM CAPE HATERAS TO CAPE
ROMAN (5).

A CHART FROM NEW YORK TO WHIMBLE SHOALS (6).

CHART FROM NEW YORK TO TIMBER ISLAND INCLUDING NANTUCKET
SHOALS (7).

A CHART OF THE BANKS OF NEWFOUNDLAND (8).

[GEORGES BANK] (9).

[COAST OF SOUTHERN MAINE] (10).

[BAY OF FUNDY] (11).

[GULPH OF ST. LAWRENCE] (12).

E-26168
Smith, Daniel. A Short Description of the Tennassee Government.
Philadelphia: Mathew Carey, 1793.

MAP OF THE TENNASSEE GOVERNMENT, FORMERLY PART OF NORTH
CAROLINA, FROM SURVEYS BY GEN. D. SMITH AND OTHERS (B).

E-26268
Toulmin, Henry. <u>A Description of Kentucky in North America</u>.
    Lexington: John Bradford, 1793.

    [KENTUCKY] (67).

E-26478
A MAP OF THE STATE OF VERMONT. James Whitelaw. Boston: s.n.,
    1793.

E-26481
Whitney, Peter. <u>The History of the County of Worcester, in the</u>
    <u>Commonwealth of Massachusetts</u>. Worcester, MA: Isaiah Thomas,
    1793.

    A MAP OF THE COUNTY OF WORCESTER. Joseph Seymour, for
        Charles Baker and John Peirce (F).

E-26509
Workman, Benjamin. <u>Elements of Geography</u>. 4th ed. Philadelphia:
    John M'Culloch, 1793.

    WORLD (F).

    THE SOLAR SYSTEM (6).

    NORTH AMERICA (66).

    UNITED STATES OF AMERICA (83).

    SOUTH AMERICA (106).

    EUROPE (110).

    ASIA (138).

    AFRICA (142).

E-26616
A MAP OF KENTUCKY FROM ACTUAL SURVEY. Elihu Barker. Philadelphia:
    Mathew Carey, 1794.

E-26732
Carey, Mathew. <u>A Short Account of Algiers</u>. Philadelphia: John
    Parker, for Mathew Carey, 1794.

        A MAP OF BARBARY, COMPREHENDING MOROCCO, FEZ, ALGIERS, TUNIS
            AND TRIPOLI. Joseph Scott (F).

E-26733
Carey, Mathew. A Short Account of Algiers. 2nd ed. Philadelphia:
    John Parker, for Mathew Carey, 1794.

        A MAP OF BARBARY, COMPREHENDING MOROCCO, FEZ, ALGIERS, TUNIS
            AND TRIPOLI. Joseph Scott (F).

E-26734
Carey, Mathew. Eine Kurze Nachricht von Algier. Philadelphia:
    Steiner and Kammerer, 1794.

        A MAP OF BARBARY, COMPREHENDING MOROCCO, FEZ, ALGIERS, TUNIS
            AND TRIPOLI. Joseph Scott (F).

E-26741
Carey, Mathew. A General Atlas for the Present War. Philadelphia:
    Mathew Carey, 1794.

        THE SEVEN UNITED PROVINCES OF HOLLAND, FRIESLAND, GRONINGEN,
            OVERYSSEL, GELDERS, UTRECHT, AND ZEALAND. Cornelius
            Tiebout (1).

        THE AUSTRIAN, FRENCH, AND DUTCH NETHERLANDS. Joseph Scott
            (2).

        FRANCE DIVIDED INTO CIRCLES AND DEPARTMENTS. William Barker
            (3).

        SPAIN AND PORTUGAL FROM THE BEST AUTHORITIES. Cornelius
            Tiebout (4).

        THE EMPIRE OF GERMANY AND THE 13 CANTONS OF SWITZERLAND FROM
            THE BEST AUTHORITIES. Joseph Scott (5).

        ITALY AND SARDINIA FROM THE BEST AUTHORITIES. Cornelius
            Tiebout (6).

        A CHART OF THE WEST INDIES FROM THE LATEST MARINE JOURNALS
            AND SURVEYS. William Barker (7).

E-26781
Colles, Christopher. The Geographical Ledger and Systemized
    Atlas. New York: John Buell, 1794.

    FROM NEW YORK TO ELIZABETHTOWN (1).

FROM NEW YORK TO BRUNSWICK (2 sheets) (2).

FROM NEW YORK TO KINGSTON (3).

FROM NEW YORK TO TRENTON (4).

FROM NEW YORK TO BRISTOL (5).

FROM NEW YORK TO FRANKFORT (6).

E-26853
Davies, Benjamin. Some Account of the City of Philadelphia, the
    Capital of Pennsylvania, and the Seat of the Federal
    Congress. Philadelphia: Richard Folwell, 1794.

    A GROUND PLAN OF THE CITY AND SUBURBS OF PHILADELPHIA, TAKEN
        FROM ACTUAL SURVEY; CONTAINING AN EXACT DESCRIPTION OF
        ALL THE SQUARES, STREETS AND ALLEYS IN THE CITY AND
        LIBERTIES; OF THE SITUATION OF ALL THE PRINCIPAL PUBLIC
        BUILDINGS; OF THE RIVULETS AND AS MUCH OF THE CANAL AS
        LIES WITHIN THE COMPASS OF THE DRAFT. A.P. Folie (B).

E-26919
Duncan, William. The New York Directory, Register, for the Year
    1794. New York: Swords and Swords, 1794.

    PLAN OF THE CITY OF NEW YORK (F).

E-27011
Fraser, Donald. The Young Gentleman and Lady's Assistant. 2nd ed.
    Danbury, CT: Nathan Douglas, 1794.

    THE WORLD (F).

    THE SOLAR SYSTEM (11).

E-27061
Gordon, William. The History of the Rise, Progress, and
    Establishment of the Independence of the United States of
    America. 2nd ed. 3 volumes. New York: Samuel Campbell, 1794.

    A NEW MAP OF THE STATES OF PENNSYLVANIA NEW JERSEY NEW YORK
        CONNECTICUT RHODE ISLAND MASSACHUSETTS AND NEW
        HAMPSHIRE INCLUDING NOVA SCOTIA AND CANADA FROM THE
        LATEST AUTHORITIES. Cornelius Tiebout. Volume 1 (F).

30

NEW MAP OF THE STATES OF GEORGIA SOUTH AND NORTH CAROLINA
VIRGINIA AND MARYLAND INCLUDING THE SPANISH PROVINCES
OF WEST AND EAST FLORIDA FROM THE LATEST SURVEYS.
Volume 2 (F).

E-27089
Hardie, James. The Philadelphia Directory and Register. 2nd ed.
Philadelphia: Jacob Johnson, 1794.

A PLAN OF THE CITY OF PHILADELPHIA (E).

E-27090
Hardie, James. A Short Account of the City of Philadelphia.
Philadelphia: Jacob Johnson, 1794.

A PLAN OF THE CITY OF PHILADELPHIA (F).

E-27162
Jefferson, Thomas. Notes on the State of Virginia. 2nd American
ed. Philadelphia: Mathew Carey, 1794.

THE STATE OF VIRGINIA (F).

E-27209
Lear, Tobias. Observations on the River Potomack. 2nd ed. New
York: Loudon and Brewer, 1794.

PLAN OF THE CITY OF WASHINGTON. Andrew Ellicott (F).

E-27341
Moore, John. A Journal During a Residence in France, from the
Beginning of August, to the Middle of December, 1792.
Volume 2. New York: Childs and Swaine, for Francis Childs;
Berry, Rogers and Berry; and Thomas Allen, 1794.

A MAP OF GENERAL DUMOURIER'S CAMPAIGN ON THE MEUSE, IN 1792.
(F).

E-27351
Morse, Jedidiah. Geography Made Easy. 4th ed. Boston: Thomas and
Andrews, 1794.

THE WORLD (F).

ARTIFICIAL SPHERE (17).

COPERNICAN SYSTEM [SOLAR SYSTEM] (17).

EUROPE (312).

ASIA (364).

A MAP OF THE TRAVELS & VOYAGES OF ST. PAUL (367).

PALESTINE OR THE HOLY LAND (371).

THE JOURNEYINGS OF OUR SAVIOR JESUS CHRIST (372).

AFRICA (393)

E-27743
Stiles, Ezra. A History of the Three Judges of King Charles I.
    Hartford, CT: Elisha Babcock, 1794.

A MAP OF NEW HAVEN (28).

[MILFORD AND GUILFORD, CONNECTICUT] (80).

GRAVES OF THE JUDGES IN NEW HAVEN (114).

[NEW HAVEN] (126).

[HADLEY, MASSACHUSETTS] (202).

[KINGSTON, RHODE ISLAND AND ENVIRONS] (344).

E-27823
Truxtun, Thomas. Remarks, Instructions, and Examples Relating to
    the Latitude & Longitude. Philadelphia: Thomas Dobson, 1794.

A GENERAL CHART OF THE GLOBE (F).

E-28094
Williams, Samuel. The Natural and Civil History of Vermont.
    Walpole, NH: Thomas and Carlisle, 1794.

A MAP OF THE STATE OF VERMONT. James Whitelaw (F).

E-28191
MAP OF THE STATE OF KENTUCKY, WITH THE ADJOINING TERRITORIES.
    Alexander Anderson. New York: Smith, Reid and Wayland, 1795.

E-28390
Carey, Mathew. <u>Carey's American Atlas</u>. Philadelphia: Mathew
    Carey, 1795.

    THE BRITISH POSSESSIONS IN NORTH AMERICA FROM THE BEST
        AUTHORITIES. Samuel Lewis (1).

    THE PROVINCE OF MAINE FROM THE BEST AUTHORITIES (2).

    THE STATE OF NEW HAMPSHIRE COMPILED CHIEFLY FROM ACTUAL
        SURVEYS. Samuel Lewis (3).

    VERMONT FROM ACTUAL SURVEY. Amos Doolittle (4).

    STATE OF MASSACHUSETTS COMPILED FROM THE BEST AUTHORITIES.
        Samuel Lewis (5).

    CONNECTICUT FROM THE BEST AUTHORITIES. Amos Doolittle (6).

    THE STATE OF RHODE ISLAND COMPILED FROM THE SURVEYS AND
        OBSERVATIONS OF CALEB HARRIS. Harding Harris (7).

    THE STATE OF NEW YORK COMPILED FROM THE BEST AUTHORITIES.
        Samuel Lewis (8).

    THE STATE OF NEW JERSEY COMPILED FROM THE MOST AUTHENTIC
        INFORMATION (9).

    THE STATE OF PENNSYLVANIA REDUCED WITH PERMISSION FROM
        READING HOWELLS MAP. Samuel Lewis (10).

    DELAWARE FROM THE BEST AUTHORITIES. William Barker (11).

    THE STATE OF MARYLAND FROM THE BEST AUTHORITIES. Samuel
        Lewis (12).

    THE STATE OF VIRGINIA FROM THE BEST AUTHORITIES. Samuel
        Lewis (13).

    THE STATE OF NORTH CAROLINA FROM THE BEST AUTHORITIES, &C.
        Samuel Lewis (14).

    THE STATE OF SOUTH CAROLINA FROM THE BEST AUTHORITIES.
        Samuel Lewis (15).

    GEORGIA FROM THE LATEST AUTHORITIES. William Barker (16).

    KENTUCKY REDUCED FROM ELIHU BARKER'S LARGE MAP. William
        Barker (17).

A MAP OF THE TENNASSEE GOVERNMENT FORMERLY PART OF NORTH
CAROLINA TAKEN CHIEFLY FROM SURVEYS OF GENL. D. SMITH &
OTHERS. Joseph Scott (18).

MAP OF SOUTH AMERICA ACCORDING TO THE BEST AUTHORITIES (19).

A MAP OF THE DISCOVERIES MADE BY CAPTS. COOK AND CLERKE IN
THE YEAR 1778 AND 1779 BETWEEN THE EASTERN COAST OF
ASIA AND THE WESTERN COAST OF NORTH AMERICA WHEN THEY
ATTEMPTED TO NAVIGATE THE NORTH SEA. Joseph Scott (20).

A CHART OF THE WEST INDIES FROM THE LATEST MARINE JOURNALS
AND SURVEYS. William Barker (21).

E-28391
AN ACCURATE MAP OF THE DISTRICT OF MAINE, BEING PART OF THE
COMMONWEALTH OF MASSACHUSETTS: COMPILED PURSUANT TO AN ACT
OF THE GENERAL COURT, FROM ACTUAL SURVEYS OF THE SEVERAL
TOWNS, &C. Osgood Carleton. Boston: Thomas and Andrews,
1795.

E-28598
Duncan, William. The New York Directory, and Register, for the
Year 1795. New York: Swords and Swords, 1795.

A PLAN OF THE CITY OF NEW YORK (F).

E-28772
MAP OF THE STATE OF MARYLAND, AND THE FEDERAL TERRITORY, AS ALSO
OF THE STATE DELAWARE. Dennis Griffith. Philadelphia: John
Vallance, 1795.

E-28803
A MAP OF THE STATE OF RHODE ISLAND; TAKEN MOSTLY FROM SURVEYS BY
CALEB HARRIS. Caleb Harris. Providence: Carter and
Wilkinson, 1795.

E-28910
Josephus, Flavius. The Whole Genuine and Complete Works of
Flavius Josephus. Philadelphia: Woodruff and Pechin, 1795.

A CORRECT MAP OF THE COUNTRIES SURROUNDING THE GARDEN OF
EDEN, OR PARADISE (15).

JERUSALEM (B).

E-29111
Morse, Jedidiah. <u>The History of America</u>. 2nd ed. Philadelphia:
    Thomas Dobson, 1795.

    A GENERAL MAP OF NORTH AMERICA (F).

    SOUTH AMERICA (F).

E-29112
Morse, Jedidiah. <u>Elements of Geography</u>. Boston: Thomas and
    Andrews, 1795.

    CHART OF THE WORLD ON MERCATORS PROJECTION (F).

    A MAP OF THE UNITED STATES OF AMERICA (74).

E-29218
Nicholson, William. <u>An Introduction to Natural Philosophy</u>. New
    ed. 2 volumes. Philadelphia: Thomas Dobson, 1795.

    THE TELESCOPIC APPEARANCE OF THE MOON. Volume 1 (172).

    NORTHERN HEMISPHERE [CELESTIAL CHART]. Volume 1 (196).

    SOUTHERN HEMISPHERE [CELESTIAL CHART]. Volume 1 (196).

E-29351
Price, Jonathan. <u>A Description of Occacock Inlet, and of Its
    Coasts, Islands, Shoals, and Anchorages....</u>. Newbern, TN:
    Francois Martin, 1795.

    OCCACOCK FROM ACTUAL SURVEY (F).

E-29474
<u>An Historical Account of the Rise, Progress and Present State of
    the Canal Navigation in Pennsylvania</u>. Philadelphia:
    Zachariah Poulson, 1795.

    TO THE LEGISLATURE AND THE GOVERNOR OF PENNSYLVANIA THIS MAP
        IS RESPECTFULLY INSCRIBED BY READING HOWELL. Reading
        Howell (B).

E-29476
Scott, Joseph. <u>The United States Gazetteer</u>. Philadelphia: Bailey
    and Bailey, 1795.

    A MAP OF THE UNITED STATES (1).

CONNECTICUT (2).

DELAWARE (3).

GEORGIA (4).

NEW JERSEY (5).

KENTUCKY (6).

MAINE (7).

MARYLAND (8).

MASSACHUSETTS (9).

NEW HAMPSHIRE (10).

NEW YORK (11).

NORTH CAROLINA (12).

PENNSYLVANIA (13).

RHODE ISLAND (14).

SOUTH CAROLINA (15).

NW TERRITORY (16).

SW TERRITORY (17).

STATE OF VERMONT (18).

VIRGINIA (19).

E-29513
Sierra Leone Company. Substance of the Report Delivered by the
    Court of Directors of the Sierra Leone Company, to the
    General Court of Proprietors, on Thursday, March 27th, 1794.
    Philadelphia: Thomas Dobson, 1795.

    PLAN OF SIERRA LEONE AND THE PARTS ADJACENT (F).

E-29521
Smith, Charles. Universal Geography Made Easy. New York: Wayland
    and Davis, 1795.

    THE WORLD (F).

EUROPE (20).

ASIA (84).

AFRICA (104).

NORTH AMERICA (124).

THE UNITED STATES OF AMERICA (132).

SOUTH AMERICA (172).

E-29589
Sullivan, James. The History of the District of Maine. Boston: Thomas and Andrews, 1795.

A MAP OF THOSE PARTS OF THE COUNTRY MOST FAMOUS FOR BEING HARRASED BY THE INDIANS, ON AND LONG AFTER THEIR FIRST SETTLEMENT AND MORE PARTICULARLY TREATED OF IN JUDGE SULLIVAN'S HISTORY OF THE DISTRICT OF MAINE (F).

A MAP OF THE DISTRICT OF MAINE, DRAWN FROM THE LATEST SURVEYS AND OTHER BEST AUTHORITIES. Osgood Carleton (F).

E-29907
Winchester, Elhanan. A Course of Lectures, on the Prophecies that Remain to be Fulfilled. Volume 2. Norwich, CT: Thomas Hubbard, 1795.

A SMALL MAP OF EUROPE ASIA AND AFRICA TO SHOW THAT JERUSALEM IS THE MOST CENTRICAL AND CONVENIENT FOR A PLACE OF GENERAL RESORT FROM EVERY POINT OF THE WORLD. James Purves (110).

A VIEW OF THE DIVISION OF THE LAND OF CANAAN AMONG THE TWELVE TRIBES OF ISRAEL THE SITUATION OF THE CITY AND SANCTUARY &C AS DESCRIBED BY THE PROPHET EZEKIAL. James Purves (110).

E-29924
Workman, Benjamin. Elements of Geography. Philadelphia: John M'Culloch, 1795.

THE WORLD (F).

THE SOLAR SYSTEM (6).

NORTH AMERICA (66).

UNITED STATES OF AMERICA (82).

SOUTH AMERICA (106).

EUROPE (110).

ASIA (138).

AFRICA (142).

E-30122
A MAP OF THE UNITED STATES EXHIBITING POST ROADS AND DISTANCES.
Abraham Bradley. PHILADELPHIA: s.n., 1795.

E-30123
A MAP OF THE UNITED STATES EXHIBITING THE POST-ROADS THE
SITUATIONS, CONNECTIONS & DISTANCES OF THE POST OFFICES
STAGE ROADS COUNTIES PORTS OF ENTRY AND DELIVERY FOR FOREIGN
VESSELS AND THE PRINCIPAL RIVERS. Abraham Bradley.
Philadelphia: s.n., 1795.

E-30161
Carey, Mathew. The American Pocket Atlas. Philadelphia: Mathew
Carey, 1796.

THE UNITED STATES OF AMERICA (F).

VERMONT (16).

THE STATE OF NEW HAMPSHIRE (22).

PROVINCE OF MAINE (22).

MASSACHUSETTS (26).

RHODE ISLAND (33).

CONNECTICUT (40).

NEW YORK (46).

NEW JERSEY (52).

PENNSYLVANIA (58).

DELAWARE (82).

NW TERRITORY (84).

MARYLAND (90).

VIRGINIA (94).

KENTUCKEY (98).

NORTH CAROLINA (102).

TENNASSEE LATELY THE SW TERRITORY (106).

SOUTH CAROLINA (110).

GEORGIA (114).

E-30162
Carey, Mathew. <u>Carey's General World Atlas for the Present War</u>.
    Philadelphia: Mathew Carey, 1796.

MAP OF THE WORLD (1).

CHART OF THE WORLD ACCORDING TO MERCATOR'S PROJECTION,
    SHEWING THE LATEST DISCOVERIES OF CAPTAIN COOK (2).

AN ACCURATE MAP OF EUROPE (3).

SWEDEN, DENMARK, NORWAY AND FINLAND (4).

THE RUSSIAN EMPIRE IN EUROPE AND ASIA (5).

SCOTLAND WITH PRINCIPAL ROADS (6).

AN ACCURATE MAP OF ENGLAND AND WALES (7).

MAP OF IRELAND (8).

THE SEVEN UNITED PROVINCES (9).

AUSTRIAN, FRENCH AND DUTCH NETHERLANDS (10).

THE EMPIRE OF GERMANY WITH THE 13 CANTONS OF SWITZERLAND
    (11).

FRANCE DIVIDED INTO CIRCLES (12).

A MAP OF THE SEAT OF WAR IN FRANCE (13).

TURKEY IN EUROPE AND HUNGARY (14).

SPAIN AND PORTUGAL (15).

ITALY AND SARDINIA (16).

SWITZERLAND (17).

POLAND, SHEWING THE CLAIMS OF RUSSIA, PRUSSIA AND AUSTRIA
(18).

ASIA (19).

CHINA DIVIDED INTO ITS GREAT PROVINCES (20).

AN ACCURATE MAP OF HINDOSTAN OR INDIA (21).

AFRICA (22).

BRITISH SETTLEMENTS IN AMERICA (23).

UNITED STATES (24).

VERMONT (25).

THE STATE OF NEW HAMPSHIRE (26).

THE PROVINCE OF MAINE (27).

THE STATE OF MASSACHUSETTS (28).

THE STATE OF RHODE ISLAND (29).

CONNECTICUT (30).

THE STATE OF NEW YORK (31).

THE STATE OF NEW JERSEY (32).

THE STATE OF PENNSYLVANIA (33).

DELAWARE (34).

THE STATE OF MARYLAND. Samuel Lewis (35).

THE STATE OF VIRGINIA. Samuel Lewis (36).

THE STATE OF NORTH CAROLINA. Samuel Lewis (37).

THE STATE OF SOUTH CAROLINA. Samuel Lewis (38).

GEORGIA (39).

KENTUCKY (40).

MAP OF THE TENNASSEE STATE FORMERLY PART OF NORTH CAROLINA (41).

A MAP OF SOUTH AMERICA (42).

A CHART OF THE WEST INDIES (43).

A MAP OF THE COUNTRIES SITUATED AT THE NORTH POLE (44).

A MAP OF THE DISCOVERIES MADE BY CAPTS. COOK AND CLERKE IN THE YEAR 1778 AND 1779 BETWEEN THE EASTERN COAST OF ASIA AND THE WESTERN COAST OF NORTH AMERICA (45).

E-30164
A PLAN OF THE TOWN OF BOSTON AND ITS VICINITY. Osgood Carleton. Boston: Manning and Loring, for John West, 1796.

E-30274
Cook, James. A Voyage to the Pacific Ocean for Making Discoveries in the Northern Hemisphere. 4 volumes. New York: Tiebout and O'Brien, for Benjamin Gomez, 1796.

A GENERAL CHART EXHIBITING THE DISCOVERIES MADE BY CAPTN. JAMES COOK IN THIS AND HIS TWO PRECEEDING VOYAGES; WITH THE TRACKS OF THE SHIPS UNDER HIS COMMAND. Volume 1 (xxxiv).

SKETCH OF KARAKAKOOA BAY. Volume 3 (148).

CHART OF THE SANDWICH ISLANDS. Volume 3 (148).

E-30338
A Description of the River Susquehana. Philadelphia: Zachariah Poulson, 1796.

[PENNSYLVANIA] (F).

E-30447
Fraser, Donald. The Young Gentleman and Lady's Assistant. 3rd ed. New York: Swords and Swords, 1796.

THE WORLD (F).

THE SOLAR SYSTEM (18).

E-30602
Hume, David. The History of England, from the Invasion of Julius
    Caesar to the Revolution in MDCLXXXVIII. Volume 6.
    Philadelphia: Heinrich Schweitzer, for Robert Campbell,
    1796.

    EAST INDIES. Thomas Hutchin (48).

E-30691
A MAP OF THE N.W. TERRITORY OF THE UNITED STATES: COMPILED FROM
    ACTUAL SURVEYS AND THE BEST AUTHORITIES. Samuel Lewis.
    Philadelphia: William Barker, for Mathew Carey, 1796.

E-30805
PLAN OF THE TOWN OF ERIE ON LAKE ERIE. Frederic Molineux.
    Philadelphia: s.n., 1796.

E-30817
Moreau de St. Mery, Mederic. Description Topographique et
    Politique de la Partie Espagnole de l'Isle Saint Domingue.
    2 volumes. Philadelphia: Mederic Moreau de St. Mery, 1796.

    CARTE DE L'ISLE ST. DOMINGUE. Volume 2 (B).

E-30818
Moreau de St. Mery, Mederic. A Topographical and Political
    Description of the Spanish Part of Saint Domingo. 2 volumes.
    Philadelphia: Mederic Moreau de St. Mery, 1796.

    CARTE DE L'ISLE ST. DOMINGUE. Volume 2 (B).

E-30823
Morse, Jedidiah. The American Universal Geography. Part 2, 2nd
    ed. Boston: Thomas and Andrews, 1796.

    EUROPE (F).

    ENGLAND, SCOTLAND, IRELAND AND WALES (98).

    POLAND, SHEWING THE CLAIMS OF RUSSIA, PRUSSIA AND AUSTRIA
        (254).

    SWITZERLAND WITH ITS SWISS ALLIES (304).

    NETHERLANDS (342).

    FRANCE DIVIDED INTO CIRCLES AND DEPARTMENTS (348).

ASIA FROM THE BEST AUTHORITIES (456).

PALESTINE OR THE HOLY LAND (472).

HINDOSTAN OR INDIA (532).

AFRICA (596).

E-30824
Morse, Jedidiah. <u>The American Universal Geography</u>. Part 1,
3rd ed. Boston: Thomas and Andrews, 1796.

MAP OF THE WORLD FROM THE BEST AUTHORITIES (F).

ARTIFICIAL SPHERE (39).

COPERNICAN SYSTEM [SOLAR SYSTEM] (39)

A GENERAL MAP OF NORTH AMERICA (128).

A MAP OF THE STATES OF NEW HAMPSHIRE AND VERMONT. John
    Denison (348).

A MAP OF THE DISTRICT OF MAINE WITH NEW BRUNSWICK & NOVA
    SCOTIA (379).

A MAP OF MASSACHUSETTS FROM THE BEST AUTHORITIES. John
    Denison (393).

RHODE ISLAND AND CONNECTICUT. Harding Harris (433).

MAP OF THE STATE OF NEW YORK. John Denison (476).

NEW JERSEY (515).

PENNSYLVANIA DRAWN FROM THE BEST AUTHORITIES. Cyrus Harris
    (533).

MAP OF THE STATES OF MARYLAND AND DELAWARE. John Denison
    (566).

A MAP OF THE NORTH WESTERN TERRITORY (573).

VIRGINIA (602).

A MAP OF THE STATE OF KENTUCKY AND THE TENNESSEE GOVERNMENTS
    COMPILED FROM THE BEST AUTHORITIES. Cyrus Harris (633).

MAP OF NORTH AND SOUTH CAROLINA. John Denison (640).

A MAP OF GEORGIA AND THE TWO FLORIDAS FROM THE BEST
AUTHORITIES. Amos Doolittle (693).

WEST INDIES FROM THE BEST AUTHORITIES. Amos Doolittle (760).

CHART OF THE WORLD ON MERCATORS PROJECTION. Amos Doolittle
(786).

E-30826
Morse, Jedidiah. Elements of Geography. 2nd ed. Boston: Thomas
and Andrews, 1796.

CHART OF THE WORLD ON MERCATORS PROJECTION (F).

MAP OF THE UNITED STATES (74).

E-30827
Morse, Jedidiah. Geography Made Easy. 5th ed. Boston: Thomas and
Andrews, 1796.

THE WORLD (F).

ARTIFICIAL SPHERE (17).

COPERNICAN SYSTEM [SOLAR SYSTEM] (17).

MAP OF THE UNITED STATES (66).

EUROPE (312).

ASIA (364).

A MAP OF THE TRAVELS AND VOYAGES OF ST. PAUL (367).

PALESTINE OR THE HOLY LAND (371).

THE JOURNEYINGS OF OUR SAVIOR JESUS CHRIST (372).

AFRICA (393).

E-31078
Reid, John. The American Atlas. New York: John Reid, 1796.

A GENERAL MAP OF NORTH AMERICA DRAWN FROM THE BEST SURVEYS
(1).

A GENERAL MAP OF SOUTH AMERICA FROM THE BEST SURVEYS (2).

AN ACCURATE MAP OF THE UNITED STATES OF AMERICA ACCORDING TO THE TREATY OF PEACE OF 1783 (3).

THE STATE OF NEW HAMPSHIRE COMPILED CHIEFLY FROM ACTUAL SURVEYS (4).

THE PROVINCE OF MAINE FROM THE BEST AUTHORITIES (5).

THE STATE OF MASSACHUSETTS FROM THE BEST INFORMATION (6).

VERMONT FROM THE LATEST AUTHORITIES (7).

THE STATE OF RHODE ISLAND FROM THE LATEST SURVEYS (8).

CONNECTICUT FROM THE BEST AUTHORITIES (9).

THE STATE OF NEW YORK COMPILED FROM THE MOST AUTHENTIC INFORMATION (10).

THE STATE OF NEW JERSEY COMPILED FROM THE MOST ACCURATE SURVEYS (11).

THE STATE OF PENNSYLVANIA FROM THE LATEST SURVEYS (12).

THE STATES OF MARYLAND AND DELAWARE FROM THE LATEST SURVEYS (13).

THE STATE OF VIRGINIA FROM THE BEST AUTHORITIES (14).

MAP OF THE STATE OF KENTUCKY WITH THE ADJOINING TERRITORIES (15).

THE STATE OF NORTH CAROLINA FROM THE BEST AUTHORITIES (16).

THE STATE OF SOUTH CAROLINA FROM THE BEST AUTHORITIES (17).

A MAP OF THE TENNASSEE GOVERNMENT FORMERLY PART OF NORTH CAROLINA FROM THE LATEST SURVEYS (18).

GEORGIA FROM THE LATEST AUTHORITIES (19).

AN ACCURATE MAP OF THE WEST INDIES WITH THE ADJACENT COAST OF AMERICA (20).

PLAN OF THE CITY OF WASHINGTON IN THE TERRITORY OF COLUMBIA CEDED BY THE STATES OF VIRGINIA AND MARYLAND TO THE UNITED STATES OF AMERICA AND BY THEM ESTABLISHED AS THE SEAT OF THEIR GOVERNMENT AFTER THE YEAR 1800 (21).

E-31158
Samoual, Jean Baptiste. Description of a Plantation Situated at
     Petit St. Louis, Near Port-de-Paix, in the Northern Part of
     Hispaniola. Boston: s.n., 1796.

     PLAN OF THE PLANTATION OF M. SAMOUAL SITUATED IN THE
          DISTRICT OF THE RIVER BARE AT PORT ST. LOUIS OF THE
          NORTH (B).

E-31235
Stephens, Thomas. Stephen's Philadelphia Directory for 1796.
     Philadelphia: William Woodward, 1796.

     STEPHEN'S PLAN OF THE CITY OF PHILADELPHIA (B).

E-31517
Volney, Constantin. The Ruins. New York: William Davis, 1796.

     [WORLD: EASTERN HEMISPHERE] (12).

     A VIEW OF THE ASTROLOGICAL HEAVEN OF THE ANCIENTS TO EXPLAIN
          THE MYSTERIES OF THE PERSIAN, JEWISH & CHRISTIAN
          RELIGIONS (12).

E-31619
West, John. The Boston Directory. Boston: Manning and Loring, for
     John West, 1796.

     A PLAN OF BOSTON. Osgood Carleton (B).

E-31626
A CORRECT MAP OF THE STATE OF VERMONT FROM ACTUAL SURVEY:
     EXHIBITING THE COUNTY AND TOWN LINES, RIVERS, LAKES, PONDS,
     MOUNTAINS, MEETING HOUSES, MILLS, PUBLIC ROADS, ETC. James
     Whitelaw. Rutland, VT: Samuel Williams, 1796.

E-31647
Winterbotham, William. An Historical, Geographical, Commercial,
     and Philosophical View of the United States of America, and
     of the European Settlements in America and the West Indies.
     Volume 3. New York: Tiebout and O'Brien, for John Reid,
     1796.

     PLAN OF LYSTRA, IN NELSON COUNTY, KENTUCKY (142).

     PLAN OF FRANKLINVILLE IN MASON COUNTY, KENTUCKY (144).

E-31661
Workman, Benjamin. Elemants of Geography. 6th ed. Philadelphia:
    John M'Culloch, 1796.

    WORLD (F).

    THE SOLAR SYSTEM (6).

    NORTH AMERICA (67).

    UNITED STATES (83).

    SOUTH AMERICA (107).

    EUROPE (111).

    ASIA (139).

    AFRICA (143).

E-31664
The World Displayed. Volume 8. Philadelphia: John Thompson, for
    Dobelbower, Key, and Simpson, 1796.

    A CHART OF THE SOUTHERN HEMISPHERE, SHEWING THE TRACT OF
        CAPTAIN COOK'S LAST VOYAGE (36).

E-31860
Braam Houckgeest, Andreas Everard van. Voyage de l'Ambassade
    de la Compagnie des Indes Orientales Hollandaises, Vers
    l'Empereur de la Chine, Dans les Années 1794 & 1795.
    Philadelphia: s.n., 1797.

    DE LA CHINE DRESSEE POUR SERVIR AU VOYAGE DE L'AMBASSADE DE
        LA COMPAGNIE DES INDES HOLLANDAISES VERS L'EMPEREUR DE
        LA CHINE (B).

    A MAP OF CHINA DESIGNED FOR THE VOYAGE OF THE EMBASSY OF THE
        DUTCH EAST INDIA COMPANY TO THE EMPEROR OF CHINA (B).

E-32253
THIS PLAN OF THE CITY OF PHILADELPHIA AND ITS ENVIRONS IS
    DEDICATED TO THE MAYOR, ALDERMEN AND CITIZENS THEREOF. John
    Hills. Philadelphia: John Hills, 1797.

E-32378
MAP OF THE UNITED STATES: COMPILED CHIEFLY FROM THE STATE, MAPS
    AND OTHER AUTHENTIC INFORMATION. Samuel Lewis. Philadelphia:
    Mathew Carey, 1797.

E-32399
M'Culloch, John. A Concise History of the United States, from the
    Discovery of America Till 1795. Philadelphia, John
    M'Culloch, 1797.

    THE UNITED STATES OF AMERICA (F).

E-32415
Malham, John. The Naval Gazetteer. 2 volumes. Boston: Samuel
    Etheridge, for Spotswood and Nancrede, 1797.

    A GENERAL CHART OF THE WORLD ON MERCATOR'S PROJECTION,
        EXHIBITING ALL THE NEW DISCOVERIES AND THE TRACKS OF
        THE DIFFERED CIRCUMNAVIGATORS. Volume 1 (F).

    A CORRECT CHART OF THE WEST COAST OF AFRICA. Volume 1 (14).

    A CORRECT CHART OF THE SOUTHERN COASTS OF AFRICA FROM THE
        EQUATOR TO THE CAPE OF GOOD HOPE. Volume 1 (14)

    A CORRECT CHART OF THE EAST COAST OF NORTH AMERICA. Volume 1
        (30).

    A CORRECT CHART OF THE WEST COAST OF NORTH AMERICA FROM
        BHERING'S STRAITS TO NOOTKA SOUND. Volume 1 (30).

    A CORRECT CHART OF THE COASTS OF SOUTH AMERICA FROM THE
        EQUATOR TO CAPE HORN. Volume 1 (32).

    A CORRECT CHART OF THE BALTIC SEA. Volume 1 (70).

    A CORRECT CHART OF THE BAY OF BISCAY. Volume 1 (102).

    A CORRECT CHART OF THE ENGLISH CHANNEL. Volume 1 (192).

    A CORRECT CHART OF THE WEST INDIA ISLANDS. Volume 1 (524).

    A CORRECT CHART OF THE IRISH SEA, WITH ST. GEORGES CHANNEL.
        Volume 1 (526).

    A CORRECT CHART OF THE COAST OF PORTUGAL. Volume 2 (49).

    A CORRECT CHART OF THE COASTS OF HINDOSTAN. Volume 2 (92).

A CORRECT CHART OF THE MEDITERRANEAN SEA. Volume 2 (132).

A CORRECT CHART OF THE NORTH SEA. Volume 2 (202).

A CORRECT CHART OF THE INDIAN OCEAN. Volume 2 (208).

A CORRECT CHART OF THE GERMAN SEA. Volume 2 (488).

E-32493
Moore, John. A Journal During a Residence in France, from the
    Beginning of August, to the Middle of December, 1792.
    Chambersburg, PA: Andrew Dover, for Mathew Carey, 1797.

    A MAP OF GENERAL DUMOURIER'S CAMPAIGN IN THE MEUSE IN 1792
        (B).

E-32504
Moreau de St. Mery, Mederic. Description Topographique,
    Physique, Civile, Politique et Historique de la Partie
    Francaise de l'Isle Saint Domingue. Philadelphia: Mederic
    Moreau de St. Mery, 1797.

    CARTE DE L'ISLE ST. DOMINGUE (F).

E-32509
Morse, Jedidiah. The American Gazetteer. Boston: Samuel Hall and
    Thomas and Andrews, 1797.

    A NEW MAP OF NORTH AMERICA SHEWING ALL THE NEW DISCOVERIES
        (F).

    A MAP OF SOUTH AMERICA AND THE THE ADJACENT ISLANDS (UP).

    A CORRECT MAP OF THE GEORGIA WESTERN TERRITORY (UP).

    MAP OF THE NORTHERN PARTS OF THE UNITED STATES OF AMERICA.
        Abraham Bradley (UP).

    MAP OF THE SOUTHERN PARTS OF THE UNITED STATES OF AMERICA.
        Abraham Bradley (UP).

    CHART OF THE NEW DISCOVERIES EAST OF NEW HOLLAND AND NEW
        GUINEA (UP).

    WEST INDIES FROM THE BEST AUTHORITIES (UP).

E-32510
Morse, Jedidiah. <u>A Description of the Soil, Productions,</u>
    <u>Commercial Agricultural and Local Advantages of the Georgia</u>
    <u>Western Territory</u>. Boston: Thomas and Andrews, 1797.

    A CORRECT MAP OF THE GEORGIA TERRITORY (F).

E-32796
Saint Pierre, Jacques. <u>Studies of Nature</u>. Volume 1. Worcester,
    MA: Isaiah Thomas, for Joseph Nancrede, 1797.

    ATLANTIC HEMISPHERE, WITH ITS CHANNEL, ITS ICES, ITS
        CURRENTS AND ITS TIDES IN THE MONTHS OF JANUARY AND
        FEBRUARY (218).

E-32797
Saint Pierre, Jacques. <u>A Vindication of Divine Providence</u>.
    2 volumes. Worcester, MA: Isaiah Thomas, for Joseph
    Nancrede, 1797.

    ATLANTIC HEMISPHERE, WITH ITS CHANNEL, ITS ICES, ITS
        CURRENTS AND ITS TIDES IN THE MONTHS OF JANUARY AND
        FEBRUARY. Volume 1 (54).

E-32841
Smith, Charles. <u>The American Gazetteer</u>. New York: Alexander
    Menut, for Charles Smith, 1797.

    UNITED STATES OF AMERICA (B).

E-32842
Smith, Charles. <u>The American War from 1775 to 1783</u>. New York:
    Charles Smith, 1797.

    A PLAN OF THE ACTION AT BREEDS HILL ON THE 17TH OF JUNE 1775
        BETWEEN THE AMERICAN FORCES AND THE BRITISH TROOPS (5).

    MAP OF THE CITY OF QUEBEC (16).

    THE ENGAGEMENT ON THE WHITE PLAINS THE 28TH OF OCTOBER 1776,
        BETWEEN THE THE AMERICAN AND BRITISH FORCES (37).

    PLAN OF THE SIEGE OF SAVANNAH (88).

    PLAN OF THE POSITION WHICH THE ARMY UNDER THE LT. GENL.
        BURGOINE TOOK AT SARATOGA ON THE 10TH OF SEPTEMBER 1777
        AND IN WHICH IT REMAINED TILL THE CONVENTION WAS SIGNED
        (56).

PLAN OF THE SIEGE OF CHARLESTOWN IN SOUTH CAROLINA (100).

A PLAN OF THE INVESTMENT OF YORK AND GLOUCESTER VIRGINIA (166).

E-32868
Stafford, Cornelius. The Philadelphia Directory, for 1797.
Philadelphia: William Woodward, for Cornelius Stafford, 1797.

PLAN OF THE CITY OF PHILADELPHIA (F).

E-32942
Trumbull, Benjamin. A Complete History of Connecticut. Hartford, CT: Hudson and Goodwin, 1797.

A CORRECT MAP OF CONNECTICUT FROM ACTUAL SURVEY. Amos Doolittle (F).

E-33448
Braam Houckgeest, Andreas Everard van. Voyage de L'Ambassade de la Compagnie des Indes Orientales Hollandaises, vers L'Empereur de la Chine, dans les Annees 1794 & 1795. Philadelphia: s.n., 1797.

PLAN OF THE CITY OF MACAO IN CHINA POSSESSED BY THE PORTUGUESE (B).

E-33682
Encyclopaedia; or, a Dictionary of Arts, Sciences, and Miscellaneous Literature. Volume 7. Philadelphia: Thomas Dobson, 1798.

EUROPE (40).

FRANCE (446).

[DESCRIPTION OF THE TERRESTRIAL GLOBE, WITH FOUR VIEWS] (650).

A MAP OF THE WORLD IN THREE SECTIONS DESCRIBING THE POLAR REGION TO THE TROPICS (662).

MAP OF THE WORLD COMPREHENDING THE LATEST DISCOVERIES (662).

E-33684
Encyclopaedia; or, a Dictionary of Arts, Sciences, and
    Miscellaneous Literature. Volume 9. Philadelphia: Thomas
    Dobson, 1798.

    EAST INDIES (218).

    WEST INDIES (218).

    IRELAND (344).

    ITALY (390).

E-33692
Encyclopaedia; or, a Dictionary of Arts, Sciences, and
    Miscellaneous Literature. Volume 17. Philadelphia: Thomas
    Dobson, 1798.

    SPAIN AND PORTUGAL (620).

E-33753
THE PLAN OF THE FRENCH INVASION OF ENGLAND AND IRELAND, BY THE
    COMBINED NAVAL AND MILITARY FORCE OF FRANCE, SPAIN, AND
    HOLLAND. Philadelphia: James Carey, 1798.

E-33794
Gibson, James. Atlas Minimus. Philadelphia: Mathew Carey, 1798.

    THE WORLD. Joseph Scott (1).

    EUROPE (2).

    ASIA (3).

    AFRICA (4).

    NORTH AMERICA (5).

    SOUTH AMERICA (6).

    BRITAIN AND IRELAND (7).

    ENGLAND AND WALES (8).

    SCOTLAND (9).

    IRELAND (10).

    THE UNITED PROVINCES (11).

NETHERLANDS (12).

FRANCE DIVIDED INTO DEPARTMENTS (13).

SPAIN AND PORTUGAL (14).

ITALY (15).

SWITZERLAND WITH ITS ALLIES (16).

GERMANY DIVIDED INTO CIRCLES (17).

THE NORTH EAST PART OF GERMANY (18).

THE NORTH WEST PART OF GERMANY (19).

THE SOUTH EAST PART OF GERMANY (20).

THE SOUTH WEST PART OF GERMANY (21).

HUNGARY (22).

POLAND (23).

PRUSSIA (24).

DENMARK (25).

SWEDEN AND NORWAY (26).

RUSSIA IN EUROPE (27).

TURKEY IN EUROPE (28).

NAPLES AND SICILY (29).

TURKEY IN ASIA (30).

PERSIA (31).

INDIA ON BOTH SIDES OF THE GANGES (32).

EAST INDIA ISLANDS (33).

RUSSIA IN ASIA (34).

CHINA (35).

BARBARY (36).

NEGROLAND AND GUINEA (37).

EGYPT, NUBIA AND ABISSINIA (38).

BRASIL (39).

PARAGUAY AND TUCUMAN (40).

PERU (41).

E-33796
Gifford, John. The History of France: From the Earliest Times,
    to the Complete Establishment of the Republic. Volume 4.
    Philadelphia: Stewart and Rowson, 1798.

    FRANCE DIVIDED INTO CIRCLES AND DEPARTMENTS (F).

    SKETCH OF THE HARBOUR AND ENVIRONS OF TOULON (422).

E-34137
Moreau de St. Mery, Mederic. Description Topographique,
    Physique, Civile, Politique et Historique de la Partie
    Francaise de L'Isle Saint Dominique. 2 volumes.
    Philadelphia: Mederic Moreau de St. Mery, 1798.

    CARTE DE L'ISLE ST. DOMINGUE. Volume 2 (B).

E-34138
Moreau de St. Mery, Mederic. A Topographical and Political
    Description of the Spanish Part of Saint Domingo. 2 volumes.
    Philadelphia: Mederic Moreau de St. Mery, 1796.

    CARTE DE L'ISLE ST. DOMINGUE. Volume 2 (B).

E-34143
Morse, Jedidiah. An Abridgement of the American Gazetteer.
    Boston: Thomas and Andrews, 1798.

    A MAP OF NORTH AMERICA FROM THE LATEST DISCOVERIES (F).

E-34145
Morse, Jedidiah. Elements of Geography. 3rd ed. Boston: Thomas
    and Andrews, 1798.

    CHART OF THE WORLD ON MERCATORS PROJECTION (F).

    A MAP OF THE UNITED STATES OF AMERICA (74).

E-34146
Morse, Jedidiah. Geography Made Easy. 6th ed. Boston: Thomas and
    Andrews, 1798.

    A NEW MAP OF THE WORLD: WITH THE LATEST DISCOVERIES (F).

    A MAP OF NORTH AMERICA FROM THE LATEST DISCOVERIES (76).

E-34147
Morse, Jedidiah. The History of America. 3rd ed. Philadelphia:
    Thomas Dobson, 1798.

    SOUTH AMERICA FROM THE BEST AUTHORITIES (F).

    A GENERAL MAP OF NORTH AMERICA FROM THE BEST AUTHORITIES
        (141).

E-34316
Payne, John. A New and Complete System of Universal Geography.
    Volume 1. New York: John Low, 1798.

    THE WORLD FROM THE BEST AUTHORITIES (F).

    GENERAL CHART ON MERCATORS PROJECTION (v).

    ASIA FROM THE LATEST AUTHORITIES (3).

    EAST INDIES FROM THE BEST AUTHORITIES (312).

E-34317
A MAP OF THE CONNECTICUT WESTERN RESERVE, FROM ACTUAL SURVEY.
    Seth Pease. New Haven, CT: Amos Doolittle, 1798.

E-34421
Proud, Robert. The History of Pennsylvania, in North America.
    Volume 2. Philadelphia: Zachariah Poulson, 1798.

    A MAP OF PENNSYLVANIA DELAWARE NEW JERSEY & MARYLAND, WITH
        THE PARTS ADJACENT (F).

E-35005
West, John. The Boston Directory. Boston: Rhoades and Laughton,
    1798.

    A PLAN OF BOSTON, FROM ACTUAL SURVEY. John West, for Osgood
        Carleton (F).

E-35033
Williamson, Charles. Description of the Genesee Country. Albany:
    Ebenezer Andrews, 1798.

    A MAP OF THE MIDDLE STATES SHEWING THE SITUATION OF THE
        GENESEE LANDS AND THEIR CONNECTION WITH THE ATLANTIC
        COAST (B).

    MAP OF ONTARIO AND STEUBEN COUNTIES (B).

E-35834
Moore, John Hamilton. The New Practical Navigator. Newburyport:
    Edmund Blunt, 1799.

    THE SOLAR SYSTEM (51).

    GEOGRAPHICAL CIRCLES AND ZONES: THE ARTIFICIAL SPHERE OR
        GLOBE (54).

    A CHART FROM ENGLAND TO THE CAPE VERDE ISLANDS (126).

    CITY AND BAY OF GAYETTE (278).

E-36047
Payne, John. New and Complete System of Universal Geography.
    Volumes 3 and 4. New York: John Low, 1799.

    EUROPE. Volume 3 (3).

    RUSSIA OR MUSCOVY IN EUROPE FROM THE LATEST AUTHORITIES.
        Volume 3 (22).

    POLAND. Volume 3 (63).

    SWEDEN DENMARK & NORWAY FROM THE LATEST AUTHORITIES.
        Volume 3 (75).

    GERMANY AND THE NETHERLANDS, FROM THE LATEST AUTHORITIES.
        Volume 3 (148).

    SWITZERLAND. Volume 3 (224).

    ITALY. Volume 3 (241).

    SPAIN AND PORTUGAL. Volume 3 (298).

    THE SEVEN UNITED PROVINCES. Volume 3 (358).

A NEW MAP OF SCOTLAND FROM THE LATEST AUTHORITIES.
Volume 3 (377).

ENGLAND AND WALES. Volume 3 (414).

IRELAND FROM THE LATEST AUTHORITIES. Volume 3 (577).

A NEW AND ACCURATE MAP OF FRANCE DIVIDED INTO DEPARTMENTS,
WITH THE NETHERLANDS, &C. Volume 3 (607).

DISPOSITION OF THE ENGLISH & FRENCH FLEETS AT THE
COMMENCEMENT OF THE ACTION, AUGUST 1ST, 1798. Volume 3
(698).

EGYPT FROM THE BEST AUTHORITIES. Volume 3 (701).

THE NETHERLANDS WITH ROADS FROM THE LATEST AUTHORITIES.
Volume 3 (708).

A MAP OF NORTH AMERICA FROM THE LATEST AUTHORITIES. Volume 4
(11).

THE UNITED STATES OF AMERICA. Volume 4 (50).

VERMONT FROM THE LATEST AUTHORITIES. Volume 4 (229*).

THE STATE OF NEW HAMPSHIRE COMPILED CHIEFLY FROM ACTUAL
SURVEYS. Volume 4 (229).

THE STATE OF MASSACHUSETTS FROM THE BEST INFORMATION.
Volume 4 (235).

THE PROVINCE OF MAINE FROM THE BEST AUTHORITIES. Volume 4
(253).

RHODE ISLAND. Volume 4 (258).

A NEW MAP OF CONNECTICUT FROM THE BEST AUTHORITIES. Volume 4
(270).

THE STATE OF NEW YORK FROM THE BEST INFORMATION. Volume 4
(296).

THE STATE OF NEW JERSEY. Volume 4 (320).

THE STATE OF PENNSYLVANIA FROM THE LATEST SURVEYS. Volume 4
(329).

THE STATES OF MARYLAND AND DELAWARE FROM THE LATEST SURVEYS.
Volume 4 (344).

THE STATE OF VIRGINIA FROM THE BEST AUTHORITIES. Volume 4
     (385).

THE STATE OF KENTUCKY WITH THE ADJOINING TERRITORIES FROM
     THE LATEST AUTHORITIES. Volume 4 (404).

NORTH CAROLINA FROM THE BEST AUTHORITIES. Volume 4 (414).

MAP OF THE TENNASSEE GOVERNMENT FROM THE LATEST AUTHORITIES.
     Volume 4 (422).

THE STATE OF SOUTH CAROLINA FROM THE BEST AUTHORITIES.
     Volume 4 (429).

GEORGIA FROM THE LATEST AUTHORITIES. Volume 4 (438).

SOUTH AMERICA FROM THE BEST SURVEYS. Volume 4 (461).

WEST INDIES. Volume 4 (486).

A CHART SHEWING THE TRACT OF CAPTAIN COOK'S LAST VOYAGE.
     Volume 4 (521).

E-36122
Pinckney, Charles. Three Letters, Addressed to the People of the
     United States. Charleston, SC: Thomas Cox, 1799.

     [NORTH ATLANTIC OCEAN] (B).

E-36202
Remmey, John. An Account of the Present State of Egypt. New York:
     Davis and Davis, 1799.

     EGYPT FROM THE BEST AUTHORITIES (8).

     DISPOSITION OF THE ENGLISH AND FRENCH FLEETS, AT THE
          COMMENCEMENT OF THE ACTION, AUGUST 1ST, 1798 (96).

E-36282
Scott, Joseph. The New and Universal Gazetteer. Volumes 1 and 2.
     Philadelphia: Bailey and Bailey, 1799.

     A NEW MAP OF THE WORLD WITH THE LATEST DISCOVERIES. Volume 1
          (F).

     A NEW MAP OF AFRICA FROM THE BEST AUTHORITIES. Volume 1
          (UP).

A NEW MAP OF NORTH AMERICA SHEWING ALL THE NEW DISCOVERIES.
Volume 1 (UP).

A NEW MAP OF SOUTH AMERICA FROM THE LATEST DISCOVERIES.
Volume 1 (UP).

A NEW MAP OF ASIA DRAWN FROM THE BEST AUTHORITIES. Volume 1
(UP).

CONNECTICUT. Volume 2 (UP).

DELAWARE. Volume 2 (UP).

AN ACCURATE MAP OF EUROPE COMPILED FROM THE BEST
AUTHORITIES. Volume 2 (UP).

GEORGIA. Volume 2 (UP).

E-36397
Tatham, William. The Political Economy of Inland Navigation,
Irrigation and Drainage. Philadelphia: s.n., 1799.

PLAN OF THE RIVER WITH THE PROPOSED DOCKS (176).

THE LONDON DOCKS (204).

THE LONDON DOCKS (282).

PLAN OF THE COMMERCIAL BASIN (364).

E-36661
Volney, Constantin. The Ruins. Philadelphia: James Lyons, 1799.

[AFRICA, ASIA AND EUROPE] (40).

A VIEW OF THE ASTROLOGICAL HEAVEN OF THE ANTIENTS TO EXPLAIN
THE MYSTERIES OF THE PERSIAN JEWISH & CHRISTIAN
RELIGIONS (292).

E-36720
Wilkinson, Eliab. The New England Calendar, and Ephemeris, for
the Year of Our Lord 1800. Warren, RI: Nathaniel Phillips,
1799.

[NORTH ATLANTIC OCEAN] (B).

E-36721
Wilkinson, Eliab. The New England Calendar, and Ephemeris, for
    the Year of Our Lord 1800. Warren, RI: Nathaniel Phillips,
    for Jacob Richardson, 1799.

    [NORTH ATLANTIC OCEAN] (B).

E-36727
Williamson, Charles. Description of the Settlement of the Genesee
    Country, in the State of New York. New York: Swords and
    Swords, 1799.

    MAP OF THE MIDDLE STATES OF NORTH AMERICA (F).

E-36740
Workman, Benjamin. Elements of Geography. 7th ed. Philadelphia:
    John M'Culloch, 1799.

    WORLD (F).

    THE SOLAR SYSTEM (6).

    NORTH AMERICA (67).

    THE UNITED STATES OF AMERICA (80).

    SOUTH AMERICA (101).

    EUROPE (111).

    ASIA (138).

    AFRICA (143).

E-37024
The Boston Directory. Boston: John Russell, for John West, 1800.

    A PLAN OF BOSTON FROM ACTUAL SURVEY. Osgood Carleton (B).

E-37096
Carey, Mathew. Carey's American Atlas. Philadelphia: Mathew
    Carey, 1800.

    THE BRITISH POSSESSIONS IN NORTH AMERICA. Samuel Lewis (1).

    VERMONT FROM ACTUAL SURVEY (2).

    THE STATE OF NEW HAMPSHIRE COMPILED FROM ACTUAL SURVEYS (3).

THE PROVINCE OF MAINE FROM THE BEST AUTHORITIES (4).

THE STATE OF MASSACHUSETTS COMPILED FROM THE BEST
    AUTHORITIES (5).

THE STATE OF RHODE ISLAND COMPILED FROM THE SURVEYS AND
    OBSERVATIONS OF CALEB HARRIS. Harding Harris (6).

CONNECTICUT FROM THE BEST AUTHORITIES (7).

THE STATE OF NEW YORK COMPILED FROM THE BEST AUTHORITIES.
    Samuel Lewis (8).

THE STATE OF NEW JERSEY COMPILED FROM THE MOST AUTHENTIC
    INFORMATION (9).

THE STATE OF PENNSYLVANIA REDUCED WITH PERMISSION FROM
    READING HOWELL'S MAP (10).

DELAWARE FROM THE BEST AUTHORITIES (11).

THE STATE OF MARYLAND FROM THE BEST AUTHORITIES (12).

THE STATE OF VIRGINIA FROM THE BEST AUTHORITIES (13).

THE STATE OF NORTH CAROLINA FROM THE BEST AUTHORITIES, &C.
    (14).

THE STATE OF SOUTH CAROLINA FROM THE BEST AUTHORITIES (15).

GEORGIA FROM THE BEST AUTHORITIES (16).

KENTUCKY REDUCED FROM ELIHU BARKER'S LARGE MAP (17).

A MAP OF THE TENNASSEE STATE FORMERLY PART OF NORTH CAROLINA
    (18).

A MAP OF SOUTH AMERICA ACCORDING TO THE BEST AUTHORITIES
    (19).

A CHART OF THE WEST INDIES FROM THE LATEST MARINE JOURNALS
    AND SURVEYS (20).

A MAP OF THE COUNTRIES SITUATED ABOUT THE NORTH POLE (21).

A MAP OF THE DISCOVERIES MADE BY CAPTAINS COOK AND CLERKE IN
    THE YEAR 1778 AND 1779 BETWEEN THE EASTERN COAST OF
    ASIA AND THE WESTERN COAST OF NORTH AMERICA (22).

A MAP OF THE AMERICAN LAKES AND ADJOINING COUNTRY. Isaac
    Brock (23).

61

E-37097
Carey, Mathew. <u>Carey's General Atlas</u>. Philadelphia: Mathew Carey, 1800.

A MAP OF THE WORLD FROM THE BEST AUTHORITIES (1).

A CHART OF THE WORLD ACCORDING TO MERCATORS PROJECTION SHEWING THE LATEST DISCOVERIES OF CAPTAIN COOK (2).

AN ACCURATE MAP OF EUROPE FROM THE BEST AUTHORITIES (3).

SWEDEN, DENMARK, NORWAY AND FINLAND FROM THE BEST AUTHORITIES (4).

THE RUSSIAN EMPIRE IN EUROPE AND ASIA (5).

SCOTLAND WITH THE PRINCIPAL ROADS FROM THE BEST AUTHORITIES (6).

AN ACCURATE MAP OF ENGLAND AND WALES WITH THE PRINCIPAL ROADS FROM THE BEST AUTHORITIES (7).

A MAP OF IRELAND ACCORDING TO THE BEST AUTHORITIES (8).

THE SEVEN UNITED PROVINCES OF HOLLAND, FREISLAND, GRONINGEN, GELDERS, UTRECHT, OVERYSSEL AND ZEALAND (9).

THE AUSTRIAN, FRENCH AND DUTCH NETHERLANDS FROM THE BEST AUTHORITIES (10).

THE EMPIRE OF GERMANY WITH THE 13 CANTONS OF SWITZERLAND FROM THE BEST AUTHORITIES (11).

FRANCE DIVIDED INTO CIRCLES AND DEPARTMENTS (12).

A MAP OF THE SEAT OF WAR IN FRANCE, WITH THE COUNTRY DIVIDED INTO ITS SEVERAL DEPARTMENTS (13).

TURKEY IN EUROPE AND HUNGARY, FROM THE BEST AUTHORITIES (14).

SPAIN AND PORTUGAL FROM THE BEST AUTHORITIES (15).

ITALY, AND SARDINIA, FROM THE BEST AUTHORITIES (16).

POLAND, SHEWING THE CLAIMS OF RUSSIA, PRUSSIA AND AUSTRIA UNTIL THE LATE DEPREDATIONS (17).

ASIA, ACCORDING TO THE BEST AUTHORITIES (19).

CHINA, DIVIDED INTO ITS GREAT PROVINCES, ACCORDING TO THE BEST AUTHORITIES (20).

AN ACCURATE MAP OF HINDOSTAN OR INDIA FROM THE BEST
    AUTHORITIES (21).

AFRICA, ACCORDING TO THE BEST AUTHORITIES (22).

THE BRITISH POSSESSIONS IN NORTH AMERICA FROM THE BEST
    AUTHORITIES (23).

A MAP OF THE UNITED STATES, COMPILED CHIEFLY FROM THE STATE
    MAPS AND OTHER AUTHENTIC INFORMATION. Samuel Lewis
    (24).

VERMONT FROM ACTUAL SURVEY (25).

THE STATE OF NEW HAMPSHIRE COMPILED CHIEFLY FROM ACTUAL
    SURVEYS. Samuel Lewis (26).

THE PROVINCE OF MAINE FROM THE BEST AUTHORITIES (27).

THE STATE OF MASSACHUSETTS COMPILED FROM THE BEST
    AUTHORITIES (28).

THE STATE OF RHODE ISLAND COMPILED FROM THE SURVEYS AND
    OBSERVATIONS OF CALEB HARRIS (29).

CONNECTICUT FROM THE BEST AUTHORITIES (30).

THE STATE OF NEW YORK COMPILED FROM THE BEST AUTHORITIES.
    Samuel Lewis (31).

THE STATE OF NEW JERSEY COMPILED FROM THE MOST AUTHENTIC
    INFORMATION (32).

THE STATE OF PENNSYLVANIA REDUCED WITH PERMISSION FROM
    READING HOWELL'S MAP. Samuel Lewis (33).

DELAWARE FROM THE BEST AUTHORITIES (34).

THE STATE OF MARYLAND FROM THE BEST AUTHORITIES (35).

THE STATE OF VIRGINIA FROM THE BEST AUTHORITIES. Samuel
    Lewis (36).

THE STATE OF NORTH CAROLINA FROM THE BEST AUTHORITIES, &C
    (37).

THE STATE OF SOUTH CAROLINA FROM THE BEST AUTHORITIES (38).

GEORGIA FROM THE LATEST AUTHORITIES (39).

KENTUCKY, REDUCED FROM ELIHU BARKER'S LARGE MAP (40).

A MAP OF THE TENNASSEE STATE FORMERLY PART OF NORTH CAROLINA TAKEN CHIEFLY FROM THE SURVEY BY GENERAL S. SMITH AND OTHERS (41).

A MAP OF SOUTH AMERICA ACCORDING TO THE BEST AUTHORITIES (42).

A CHART OF THE WEST INDIES, FROM THE LATEST MARINE JOURNALS AND SURVEYS (43).

A MAP OF THE COUNTRIES SITUATED ABOUT THE NORTH POLE (44).

A MAP OF THE DISCOVERIES MADE BY CAPTAINS COOK AND CLERKE IN THE YEAR 1778 AND 1779 BETWEEN THE EASTERN COAST OF ASIA AND THE WESTERN COAST OF NORTH AMERICA (45).

PART OF THE SEVEN RANGES OF TOWNSHIPS BEING PART OF THE TERRITORY OF THE UNITED STATES, NW OF THE RIVER OHIO (46).

A MAP OF PART OF THE NW TERRITORY OF THE UNITED STATES COMPILED FROM ACTUAL SURVEYS AND THE BEST INFORMATION (47).

A MAP OF THE FRENCH PART OF ST. DOMINGO (48).

A MAP OF THOSE COUNTRIES IN WHICH THE APOSTLES TRAVELLED, IN PROPAGATING CHRISTIANITY (49).

E-37991
Moore, John Hamilton. The New and Practical Navigator. 2nd ed. Newburyport, MA: Edmund Blunt, 1800.

THE SOLAR SYSTEM (48).

GEOGRAPHICAL CIRCLES AND ZONES THE ARTIFICIAL SPHERE AND GLOBE (50).

A CHART FROM ENGLAND TO THE CAPE VERDE ISLANDS (109).

CITY AND BAY OF GAYETTE (259).

E-38004
Morse, Jedidiah. Geography Made Easy. 7th ed. Boston: Thomas and Andrews, 1800.

A NEW MAP OF THE WORLD WITH THE LATEST DISCOVERIES (F).

A MAP OF NORTH AMERICA FROM THE LATEST DISCOVERIES (67).

E-38188
Park, Mungo. <u>Travels in the Interior Parts of Africa</u>.
    Philadelphia: James Humphreys, 1800.

    THE ROUTE OF MR. MUNGO PARK, FROM PISANIA IN THE RIVER
        GAMBIA TO SILLA, ON THE RIVER JOLIBA OR NIGER. J.
        Renuell (F).

E-38189
Park, Mungo. <u>Travels in the Interior Parts of Africa</u>. New York:
    John Tiebout, 1800.

    THE ROUTE OF MR. MUNGO PARK, FROM PISANIA IN THE RIVER
        GAMBIA TO SILLA, ON THE RIVER JOLIBA OR NIGER. J.
        Renuell (F).

E-38199
Payne, John. <u>New and Complete System of Universal Geography</u>.
    Volume 2. New York: John Low, 1800.

    AFRICA FROM THE BEST AUTHORITIES (3).

    A CORRECT MAP OF THE MEDITERRANEAN SEA WITH THE COUNTRIES
        ADJACENT (346).

E-38473
Scott, Joseph. <u>The New and Universal Gazetteer</u>. Volumes 3 and 4.
    Philadelphia: Patterson and Cochran, 1800.

    KENTUCKY. Volume 3 (UP).

    MAINE. Volume 3 (UP).

    MARYLAND. Volume 3 (UP).

    MASSACHUSETTS. Volume 3 (UP).

    NEW HAMPSHIRE. Volume 4 (UP).

    NEW JERSEY. Volume 4 (UP).

    NEW YORK. Volume 4 (UP).

    NORTH CAROLINA. Volume 4 (UP).

    PENNSYLVANIA. Volume 4. (UP).

    RHODE ISLAND. Volume 4 (UP).

SOUTH CAROLINA. Volume 4 (UP).

TENNASSEE. Volume 4 (UP).

N.W. TERRITORY. Volume 4 (UP).

THE UNITED STATES OF AMERICA. William Barker. Volume 4 (UP).

STATE OF VERMONT. Volume 4 (UP).

VIRGINIA. Volume 4 (UP).

E-39109
Williamson, Charles. Observations on the Proposed State Road,
    from Hudson's River...to Lake Erie. New York: Swords and
    Swords, 1800.

    MAP OF THE MIDDLE STATES OF NORTH AMERICA (F).

E-39117
Winchester, Elhanan. A Course of Lectures on the Prophecies that
    Remain to be Fulfilled. Volume 2. Walpole, NH: David
    Carlisle, for Thomas and Thomas, 1800.

    A VIEW OF THE DIVISION OF THE LAND OF CANAAN AMONG THE 12
        TRIBES OF ISRAEL (F).

E-40647
At a Meeting of the Proprietors of the Township of Brunswick in
    the County of York. Boston: s.n., 1753.

    A TRUE COPY FROM AN ACTUAL PLAN OF E. HUTCHINSON'S ENGRAVING
        [BRUNSWICK, ME] (B).

E-41172
TO HIS EXCELLENCY EDWD CORNWALLIS...THIS MAP... OF NOVA SCOTIA
    AND PARTS ADJACENT IS HUMBLY PRESENTED. 2nd ed. James
    Turner. Philadelphia: Andrew Hook, 1760.

E-42370
Remarks: The Common Rates of Land Carriage. Philadelphia: s.n.,
    1772.

    [MIDDLE STATES OF THE UNITED STATES SHOWING ROADS AND
        CANALS] (F).

E-42702
Smith, William. An Examination of the Connecticut Claim to Lands
in Pennsylvania. Philadelphia: Joseph Crukshank, 1774.

[CONNECTICUT, NEW YORK AND PENNSYLVANIA] (31).

E-42771
Bickerstaff's Albany Almanack for the Year of Our Lord, 1776.
Albany: Alexander and Robertson, 1775.

PLAN OF BOSTON (1).

E-43142
A PLAN OF THE ATTACK OF FORT SULLIVAN, THE KEY OF CHARLESTOWN IN
SOUTH CAROLINA ON THE 28TH DAY OF JUNE 1776. Philadelphia:
Styner and Cist, for Daniel Humphreys, 1776.

E-43551
THE TOWNSHIPS OR GRANTS EAST OF LAKE CHAMPLAIN ARE LAID DOWN AS
GRANTED BY THE STATE OF NEW HAMPSHIRE. Bernard Romans. New
Haven, CT: s.n., 1778.

E-43609
A CHOROGRAPHICAL MAP OF THE NORTHERN DEPARTMENT OF NORTH AMERICA
DRAWN FROM THE LATEST AND MOST ACCURATE OBSERVATIONS [NEW
HAMPSHIRE GRANTS IN VERMONT]. Amos Doolittle. New Haven, CT:
Amos Doolittle, 1779.

E-44888
Franklin, Benjamin. Maritime Observations. Philadelphia: Robert
Aitken, 1786.

A CHART OF THE GULF STREAM (B).

E-46214
MAP OF THE MIDDLE STATES OF NORTH AMERICA WITH PART OF CANADA
SHEWING THE SITUATION OF THE PRINCIPAL TOWNS VIZ COLUMBIA,
BALTIMORE, PHILADELPHIA, NEW YORK, NEWPORT, (RHODE ISLAND)
BOSTON & MONTREAL ALSO THEIR SEVERAL COMMUNICATIONS WITH
RESPECT TO LAKE ONTARIO. s.l.: s.n., 1791.

E-46437
PLAN OF THE CITY OF WASHINGTON IN THE TERRITORY OF COLUMBIA CEDED
BY THE STATES OF VIRGINIA AND MARYLAND. Andrew Ellicott.
Boston: Samuel Hill, 1792.

E-47117
Moore, John. <u>A Journal During a Residence in France, from the Beginning of August, to the Middle of December, 1792</u>. Volume 2. New York: Thomas and Swords, for Berry, Rogers and Berry; Francis Childs; and Thomas Allen, 1794.

A MAP OF GENERAL DUMOURIER'S CAMPAIGN ON THE MEUSE, IN 1792. (F).

E-47413
PLAN OF THE CITY OF WASHINGTON IN THE TERRITORY OF COLUMBIA CEDED BY THE STATES OF VIRGINIA AND MARYLAND. Andrew Ellicott. New York: Reid, Wayland and Smith, 1795.

E-47908
Scott, Joseph. <u>An Atlas of the United States</u>. Philadelphia: Bailey and Bailey, 1796.

A MAP OF THE UNITED STATES (1).

MAINE (2).

NEW HAMPSHIRE (3).

STATE OF VERMONT (4).

MASSACHUSETTS (5).

RHODE ISLAND (6).

CONNECTICUT (7).

NEW YORK (8).

NEW JERSEY (9).

PENNSYLVANIA (10).

DELAWARE (11).

MARYLAND (12).

VIRGINIA (13).

NORTH CAROLINA (14).

SOUTH CAROLINA (15).

GEORGIA (16).

SW TERRITORY (17).

KENTUCKY (18).

NW TERRITORY (19).

E-48394
PLAN OF THE TOWN OF ALEXANDRIA IN THE DISTRICT OF COLUMBIA.
Philadelphia: Thomas Clarke, for Isaiah Thomas, 1798.

E-48414
Duane, William. <u>A History of the French Revolution, from Its
Commencement to the Complete Establishment of the Republic</u>.
Philadelphia: Stewart and Rowson, 1798.

FRANCE DIVIDED INTO CIRCLES AND DEPARTMENTS (F).

SKETCH OF THE HARBOUR AND ENVIRONS OF TOULON (326).

E-48553
Norman, William. <u>The American Pilot</u>. Boston: William Norman,
1798.

A CHART OF NANTUCKET SHOALS SURVEYED BY CAPT. PAUL PINKHAM
(B).

A NEW GENERAL CHART OF THE WEST INDIES FROM THE LATEST
MARINE JOURNALS AND SURVEYS. Osgood Carleton (B).

A CHART OF SOUTH CAROLINA AND GEORGIA (B).

A CHART OF THE COAST OF AMERICA FROM CAPE HATERAS TO CAPE
ROMAN (B).

A NEW AND ACCURATE CHART OF THE BAY OF CHESAPEAKE INCLUDING
DELAWARE BAY (B).

A TIDE TABLE FOR DELAWARE BAY AND RIVER (B).

OBSERVATIONS ON THE NORTH EAST CURRENT ON THE COAST OF
VIRGINIA (B).

OBSERVATIONS IN THE RIVER PATOWALICK (B).

DIRECTIONS FOR THE JAMES RIVER (B).

DIRECTIONS FOR SAILING BETWEEN THE MIDDLE GROUND AND THE
HORSE SHOE CAPE HENRY (B).

E-48580
PLAN OF THE FRENCH INVASION OF ENGLAND AND IRELAND, &C.
    Philadelphia: James Carey, 1798.

--ooOoo--

PART II:

THE AMERICAN BIBLIOGRAPHY,
1801–1819:

THE SHAW/SHOEMAKER BIBLIOGRAPHY

S-00277
Carey, Mathew. Carey's American Pocket Atlas. 2nd ed.
    Philadelphia: Heinrich Schweitzer, for Mathew Carey, 1801.

    THE UNITED STATES OF AMERICA (1).

    VERMONT FROM ACTUAL SURVEYS. Samuel Lewis (14).

    THE STATE OF NEW HAMPSHIRE. Samuel Lewis (18).

    PROVINCE OF MAINE (22).

    MASSACHUSETTS (26).

    RHODE ISLAND (34).

    CONNECTICUT (40).

    NEW YORK (46).

    NEW JERSEY (56).

    PENNSYLVANIA (62).

    DELAWARE (69).

    N.W. TERRITORY (72).

    MARYLAND (78).

    VIRGINIA (82).

    KENTUCKEY (86).

    NORTH CAROLINA (92).

    TENNASSEE: LATELY THE S.W. TERRITORY (96).

    SOUTH CAROLINA (100).

    GEORGIA (104).

S-00720
Jefferson, Thomas. Notes on the State of Virginia. Philadelphia:
    Robert Rawle, 1801.

    A MAP OF THE STATE OF VIRGINIA (F).

    AN EYE DRAUGHT OF MADISON'S CAVE (40).

    [PITTSBURG AND ENVIRONS] (41).

73

S-00721
Jefferson, Thomas. <u>Notes on the State of Virginia</u>. 3rd American
     ed. Newark: Pennington and Gould, 1801.

     A MAP OF THE STATE OF VIRGINIA (F).

     AN EYE DRAUGHT OF MADISON'S CAVE (40).

     [PITTSBURGH AND ENVIRONS] (41).

S-00722
Jefferson, Thomas. <u>Notes on the State of Virginia</u>. 3rd American
     ed. New York: Davis and Davis, for Furman and Loudon, 1801.

     A MAP OF THE STATE OF VIRGINIA (F).

     AN EYE DRAUGHT OF MADISON'S CAVE (40).

     [PITTSBURGH AND ENVIRONS] (41).

S-00723
Jefferson, Thomas. <u>Notes on the State of Virginia</u>. 4th American
     ed. New York: Jansen and Jansen, 1801.

     A MAP OF THE STATE OF VIRGINIA (F).

     AN EYE DRAUGHT OF MADISON'S CAVE (40).

     [PITTSBURGH AND ENVIRONS] (41).

S-00724
Jefferson, Thomas. <u>Notes on the State of Virginia</u>. 8th American
     ed. Boston: David Carrington, for Thomas and Andrews, 1801.

     A MAP OF THE STATE OF VIRGINIA (F).

     AN EYE DRAUGHT OF MADISON'S CAVE (40).

     [PITTSBURGH AND ENVIRONS] (41).

S-00957
Morse, Jedidiah. <u>The American Universal Geography</u>. 3rd ed.
     Boston: Thomas and Andrews, 1801.

     EUROPE FROM THE BEST AUTHORITIES (F).

     ENGLAND, SCOTLAND, IRELAND AND WALES FROM THE BEST
          AUTHORITIES. Cyrus Harris (98).

POLAND SHEWING THE CLAIMS OF RUSSIA, PRUSSIA & AUSTRIA FROM
    THE BEST AUTHORITIES (254).

SWITZERLAND WITH ITS SUBJECTS & ALLIES FROM THE BEST
    AUTHORITIES (302).

NETHERLANDS FROM THE BEST AUTHORITIES (336).

FRANCE DIVIDED INTO CIRCLES AND DEPARTMENTS (344).

ASIA FROM THE BEST AUTHORITIES (474).

PALESTINE OR THE HOLY LAND (492).

HINDOSTAN OR INDIA FROM THE BEST AUTHORITIES (524).

AFRICA FROM THE BEST AUTHORITIES (590).

S-00959
Morse, Jedidiah. _Elements of Geography_. 4th ed. Boston: Thomas
    and Andrews, 1801.

CHART OF THE WORLD ON MERCATORS PROJECTION (F).

A MAP OF THE UNITED STATES OF AMERICA (74).

S-01380
Taurinius, Zacharias. _Travels Through the Interior of Africa_.
    Charlestown, MA: Samuel Etheridge, for Larkin and Larkin,
    1801.

A MAP OF AFRICA FOR C.F. DAMBERGER'S TRAVELS (F).

S-01689
Workman, Benjamin. _Elements of Geography_. 8th ed. Philadelphia:
    John M'Culloch, 1801.

THE WORLD (F).

THE SOLAR SYSTEM (6).

NORTH AMERICA (66).

THE UNITED STATES OF AMERICA (82).

SOUTH AMERICA (106).

EUROPE (111).

ASIA (138).

AFRICA (142).

S-01755
American Philosophical Society. Transactions. Volume 5.
    Philadelphia: Budd and Bartram, for Thomas Dobson, 1802.

    [WESTERN HEMISPHERE] (86).

    [NORTH ATLANTIC OCEAN SHOWING THE GULF STREAM] (103).

    [MISSISSIPPI RIVER] (220).

    [MOBILE RIVER] (236).

    [CHATOHOCHEE OR APALACHICOLA RIVER] (276).

    [OKEFENOKEE SWAMP] (300).

S-01842
Barrow, John. An Account of the Travels into the Interior of
    Southern Africa. 1st American ed. New York: George Hopkins,
    1802.

    GENERAL CHART OF THE COLONY OF THE CAPE OF GOOD HOPE (F).

S-01843
Barrow, John. An Account of the Travels into the Interior of
    Southern Africa. 1st American ed. New York: George Hopkins,
    for John Conrad, 1802.

    GENERAL CHART OF THE COLONY OF THE CAPE OF GOOD HOPE (F).

S-01878
Bible. Philadelphia: Mathew Carey, 1802.

    THE JOURNEYINGS OF THE CHILDREN OF ISRAEL FROM EGYPT THROUGH
        THE RED SEA AND WILDERNESS TO THE LAND OF CANAAN (F).

    CANAAN OR THE LAND OF PROMISE TO ABRAHAM AND HIS POSTERITY
        (8).

    CANAAN FROM THE TIME OF JOSHUA TO THE BABYLONIAN CAPTIVITY
        (148).

MAP OF THE ASSYRIAN, BABYLONIAN, MEDIAN AND PERSIAN EMPIRES
(171).

THE LAND OF MORIAH OR JERUSALEM AND THE ADJACENT COUNTRY
(725).

MAP OF THE COUNTRY TRAVELLED BY THE APOSTLES WITH THE VOYAGE
OF SAINT PAUL TO ROME (810).

S-01936
Bowditch, Nathaniel. The New American Navigator. Newburyport, MA:
Edmund Blunt, for Brown and Stansbury, 1802.

CHART OF THE ATLANTIC OCEAN (F).

THE SOLAR SYSTEM (72).

GEOGRAPHICAL CIRCLES AND ZONES: THE ARTIFICIAL SPHERE OR
GLOBE (74).

S-01937
Bowditch, Nathaniel. The New American Navigator. Newburyport, MA:
Edmund Blunt, for Caleb Bingham, 1802.

CHART OF THE ATLANTIC OCEAN (F).

THE SOLAR SYSTEM (72).

GEOGRAPHICAL CIRCLES AND ZONES: THE ARTIFICIAL SPHERE OR
GLOBE (74).

S-01938
Bowditch, Nathaniel. The New American Navigator. Newburyport, MA:
Cushing and Appleton, 1802.

CHART OF THE ATLANTIC OCEAN (F).

THE SOLAR SYSTEM (72).

GEOGRAPHICAL CIRCLES AND ZONES: THE ARTIFICIAL SPHERE OR
GLOBE (74).

S-01939
Bowditch, Nathaniel. The New American Navigator. Boston: Thomas
and Andrews, 1802.

CHART OF THE ATLANTIC OCEAN (F).

THE SOLAR SYSTEM (72).

GEOGRAPHICAL CIRCLES AND ZONES: THE ARTIFICIAL SPHERE OR
GLOBE (74).

S-02139
A MAP OF THE STATE OF NEW YORK. Simeon DeWitt. Albany: Gideon
Fairman, for Simeon DeWitt, 1802.

S-02140
A MAP OF THE STATE OF NEW YORK. Simeon DeWitt. New York: Gideon
Fairman, for Simeon DeWitt, 1802.

S-02159
Drayton, John. A View of South Carolina. Charleston, SC: William
P. Young, 1802.

[SOUTH CAROLINA] (F).

SKETCH OF THE SANTEE CANAL (156).

A PLAN OF THE ENTRANCE TO WINYAH BAY AT GEORGETOWN (B).

S-02568
Mackenzie, Alexander. Voyages from Montreal. New York: George
Hopkins, 1802.

A MAP OF AMERICA, BETWEEN LATITUDES 40 AND 70 NORTH AND
LONGITUDES 45 AND 180 WEST (F).

S-02569
Mackenzie, Alexander. Voyages from Montreal. Philadelphia: Robert
Carr, for John Morgan, 1802.

A MAP OF AMERICA, BETWEEN LATITUDES 40 AND 70 NORTH AND
LONGITUDES 45 AND 180 WEST (F).

S-02652
A PLAN OF THE COMPACT PART OF EXETER. Phineas Merrill. Exeter,
NH: Phineas Merrill, 1802.

S-02686
Moore, S.S. and Jones, T.W. The Traveller's Directory.
Philadelphia: Mathew Carey; maps engraved by Francis
Shallus, William Harrison, Jr., and John Draper, 1802.

ROAD FROM PHILADELPHIA TO NEW YORK (14 sheets) (B).

ROAD FROM PHILADELPHIA TO WASHINGTON (23 sheets) (B).

S-02698
Morse, Jedidiah. The American Universal Geography. Parts 1 and 2.
   4th ed. Boston: Thomas and Andrews, 1802.

MAP OF THE WORLD FROM THE BEST AUTHORITIES. Part 1 (F).

THE SOLAR SYSTEM. Part 1 (16).

MAP OF THE NORTHERN PLAINS OF THE UNITED STATES OF AMERICA.
   Abraham Bradley. Part 1 (302).

A MAP OF THE STATES OF NEW HAMPSHIRE AND VERMONT. John
   Denison. Part 1 (319).

MAP OF THE DISTRICT OF MAINE, PART OF MASSACHUSETTS FROM THE
   LATEST SURVEYS. Osgood Carleton. Part 1 (351).

MAP OF MASSACHUSETTS FROM THE BEST AUTHORITIES. A. Adams.
   Part 1 (365).

RHODE ISLAND AND CONNECTICUT. Harding Harris. Part 1 (415).

THE STATE OF NEW YORK COMPILED FROM THE LATEST SURVEYS.
   Part 1 (458).

MAP OF THE SOUTHERN PARTS OF THE UNITED STATES OF AMERICA.
   Abraham Bradley. Part 1 (579).

WEST INDIES FROM THE BEST AUTHORITIES. Part 1 (771).

A CHART OF THE NTH. WEST COAST OF AMERICA & THE NTH. EAST
   COAST OF ASIA, SHOWING THE DISCOVERIES THAT HAVE BEEN
   LATELY MADE IN THOSE PARTS. Part 1 (807).

EUROPE FROM THE BEST AUTHORITIES. Part 2 (F).

SWEDEN, DENMARK & NORWAY FROM THE LATEST AUTHORITIES. Part 2
   (38).

ENGLAND, SCOTLAND, IRELAND AND WALES FROM THE BEST
   AUTHORITIES. Cyrus Harris. Part 2 (98).

GERMANY AND THE NETHERLANDS FROM THE LATEST AUTHORITIES.
   Part 2 (213).

POLAND, SHOWING THE CLAIMS OF RUSSIA, PRUSSIA & AUSTRIA FROM
   THE BEST AUTHORITIES. Part 2 (254).

SWITZERLAND WITH ITS SUBJECTS & ALLIES FROM THE BEST
    AUTHORITIES. Part 2 (303).

THE SEVEN UNITED PROVINCES. Part 2 (325).

THE NETHERLANDS OR BELGIC PROVINCES, WITH THE ROADS FROM THE
    LATEST AUTHORITIES. Part 2 (337).

FRANCE DIVIDED INTO DEPARTMENTS, AGREEABLE TO THE DECREES OF
    THE NATIONAL ASSEMBLY. Part 2 (345).

SPAIN AND PORTUGAL FROM THE LATEST AUTHORITIES. Part 2
    (400).

ITALY FROM THE BEST AUTHORITIES. Part 2 (431).

TURKEY IN EUROPE, AND HUNGARY. Part 2 (463).

EUROPE FROM THE BEST AUTHORITIES. Part 2 (475).

PALESTINE OR THE HOLY LAND. Part 2 (493).

HINDOSTAN OR INDIA, FROM THE BEST AUTHORITIES. Part 2 (525).

MAP OF AFRICA WITH THE ROUTES OF THE MODERN TRAVELLERS,
    PARKE, BROWN, LE VAILIANT, &C. Part 2 (591).

A MAP OF EGYPT FROM THE BEST AUTHORITIES. Part 2 (595).

S-02699
Morse, Jedidiah. Geography Made Easy. 8th ed. Boston: Thomas and
    Andrews, 1802.

A MAP OF THE WORLD (F).

A MAP OF NORTH AMERICA FROM THE LATEST DISCOVERIES (66).

S-02700
Morse, Jedidiah. A New Gazetteer of the Eastern Continent.
    Charlestown, MA: Samuel Etheridge, 1802.

EUROPE FROM THE BEST AUTHORITIES (F).

ENGLAND, SCOTLAND, IRELAND, AND WALES FROM THE BEST
    AUTHORITIES (UP).

MAP OF AFRICA WITH THE ROUTES OF THE MODERN TRAVELLERS,
    PARKE, BROWN, LE VAILTIANT, &C. (UP).

ASIA FROM THE BEST AUTHORITIES (UP).

A MAP OF EGYPT FROM THE BEST AUTHORITIES (UP).

FRANCE DIVIDED INTO DEPARTMENTS, AGREEABLE TO THE DECREES OF THE NATIONAL ASSEMBLY (UP).

GERMANY AND THE NETHERLANDS FROM THE LATEST AUTHORITIES (UP).

HINDOSTAN OR INDIA, FROM THE BEST AUTHORITIES (UP).

TURKEY IN EUROPE, AND HUNGARY (UP).

ITALY FROM THE BEST AUTHORITIES (UP).

THE NETHERLANDS OR BELGIC PROVINCES WITH THE ROADS FROM THE LATEST AUTHORITIES (UP).

PALESTINE, OR THE HOLY LAND (UP).

POLAND, SHOWING THE CLAIMS OF RUSSIA, PRUSSIA & AUSTRIA FROM THE BEST AUTHORITIES (UP).

SPAIN AND PORTUGAL FROM THE LATEST AUTHORITIES (UP).

SWEDEN, DENMARK, & NORWAY FROM THE LATEST AUTHORITIES (UP).

SWITZERLAND WITH ITS SUBJECTS & ALLIES FROM BEST AUTHORITIES (UP).

THE SEVEN UNITED PROVINCES (UP).

S-03172
Tooke, William. The Life of Catherine II. Philadelphia: Hugh Maxwell, for William Fry, 1802.

THE RUSSIAN EMPIRE (F).

S-03667
The American Pilot. Boston: William Norman, 1803.

A CHART OF NANTUCKET (1).

A NEW GENERAL CHART OF THE WEST INDIES FROM THE LATEST MARINE JOURNALS AND SURVEYS (2).

A NEW GENERAL CHART OF THE WEST INDIES FROM THE LATEST MARINE JOURNALS AND SURVEYS (3).

A CHART OF SOUTH CAROLINA AND GEORGIA (4).

CHART OF THE COAST OF AMERICA FROM CAPE HATERAS TO CAPE
ROMAN FROM THE ACTUAL SURVEYS OF DR. DUNBIBIN (5).

A NEW AND ACCURATE CHART OF THE BAY OF CHESAPEAKE INCLUDING
DELAWARE BAY (6).

CHART FROM NEW YORK TO TIMBER ISLAND INCLUDING NANTUCKET
SHOALS FROM THE LATEST SURVEYS (7).

A CHART OF THE COAST OF NEW ENGLAND FROM THE SOUTH SHOAL TO
CAPE SABLE (8).

A CHART OF THE COAST OF AMERICA FROM WOOD ISLAND TO GOOD
HARBOUR (9).

A CHART OF THE BANKS AND PART OF THE COAST OF NEWFOUNDLAND
INCLUDING THE ISLANDS OF SABLE AND CAPE BRETON (10).

S-03789
Bible. Charlestown, MA: Samuel Etheridge, 1803.

A MAP OF PALESTINE DESCRIBING THE TRAVELS OF JESUS CHRIST
(UP).

S-03862
The Boston Directory. Boston: Ensign Lincoln, for John West,
1803.

A PLAN OF BOSTON (F).

S-04071
Denon, Dominique. Travels in Upper and Lower Egypt, During the
Campaigns of General Bonaparte in that Country. New York:
Heard and Forman, 1803.

UPPER AND LOWER EGYPT TAKEN FROM D'ANVILLE & CORRECTED BY
THE ASTRONOMICAL OBSERVATIONS OF CITIZEN NOVET. (F).

S-04079
Diaz del Castillo, Bernal. The True History of the Conquest of
Mexico. Volume 1. Salem, MA: Cushing, Cushing and Appleton,
1803.

A PLAN OF THE CITY AND LAKE OF MEXICO WITH AN ELEVATION OF
AN ANCIENT TEMPLE (F).

S-04128
An Easy Introduction to Geography. Charleston, SC: John J. Evans,
    1803.

    THE WORLD (F).

S-04147
Ellicott, Andrew. The Journal of Andrew Ellicott. Philadelphia:
    Budd and Bartram, for Thomas Dobson, 1803.

    [MAP OF THE AREA ALONG THE COURSE OF THE OHIO RIVER] (18).

    [MAP OF THE AREA ALONG THE COURSE OF THE MISSISSIPPI RIVER]
    (25).

    [MAP OF THE AREA AROUND THE MISSISSIPPI DELTA] (202).

    [MAP OF A PORTION OF THE COAST OF THE FLORIDA PANHANDLE]
    (299).

    [MAP OF THE OKEFENOKEE SWAMP] (142).

S-04406
Hubbard, John. The Rudiments of Geography. Walpole, NH: Thomas
    and Thomas, 1803.

    A NEW MAP OF THE WORLD WITH THE LATEST DISCOVERIES (F).

S-04409
Hughes, John. A Report of the Causes Determined by the Late
    Supreme Court for the District of Kentucky and by the Court
    of Appeals in Which the Titles to Land Were in Dispute.
    Lexington, KY: John Bradford, 1803.

    SURVEY OF PLATS OF VARIOUS PARCELS OF LAND IN KENTUCKY
        (41 sheets) (VP).

S-04572
Mackenzie, Alexander. Voyages from Montreal. 3rd American ed. New
    York: Lewis Nichols, for Evert Duyckinck, 1803.

    A MAP OF AMERICA BETWEEN LATITUDES 40 AND 70 NORTH, AND
        LONGITUDES 45 AND 180 WEST. (F).

S-04625
Mavor, William. An Historical Account of the Most Celebrated
     Voyages. Volume 21. New Haven, CT: William Morse, for Isaac
     Beers, 1803.

     THE WORLD ON MERCATORS PROJECTION (F).

S-04632
Mavor, William F. A Preliminary View of Universal History. New
     York: Isaac Collins, 1803.

     THE ANCIENT WORLD (336).

S-05600
Wilson, Robert. History of the British Expedition to Egypt.
     Philadelphia: Bonsal and Niles, for John Conrad, 1803.

     A PLAN OF ACTION OF THE 21ST OF MARCH FOUGHT NEAR ALEXANDRIA
          (xxvi).

     A PLAN OF THE AFFAIR OF RAHMANIE IN EGYPT BETWEEN THE
          OLTOMAN AND BRITISH ARMIES (302).

S-05619
Workman, Benjamin. Elements of Geography. 9th ed. Philadelphia:
     William Young, for John M'Culloch, 1803.

     WORLD (F).

     THE SOLAR SYSTEM (4).

     NORTH AMERICA (66).

     THE UNITED STATES OF AMERICA (82).

     SOUTH AMERICA (106).

     EUROPE (111).

     ASIA (138).

     AFRICA (144).

S-05726
Arrowsmith, Aaron. A New and Elegant General Atlas. Boston:
     Thomas and Andrews, 1804.

     THE WORLD (1).

THE WORLD ON MERCATORS PROJECTION (2).

EUROPE (3).

UNITED KINGDOMS OF GREAT BRITAIN AND IRELAND (4).

ENGLAND AND WALES (5).

SCOTLAND (6).

IRELAND (7).

REMOTE BRITISH ISLES (8).

FRANCE (9).

NETHERLANDS (10).

RUSSIA IN EUROPE (11).

AUSTRIAN DOMINIONS (12).

PRUSSIAN STATES (13).

SPAIN AND PORTUGAL (14).

TURKEY IN EUROPE (15).

GREECE (16).

HOLLAND (17).

DENMARK (18).

SWEDEN AND NORWAY (19).

SWITZERLAND (20).

GERMANY, NORTH OF THE MAYN (21).

GERMANY, SOUTH OF THE MAYN (22).

ITALY (23).

ASIA (24).

ASIA MINOR (25).

CHINA (26).

CENTRAL ASIA (27).

JAPAN (28).

HINDOSTAN (29).

CHART OF THE EAST INDIA ISLANDS, EXHIBITING THE SEVERAL PASSAGES BETWEEN THE INDIAN AND PACIFIC OCEANS (30).

PERSIA (31).

NEW HOLLAND (32).

PACIFIC OCEAN (33).

NORTH AMERICA (34).

UNITED STATES (35).

NEW HAMPSHIRE (36).

MASSACHUSETTS (37).

MAINE (38).

VERMONT (39).

RHODE ISLAND (40).

CONNECTICUT (41).

NEW YORK (42).

NEW JERSEY (43).

PENNSYLVANIA (44).

DELAWARE (45).

MARYLAND (46).

VIRGINIA (47).

NORTH CAROLINA (48).

SOUTH CAROLINA (49).

GEORGIA (50).

KENTUCKY (51).

TENNESSEE (52).

OHIO (53).

MISSISSIPPI TERRITORY (54).

LOUISIANA (55).

BRITISH POSSESSIONS IN AMERICA (56).

SPANISH DOMINIONS IN NORTH AMERICA (57).

WEST INDIES (58).

AFRICA (59).

EGYPT (60).

WEST AFRICA (62).

COLONY OF THE CAPE OF GOOD HOPE (63).

S-05727
Arrowsmith, Aaron. <u>A New and Elegant General Atlas</u>. Boston:
    Thomas and Andrews, 1804.

THE WORLD (1).

THE WORLD ON MERCATORS PROJECTION (2).

EUROPE (3).

UNITED KINGDOMS OF GREAT BRITAIN AND IRELAND (4).

ENGLAND AND WALES (5).

SCOTLAND (6).

IRELAND (7).

REMOTE BRITISH ISLES (8).

FRANCE (9).

NETHERLANDS (10).

RUSSIA IN EUROPE (11).

AUSTRIAN DOMINIONS (12).

PRUSSIAN STATES (13).

SPAIN AND PORTUGAL (14).

TURKEY IN EUROPE (15).

GREECE (16).

HOLLAND (17).

DENMARK (18).

SWEDEN AND NORWAY (19).

SWITZERLAND (20).

GERMANY, NORTH OF THE MAYN (21).

GERMANY, SOUTH OF THE MAYN (22).

ITALY (23).

ASIA (24).

ASIA MINOR (25).

CHINA (26).

CENTRAL ASIA (27).

JAPAN (28).

HINDOSTAN (29).

CHART OF THE EAST INDIA ISLANDS, EXHIBITING THE SEVERAL
    PASSAGES BETWEEN THE INDIAN AND PACIFIC OCEANS (30).

PERSIA (31).

NEW HOLLAND (32).

PACIFIC OCEAN (33).

NORTH AMERICA (34).

UNITED STATES (35).

NEW HAMPSHIRE (36).

MASSACHUSETTS (37).

MAINE (38).

VERMONT (39).

RHODE ISLAND (40).

CONNECTICUT (41).

NEW YORK (42).

NEW JERSEY (43).

PENNSYLVANIA (44).

DELAWARE (45).

MARYLAND (46).

VIRGINIA (47).

NORTH CAROLINA (48).

SOUTH CAROLINA (49).

GEORGIA (50).

KENTUCKY (51).

TENNESSEE (52).

OHIO (53).

MISSISSIPPI TERRITORY (54).

LOUISIANA (55).

BRITISH POSSESSIONS IN AMERICA (56).

SPANISH DOMINIONS IN NORTH AMERICA (57).

WEST INDIES (58).

AFRICA (59).

EGYPT (60).

WEST AFRICA (62).

COLONY OF THE CAPE OF GOOD HOPE (63).

S-05764
The Baltimore Directory, for 1804. Baltimore: Warner and Hanna,
    for James Robinson, 1804.

    IMPROVED PLAN OF THE CITY OF BALTIMORE (F).

S-05809
Barthelemy, Jean Jacques. <u>Travels of Anacharsis the Younger in
     Greece</u>. 4 volumes. Philadelphia: William M'Laughlin, for
     Jacob Johnson, 1804.

     MAP OF GREECE, AND THE GRECIAN ISLANDS; FOR THE TRAVELS OF
         ANACHARSIS. M.B. duBocage. Volume 1 (F).

S-05848
<u>Bible</u>. Philadelphia: Mathew Carey, 1804.

     MAP OF THE COUNTRY TRAVELLED BY THE APOSTLES WITH THE VOYAGE
         OF SAINT PAUL TO ROME (832).

S-05971
Caesar, Caius Julius. <u>C. Julii Caesaris Quae Extant</u>.
     Philadelphia: William Poyntell, 1804.

     GALLIA VETUS (vi).

     ITALIAE ANTIQUAE (204).

     CONSPECTUS LOCORUM BELLI AFRICANI (384).

S-05982
Carey, Mathew. <u>Carey's General Atlas</u>. Philadelphia: Mathew Carey,
     1804.

     A MAP OF THE WORLD FROM THE BEST AUTHORITIES (1).

     A CHART OF THE WORLD ACCORDING TO MERCATORS PROJECTION,
         SHOWING THE LATEST DISCOVERIES OF CAPT. COOK (2).

     AN ACCURATE MAP OF EUROPE FROM THE BEST AUTHORITIES (3).

     THE RUSSIAN EMPIRE IN EUROPE AND ASIA (4).

     SCOTLAND WITH THE PRINCIPAL ROADS FROM THE BEST AUTHORITIES
         (5).

     AN ACCURATE MAP OF ENGLAND AND WALES WITH THE PRINCIPAL
         ROADS FROM THE BEST AUTHORITIES (6).

     A MAP OF IRELAND FROM THE BEST AUTHORITIES (7).

     THE SEVEN UNITED PROVINCES OF HOLLAND FRIESLAND, GELDERS,
         UTRECHT, OVERYSSEL, GRONINGEN AND ZEALAND (8).

THE AUSTRIAN, FRENCH AND DUTCH NETHERLANDS FROM THE BEST
AUTHORITIES (9).

THE EMPIRE OF GERMANY WITH THE 13 CANTONS OF SWITZERLAND
FROM THE BEST AUTHORITIES (10).

FRANCE DIVIDED INTO CIRCLES AND DEPARTMENTS (11).

A MAP OF THE SEAT OF NORTH FRANCE WITH THE COUNTRY DIVIDED
INTO ITS SEVERAL DEPARTMENTS (12).

TURKEY IN EUROPE AND HUNGARY, FROM THE BEST AUTHORITIES
(13).

SPAIN AND PORTUGAL FROM THE BEST AUTHORITIES (14).

ITALY AND SARDINIA FROM THE BEST AUTHORITIES (15).

SWITZERLAND ACCORDING TO THE BEST AUTHORITIES (16).

POLAND SHOWING THE CLAIMS OF RUSSIA PRUSSIA & AUSTRIA, UNTIL
THE LATE DEPREDATIONS (17).

ASIA, ACCORDING TO THE BEST AUTHORITIES (18).

CHINA, DIVIDED INTO ITS GREAT PROVINCES, ACCORDING TO THE
BEST AUTHORITIES (19).

AN ACCURATE MAP OF HINDOSTAN OR INDIA, FROM THE BEST
AUTHORITIES (20).

AFRICA ACCORDING TO BEST AUTHORITIES (21).

THE BRITISH POSSESSIONS IN NORTH AMERICA FROM THE BEST
AUTHORITIES. Samuel Lewis (22).

A MAP OF THE UNITED STATES COMPILED CHIEFLY FROM THE STATE
MAPS AND OTHER AUTHENTIC INFORMATION. Samuel Lewis
(23).

THE PROVINCE OF MAINE FROM THE BEST AUTHORITIES. Samuel
Lewis (24).

THE STATE OF MASSACHUSETTS COMPILED FROM THE BEST
AUTHORITIES. Samuel Lewis (25).

THE STATE OF RHODE ISLAND, COMPILED FROM THE SURVEYS AND
OBSERVATIONS OF CALEB HARRIS. Harding Harris (25).

CONNECTICUT FROM THE BEST AUTHORITIES (27).

THE STATE OF NEW YORK COMPILED FROM THE BEST AUTHORITIES.
    Samuel Lewis (28).

THE STATE OF NEW JERSEY COMPILED FROM THE MOST AUTHENTIC
    INFORMATION (29).

THE STATE OF PENNSYLVANIA REDUCED WITH PERMISSION FROM
    READING HOWELL'S MAP. Samuel Lewis (30).

DELAWARE FROM THE BEST AUTHORITIES (31).

THE STATE OF MARYLAND FROM THE BEST AUTHORITIES. Samuel
    Lewis (32).

THE STATE OF VIRGINIA FROM THE BEST AUTHORITIES. Samuel
    Lewis (33).

THE STATE OF NORTH CAROLINA FROM THE BEST AUTHORITIES, &C.
    Samuel Lewis (34).

THE STATE OF SOUTH CAROLINA FROM THE BEST AUTHORITIES.
    Samuel Lewis (35).

GEORGIA FROM THE BEST AUTHORITIES (36).

KENTUCKY, REDUCED FROM ELIHU BARKER'S LARGE MAP. Elihu
    Barker (37).

MAP OF THE TENNESEE STATE, FORMERLY PART OF NORTH CAROLINA
    (38).

A MAP OF SOUTH AMERICA ACCORDING TO THE BEST AUTHORITIES
    (39).

A CHART OF THE WEST INDIES FROM THE LATEST MARINE JOURNALS
    AND SURVEYS (40).

A MAP OF THE COUNTRIES SITUATED ABOUT THE NORTH POLE (41).

A MAP OF THE DISCOVERIES MADE BY CAPTS. COOK AND CLERKE IN
    THE YEARS 1778 & 1779 BETWEEN THE EASTERN COAST OF ASIA
    AND THE WESTERN COAST OF NORTH AMERICA (42).

PLAT OF THE SEVEN RANGES OF TOWNSHIP BEING PART OF THE
    TERRITORY OF THE UNITED STATES, N.W. OF THE RIVER OHIO
    (43).

A MAP OF PART OF THE N.W. TERRITORY OF THE UNITED STATES
    COMPILED FROM ACTUAL SURVEYS AND THE BEST AUTHORITIES.
    Samuel Lewis (44).

A MAP OF THE FRENCH PART OF ST. DOMINGO (45).

A MAP OF THOSE COUNTRIES IN WHICH THE APOSTLES TRAVELLED IN
    PROPAGATING CHRISTIANITY (46).

S-06034
Clavigero, Abbe. The History of Mexico. 2 volumes. Philadelphia:
    Budd and Bartram, for Thomas Dobson, 1804.

    ANAHUAC, OR THE EMPIRE OF MEXICO, THE KINGDOMS OF ACOLHUACAN
        & MICHAACAN &C., AS THEY WERE IN THE YEAR 1521.
        Volume 1 (F).

    LAKES OF MEXICO. Volume 2 (F).

S-06160
A MAP OF THE STATE OF NEW YORK, CONTRACTED FROM HIS LARGE MAP OF
    THE STATE. Simeon DeWitt. s.l.: s.n., 1804.

S-06361
Furlong, Lawrence. The American Coast Pilot. 4th ed. Newburyport,
    MA: Edmund Blunt, 1804.

    PORTLAND HARBOUR (134).

    HARBOUR OF PORTSMOUTH (136).

    NEWBURYPORT HARBOUR (140).

    ANNISSQUAM HARBOUR IN IPSWICH BAY (142).

    THE EASTERN END OF THE ISLE OF SABLE, TAKEN FROM THE
        SOUTHWARD (150).

    BOSTON HARBOUR (152).

    NEWPORT (168).

    NEW YORK (176).

    THE BAY AND RIVER OF DELAWARE (182).

    THE BAY OF CHESAPEAKE FROM ITS ENTRANCE TO BALTIMORE (186).

    CHARLESTON HARBOUR (194).

S-06703
Malham, John. <u>Navy Atlas</u>. Philadelphia: William Spotswood, 1804.

A GENERAL CHART OF THE WORLD ON MERCATOR'S PROJECTION
    EXHIBITING ALL THE NEW DISCOVERIES AND THE TRAVELS OF
    DEFLERENT ARCUM--NAVIGATOR (1).

A CORRECT CHART OF THE ENGLISH CHANNEL (2).

A CORRECT CHART OF THE WEST COAST OF NORTH AMERICA FROM
    BHERING'S STRAITS TO NOOTKA SOUND (3).

A CORRECT CHART OF THE EAST COAST OF NORTH AMERICA (4).

A CORRECT CHART OF THE INDIAN OCEAN (5).

A CORRECT CHART OF THE IRISH SEA, WITH ST. GEORGES CHANNEL
    (6).

A CORRECT CHART OF THE BAY OF BISCAY (7).

A CORRECT CHART OF THE WEST COAST OF AFRICA (8).

A CORRECT CHART OF THE BALTIC SEA (9).

A CORRECT CHART OF THE WEST INDIA ISLANDS (10).

A CORRECT CHART OF THE NORTH SEA (11).

A CORRECT CHART OF THE COAST OF PORTUGAL (12).

A CORRECT CHART OF THE COASTS OF HINDOSTAN (13).

A CORRECT CHART OF THE MEDITERRANEAN SEA (14).

A CORRECT CHART OF THE COASTS OF SOUTH AMERICA FROM THE
    EQUATOR TO CAPE HORN (15).

A CORRECT CHART OF THE SOUTHERN COASTS OF AFRICA FROM THE
    EQUATOR TO THE CAPE OF GOOD HOPE (16).

A CORRECT CHART OF THE GERMAN OCEAN (17).

S-06704
A MAP SHEWING THE RELATIVE SITUATION OF A TRACT OF LAND BELONGING
    TO I.B. CHURCH [SITUATED ON THE GENESEO RIVER, AND THE SITE
    OF THE TOWN OF ANGELICA, NY]. Joseph Mangin. New York: Peter
    Maverick, 1804.

S-06759
Mavor, William. Universal History. 25 volumes. New York: Samuel
    Stansbury, 1804.

    THE ANCIENT WORLD. Volume 1 (B).

    ANCIENT GREECE. Volume 3 (F).

    ITALIAE ANTIQUAE. Volume 6 (B).

    THE ROMAN EMPIRE UNDER AUGUSTUS. Volume 7 (B).

    MAP OF AFRICA FOR DR. MAVOR'S UNIVERSAL HISTORY. Volume 13
        (B).

    ENGLAND AND WALES COMPILED FROM THE BEST AUTHORITIES. Volume
        19 (B).

    ASIA. Volume 22 (B).

S-06815
Moore, S.S. and Jones, T.W. The Traveller's Directory. 2nd ed.
    Philadelphia: Mathew Carey; maps engraved by Francis
    Shallus, William Harrison, Jr., and John Draper, 1804.

    ROAD FROM PHILADELPHIA TO NEW YORK (15 sheets) (B).

    ROAD FROM PHILADELPHIA TO WASHINGTON (23 sheets) (B).

S-06823
Morris, Richard. A Defence of the Conduct of Commodore Morris.
    New York: Isaac Riley, 1804

    MAP OF THE COUNTRIES SURROUNDING THE MEDITERRANEAN SEA (2).

S-06825
Morse, Jedidiah. The American Gazetteer. 2nd ed. Charlestown, MA:
    Samuel Etheridge, 1804.

    MAP OF NORTH AMERICA SHEWING ALL THE NEW DISCOVERIES (F).

    SOUTH AMERICA FROM THE BEST AUTHORITIES (UP).

    MAP OF THE NORTHERN PARTS OF THE UNITED STATES OF AMERICA.
        Abraham Bradley (UP).

A CHART OF THE NTH. WEST COAST OF AMERICA & THE NTH. EAST
COAST OF ASIA, SHEWING THE DISCOVERIES THAT HAVE BEEN
LATELY MADE IN THOSE PARTS (UP).

MAP OF THE SOUTHERN PARTS OF THE UNITED STATES OF AMERICA.
Abraham Bradley (UP).

WEST INDIES FROM THE BEST AUTHORITIES (UP).

S-06828
Morse, Jedidiah. The Compendious History of New England.
Charlestown, MA: Samuel Etheridge, 1804.

NEW ENGLAND (F).

S-06829
Morse, Jedidiah. Elements of Geography. 5th ed. Boston: Thomas
and Andrews, 1804.

CHART OF THE WORLD ON MERCATORS PROJECTION (F).

A MAP OF THE UNITED STATES OF AMERICA (74).

S-06831
Morse, Jedidiah. Geography Made Easy. 9th Ed. Boston: Thomas and
Andrews, 1804.

A NEW MAP OF THE WORLD WITH THE LATEST DISCOVERIES (F).

A MAP OF NORTH AMERICA FROM THE LATEST DISCOVERIES (50).

S-06836
Munro, Robert. A Description of the Genesee Country. New York:
s.n., 1804.

A MAP OF THE GENESEE COUNTRY (2).

S-06857
Neuer Hauswirthschafts Calender: Auf Das Jahr 1805. Philadelphia:
Heinrich Schweitzer, 1804.

[LOUISIANA TERRITORY] (2).

S-07675
Volney, Constantin. <u>A View of the Soil and Climate of the
    United States</u>. Philadelphia: Palmer and Palmer, for John
    Conrad, 1804.

    A MAP OF NORTH AMERICA (F).

    UNITED STATES (188).

S-07683
Wakefield, Priscilla. <u>A Family Tour Through the British Empire</u>.
    Philadelphia: Archibald Bartram, 1804.

    A MAP OF THE BRITISH EMPIRE (B).

S-07803
Workman, Benjamin. <u>Elements of Geography</u>. 10th ed. Philadelphia:
    John M'Culloch, 1804.

    WORLD (F).

    THE SOLAR SYSTEM (6).

    NORTH AMERICA (66).

    EUROPE (110).

    ASIA (138).

    AFRICA (142).

S-07884
MARYLAND. Boston: Arrowsmith and Lewis, 1805.

S-07988
<u>Bible</u>. Philadelphia: Mathew Carey, 1805.

    CANAAN OR THE LAND OF PROMISE TO ABRAHAM AND HIS POSTERITY
        (8).

    [GALILEE] (834).

    THE LAND OF MORIAH OR JERUSALEM AND THE ADJACENT COUNTRY
        (834).

S-07989
Bible. Philadelphia: Mathew Carey, 1805.

   THE JOURNEYINGS OF THE CHILDREN OF ISRAEL FROM EGYPT THROUGH
      THE RED SEA AND WILDERNESS TO THE LAND OF CANAAN (F).

S-07991
Bible. 1st American ed., from the 5th Dublin ed. Philadelphia:
   Mathew Carey, 1805.

   A MAP OF PALESTINE DESCRIBING THE TRAVELS OF JESUS CHRIST
      (F).

   THE LAND OF MORIAH OR JERUSALEM AND THE ADJACENT COUNTRY
      (772).

   A MAP OF THE COUNTRY TRAVELLED BY THE APOSTLES WITH THE
      VOYAGE OF SAINT PAUL TO ROME (96).

S-08001
Bible. Philadelphia: Mathew Carey, 1805.

   A MAP OF PALESTINE DESCRIBING THE TRAVELS OF JESUS CHRIST
      (F).

   THE LAND OF MORIAH OR JERUSALEM AND THE ADJACENT COUNTRY
      (1).

   MAP OF THE COUNTRY TRAVELLED BY THE APOSTLES WITH THE VOYAGE
      OF SAINT PAUL TO ROME (96).

S-08057
The Boston Directory. Boston: David Carlisle, for Edward Cotton,
   1805.

   A PLAN OF BOSTON, FROM ACTUAL SURVEY (F).

S-08134
Carey, Mathew. Carey's American Pocket Atlas. 3rd ed.
   Philadelphia: Mathew Carey, 1805.

   THE UNITED STATES OF AMERICA (1).

   VERMONT FROM ACTUAL SURVEY (14).

   THE STATE OF NEW HAMPSHIRE (20).

   PROVINCE OF MAINE (24).

MASSACHUSETTS (28).

RHODE ISLAND (38).

CONNECTICUT (44).

NEW YORK (50).

NEW JERSEY (60).

PENNSYLVANIA (66).

DELAWARE (72).

OHIO AND N.W. TERRITORY (76).

MARYLAND (82).

VIRGINIA (86).

KENTUCKEY (90).

NORTH CAROLINA (96).

TENNASSEE, LATELY THE S.W. TERRITORY (100).

SOUTH CAROLINA (104).

MISSISSIPPI TERRITORY AND GEORGIA (108).

LOUISIANA (116).

S-08298
Davies, Benjamin. _A New System of Modern Geography_. Philadelphia:
    Jacob Johnson, 1805.

MAP OF THE WORLD WITH THE MOST RECENT DISCOVERIES (F).

EUROPE (27).

GREAT BRITAIN AND IRELAND (30).

ASIA (124).

NORTH AMERICA (396).

A MAP OF THE UNITED STATES AND PART OF LOUISIANA (422).

SOUTH AMERICA (586).

AFRICA (600).

S-08299
Davies, Benjamin. <u>A New System of Modern Geography</u>. 2nd ed.
    2 volumes. Philadelphia: Jacob Johnson, 1805.

    MAP OF THE WORLD WITH THE MOST RECENT DISCOVERIES. Volume 1
        (F).

    EUROPE. Volume 1 (26).

    GREAT BRITAIN AND IRELAND. Volume 1 (30).

    ASIA. Volume 1 (224).

    NORTH AMERICA. Volume 2 (74).

    SOUTH AMERICA. Volume 2 (262).

    AFRICA. Volume 2 (276).

S-08418
<u>Facts and Arguments Respecting the Great Utility of an Extensive
    Plan of Inland Navigation in America</u>. Philadelphia: William
    Duane, 1805.

    A MAP OF PENNSYLVANIA, DELAWARE, NEW JERSEY & MARYLAND, WITH
        THE PARTS ADJACENT (F).

S-08435
Ferguson, Adam. <u>The History of the Progress and Termination of
    the Roman Republic</u>. 3 volumes. Philadelphia: William
    Poyntell, 1805.

    MAP REPRESENTING THE RELATIVE PORTION OF THE PRINCIPAL
        KINGDOMS & STATES ON THE COASTS OF THE MEDITERRANEAN
        SEA. Volume 1 (100).

    THEATRE OF THE CAMPAIGN ON THE SEGRA OR SICAR IS. Volume 2
        (264).

    ITALY WITH THE PROVINCES OF CAESAR AND PART OF THE PROVINCE
        POMPEY. Volume 2 (274).

    THEATRE OF THE CAMPAIGNS IN MACEDONIA & THESSALY. Volume 2
        (378).

    THEATRE OF THE CAMPAIGN IN AFRICA. Volume 2 (438).

    THE ROMAN EMPIRE EXHIBITING ITS COASTS AND INTERNAL
        DIVISIONS WITH THE PRINCIPAL NAVAL & MILITARY STATIONS
        UNDER AUGUSTUS. Volume 3 (474).

S-08518
Gibbon, Edward. <u>The History of the Decline and Fall of the Roman Empire</u>. 8 Volumes. Philadelphia: Robert Carr, for Birch and Small, 1805.

WESTERN PART OF THE ROMAN EMPIRE. Volume 7 (ix).

THE PARTS OF EUROPE AND ASIA ADJACENT TO CONSTANTINOPLE. Volume 8 (F).

EASTERN PART OF THE ROMAN EMPIRE. Volume 8 (1).

S-08587
Harris, Thaddeus Mason. <u>The Journal of a Tour into the Territory Northwest of the Alleghany Mountains</u>. Boston: Manning and Loring, 1805.

A MAP OF THE ALLEGHANY MONONGAHELA AND YOHIOGANY RIVERS (B).

MAP OF THE STATE OF OHIO (B).

A PLAT OF THE STATE OF OHIO WHICH IS APPROPRIATED FOR MILITARY SERVICES (B).

A PLAN OF PART OF MARIETTA WITH THE REMAINS OF THE ANCIENT WORKS FOUND THERE (B).

S-08658
Hubbard, John. <u>The Rudiments of Geography</u>. 2nd ed. Walpole, NH: George Nichols, for Thomas and Thomas, 1805.

MAP OF THE WORLD WITH THE LATEST DISCOVERIES (F).

S-08933
Morse, Jedidiah. <u>The American Universal Geography</u>. Part 1, 5th ed.; Part 2, 4th ed. Boston: Thomas and Andrews, 1805.

MAP OF THE WORLD. Part 1 (F).

NORTH AMERICA. Part 1 (124).

SOUTH AMERICA. Part 1 (790).

EUROPE. Part 1 (858).

ASIA. Part 2 (380).

AFRICA. Part 2 (494).

S-08971
The New and Complete American Encyclopedia. 7 Volumes, plus a
    volume of plates. New York: John Low, 1805.

    NORTHERN HEMISPHERE WITH THE FIGURES OF THE CONSTELLATIONS
        (plate xxv).

    RHODE ISLAND (UP).

    EUROPE (UP).

    AFRICA FROM THE BEST AUTHORITIES (UP).

    THE STATE OF NEW YORK FROM THE BEST INFORMATION (UP).

    ITALY (UP).

    A NEW MAP OF CONNECTICUT FROM THE BEST AUTHORITIES (UP).

    GENERAL CHART ON MERCATORS PROJECTION (UP).

    IRELAND FROM THE LATEST AUTHORITIES (UP).

    VERMONT FROM THE LATEST AUTHORITIES (UP).

    THE NETHERLANDS WITH ROADS FROM THE LATEST AUTHORITIES (UP).

    SPAIN AND PORTUGAL (UP).

    THE STATE OF SOUTH CAROLINA FROM THE BEST AUTHORITIES (UP).

    WEST INDIES (UP).

    RUSSIA OR MUSCOVY IN EUROPE FROM THE LATEST AUTHORITIES
        (UP).

    THE STATE OF PENNSYLVANIA FROM THE LATEST AUTHORITIES (UP).

    SWEDEN, DENMARK & NORWAY FROM THE LATEST AUTHORITIES (UP).

    THE STATE OF VIRGINIA FROM THE BEST AUTHORITIES (UP).

    THE WORLD FROM THE BEST AUTHORITIES (UP).

    ASIA FROM THE LATEST AUTHORITIES (UP).

    EAST INDIES FROM THE BEST AUTHORITIES (UP).

    SOUTH AMERICA FROM THE BEST SURVEYS (UP).

    A MAP OF NORTH AMERICA FROM THE LATEST AUTHORITIES (UP).

NORTH CAROLINA FROM THE BEST AUTHORITIES (UP).

GEORGIA FROM THE LATEST AUTHORITIES (UP).

THE STATE OF NEW HAMPSHIRE COMPILED CHIEFLY FROM ACTUAL
    SURVEYS (UP).

ENGLAND AND WALES (UP).

GERMANY AND THE NETHERLANDS (UP).

THE PROVINCE OF MAINE FROM THE BEST AUTHORITIES (UP).

THE BATAVIAN REPUBLIC (UP).

THE UNITED STATES OF AMERICA (UP).

THE STATE OF MASSACHUSETTS FROM THE BEST INFORMATION (UP).

THE STATES OF MARYLAND AND DELAWARE FROM THE LATEST SURVEYS
    (UP).

A NEW MAP OF SCOTLAND FROM THE BEST AUTHORITIES (UP).

THE STATE OF KENTUCKY WITH THE ADJOINING TERRITORIES FROM
    THE BEST AUTHORITIES (UP).

A MAP OF THE TENNASSEE GOVERNMENT FROM THE LATEST SURVEYS
    (UP).

EGYPT FROM THE BEST AUTHORITIES (UP).

S-08972
A New and Elegant General Atlas. Boston: Thomas and Andrews,
    1805.

THE WORLD (1).

THE WORLD ON MERCATORS PROJECTION (2).

EUROPE (3).

UNITED KINGDOMS OF GREAT BRITAIN AND IRELAND (4).

ENGLAND AND WALES (5).

SCOTLAND (6).

IRELAND (7).

REMOTE BRITISH ISLES (8).

FRANCE (9).

RUSSIA IN EUROPE (10).

AUSTRIAN DOMINIONS (11).

PRUSSIAN STATES (12).

SPAIN AND PORTUGAL (13).

TURKEY IN EUROPE (14).

GREECE (15).

HOLLAND (16).

DENMARK (17).

SWEDEN AND NORWAY (18).

SWITZERLAND (19).

GERMANY NORTH OF THE MAYN (20).

GERMANY SOUTH OF THE MAYN (21).

ITALY (22).

ASIA (23).

ASIA MINOR (24).

CHINA (25).

CENTRAL ASIA (26).

JAPAN (27).

HINDOOSTAN (28).

CHART OF THE EAST INDIA ISLANDS EXHIBITING THE SEVERAL
    PASSAGES BETWEEN THE INDIAN AND PACIFIC OCEANS (29).

PERSIA (30).

NEW HOLLAND (31).

PACIFIC OCEAN (32).

NORTH AMERICA (33).

UNITED STATES (34).

NEW HAMPSHIRE (35).

MASSACHUSETTS (36).

MAINE (37).

VERMONT (38).

RHODE ISLAND (39).

CONNECTICUT (40).

NEW YORK (41).

NEW JERSEY (42).

PENNSYLVANIA (43).

DELAWARE (44).

MARYLAND (45).

VIRGINIA (46).

NORTH CAROLINA (47).

SOUTH CAROLINA (48).

GEORGIA (49).

KENTUCKY (50).

TENNESSEE (51).

OHIO (52).

MISSISSIPPI TERRITORY (53).

LOUISIANA (54).

BRITISH POSSESSIONS IN AMERICA (55).

SPANISH DOMINIONS IN NORTH AMERICA (56).

WEST INDIES (57).

SOUTH AMERICA (58).

AFRICA (59).

EGYPT (60).

WEST AFRICA (61).

COLONY OF THE CAPE OF GOOD HOPE (62).

S-09152
Pinkerton, John. Pinkerton's Geography. Philadelphia:
    Samuel Bradford, 1805.

    A NEW MAP OF THE WORLD WITH THE LATEST DISCOVERIES (F).

S-09234
Rees, Abraham. The Cyclopaedia; or, Universal Dictionary of Arts,
    Sciences, and Literature. 41 volumes, 6 volumes of plates.
    Philadelphia: Samuel Bradford and Murray and Fairman, 1805-
    1825. (Note: all volume numbers refer to plate volumes).

    GENERAL VIEW OF THE SOLAR SYSTEM. Volume 1 (astronomy,
        plate II).

    [GULF OF BOTHNIA]. Volume 1 (astronomy, plate VI).

    [ENGLISH CHANNEL]. Volume 1 (astronomy, plate VIII).

    SOLAR SYSTEM. Volume 1 (astronomy, plate XXI).

    PROJECTION ON THE PLANE OF THE ECLIPTIC OF THE PARABOLIC
        ORBITS OF 72 COMETS WHOSE COURSES HAVE BEEN CALCUTED.
        Volume 1 (astronomy, plate XXXVIII).

    NORTHERN HEMISPHERE [CELESTIAL CHART]. Volume 1 (asronomy,
        plate I).

    SOUTHERN HEMISPHERE [CELESTIAL CHART]. Volume 1 (astronomy,
        plate II).

    ORION. Volume 1 (constellation, plate I).

    URSA MAJOR AND URSA MINOR. Volume 1 (constellation,
        plate II).

    PLAN OF THE DOCKS AT LIVERPOOL IN 1808. Volume 2 (plate I).

    PLAN OF THE DOCKS AT LONDON IN 1808. Volume 2 (plate I).

    IMPERIUM CAR. MAGN. AD FINEM SAEC. POST CHRIST viiim
        [EUROPE]. Volume 6 (ancient geography, plate I).

    ORBIS VETERIBUS COGNITI. Volume 6 (geographiae antiquae,
        plate I).

POPULI, TRIBES, &C. IN GRAECIA, THRACIA, ET ASIA, QUORUM
MEMINIT HOMERUS. Volume 6 (geographiae antiquae, plate
II).

BRITANNIA, ROMANA CUM HIBERNIA ET INSULIS ADJACENTIBUS
[ENGLAND AND IRELAND]. Volume 6 (geographiae antiquae,
plate III).

PELOPONNESUS (QUAE ANTEA APIA, PELASGIA, ET ARGUS). Volume 6
(geographiae antiquae, plate IV).

HELLAS NIVE GRAECIA PROPRIA, THESALIA ET EPIHUS. Volume 6
(geographiae antiquae, plate V).

MACEDONIA ET THRACIA. Volume 6 (geographiae antiquae,
plate VI).

ASIA PENINSULARIS CUM INSULIS ADJACENTIBUS [TURKEY].
Volume 6 (geographiae antiquae, plate VII).

AEGYPTIS, PROVINCIA ROMANA IMPERIALIS. Volume 6 (geographiae
antiquae, plate VIII).

AEGYPTI PAR MERIDIONALIS. Volume 6 (geographiae antiquae,
plate VIII).

LIBYIAE VEL AFRICAE ORA BOREALIS. Volume 6 (geographiae
antiquae, plate IX).

ITALLAE RECIO ALPINA QUAE VULGO, SED MINUS RECTE DICITUR
GALLIA CISALPINA. Volume 6 (geographiae antiquae,
plate X).

ITALIA MEDIA VEL ITALIAE PROPRIAE PARS BOREALIS. Volume 6
(geographiae antiquae, plate XI).

ITALIA ULTERIOR EUJUS PARS AUSTRALIS MAGNA GRAECIA. Volume 6
(geographiae antiquae, plate XII).

SICILIA PROVINCIA ROMANORUM CUM INSULIS ADJACENTIBUS.
Volume 6 (geographiae antiquae, plate XIII).

ITALIA IN REGIONES UNDECIM AB AUGUSTO DESCRIPTA, CUM INSULIS
CORSICA ET SARDINIA. Volume 6 (geographiae antiquae,
plate XIV).

IMPERIUM ROMANUM. Volume 6 (geographiae antiquae, plates XV
and XVI).

HISPANIA ROMANA. Volume 6 (geographiae antiquae, plate
XVII).

107

GALLIAE SICUT AB AGUSTO DIVISAE. Volume 6 (geographiae antiquae, plate XVIII).

GALLIAE SICUT AB AGUSTO DIVISAE PARS SEPTENTRIONALIS. Volume 6 (geographiae antiquae, plate XIX).

RHAETIA ET NORICUM, PROVINCIAE ROMANORUM. Volume 6 (geographiae antiquae, plate XX).

GERMANIA MAGNA QUAE NUNQUAM ROMANUS PARUIT. Volume 6 (geographiae antiquae, plate XXI).

JUDAEIA ET REGIONES FINITIMAE. Volume 6 (geographiae antiquae, plate XXII).

TERRA FILIORUM ISRAELIS. Volume 6 (geographiae antiquae, plate XXII).

(Note: the following maps are unnumbered plates which appear after, geographiae antiquae, plate XXI,I in plate volume 6)

THE WORLD (UP).

THE WORLD ON MERCATORS PROJECTION (UP).

EUROPE (UP).

BRITISH ISLES (UP).

ENGLAND AND WALES (UP).

SCOTLAND (UP).

CANALS, NAVIGATIONS, AND RAILWAYS OF GREAT BRITAIN (UP).

IRELAND (UP).

SWEDEN, DENMARK, AND NORWAY (UP).

RUSSIAN EMPIRE (UP).

SOUTH PART OF RUSSIA IN EUROPE (UP).

NORTH PART OF RUSSIA IN EUROPE (UP).

THE SEVEN UNITED PROVINCES (UP).

FRANCE (UP).

SPAIN AND PORTUGAL (UP).

PORTUGAL (UP).

SWITZERLAND (UP).

ALPINE COUNTRY (UP).

SOUTH ITALY (UP).

PRUSSIA (UP).

GERMANY EAST (UP).

GERMANY WEST (UP).

HUNGARY (UP).

ENVIRONS ON CONSTANTINOPLE (UP).

ASIA (UP).

ARABIA (UP).

PERSIA (UP).

HINDOOSTAN (UP).

CHINA (UP).

EMPIRE OF JAPAN (UP).

CHART OF THE EAST INDIA ISLANDS (UP).

CHART OF THE PACIFIC OCEAN (UP).

AFRICA (UP).

EGYPT (UP).

CAPE OF GOOD HOPE (UP).

NORTH AMERICA (UP).

SOUTH AMERICA (UP).

BRITISH POSSESSIONS IN NORTH AMERICA (UP).

WEST INDIES (UP).

UNITED STATES OF AMERICA COMPILED FROM THE LATEST & BEST
AUTHORITIES. John Melish (UP).

S-09271
Rollin, Charles. <u>The Ancient History of the Egyptians....</u>
    8 Volumes. Boston: Munroe and Francis, 1805.

    A PLAN OF THE CITY OF SYRACUSE BESIEGED BY THE ATHENIANS.
        Volume 3 (242).

    A MAP OF THE RETREAT OF THE TEN THOUSAND. Volume 3 (357).

    A MAP OF THE PLACES ADJACENT TO ISSUS TO FACILITATE THE
        UNDERSTANDING OF THE MARCHES OF ALEXANDER AND DARIUS
        TOWARDS THAT CITY. Volume 5 (120).

    A VIEW OF THE CITY AND PORT OF ALEXANDRIA AND ISLE OF
        PHAROS. Volume 5 (168).

S-09272
Rollin, Charles. <u>The Ancient History of the Egyptians....</u>
    8 Volumes. Philadelphia: Bioren and Plowman, 1805.

    A PLAN OF THE CITY OF SYRACUSE BESIEGED BY THE ATHENIANS.
        Volume 3 (242).

    A MAP OF THE RETREAT OF THE TEN THOUSAND. Volume 3 (356).

    A MAP OF THE PLACES ADJACENT TO ISSUS TO FACILITATE THE
        UNDERSTANDING OF THE MARCHES OF ALEXANDER AND DARIUS
        TOWARDS THAT CITY. Volume 5 (121).

    THE PLAN OF BABYLON (127).

S-09273
Rollin, Charles. <u>The Ancient History of the Egyptians....</u>
    Volume 3. Portland, ME: Thomas Clark, 1805.

    A PLAN OF THE CITY OF SYRACUSE BESIEGED BY THE ATHENIANS
        (243).

    A MAP OF THE RETREAT OF THE TEN THOUSAND (356).

S-09274
Rollin, Charles. <u>The Ancient History of the Egyptians....</u>
    Volumes 2 and 5. Portsmouth, NH: Treadwell and Treadwell,
    1805.

    THE PLAN OF BABYLON. Volume 2 (8).

A MAP OF THE PLACES ADJACENT TO ISSUS TO FACILITATE THE
UNDERSTANDING OF THE MARCHES OF ALEXANDER AND DARIUS
TOWARDS THAT CITY. Volume 5 (116).

A VIEW OF THE CITY AND PORT OF ALEXANDRIA AND ISLE OF
PHAROS. Volume 5 (168).

S-09325
Scott, Joseph. A Geographical Dictionary of the United States.
Philadelphia: Archibald Bartram, for Jacob Johnson, 1805.

A MAP OF THE UNITED STATES (F).

S-09326
Scott, Joseph. A Geographical Dictionary of the United States.
Philadelphia: Archibald Bartram, for Thomas Armstrong, 1805.

A MAP OF THE UNITED STATES (F).

S-09385
Snowden, Richard. The History of North and South America.
2 volumes. Philadelphia: Jacob Johnson, 1805.

NORTH AMERICA. Volume 1 (F).

SOUTH AMERICA. Volume 2 (F).

S-09385a
Snowden, Richard. The History of North and South America.
2 volumes in 1. Philadelphia: Jacob Johnson, 1805.

NORTH AMERICA. Volume 1 (F).

SOUTH AMERICA. Volume 2 (F).

S-09444
Subscribers to the Life of Washington. Philadelphia: s.n., 1805.

A MAP OF PART OF RHODE ISLAND, SHEWING THE POSITIONS OF THE
AMERICAN AND BRITISH ARMIES AT THE SIEGE OF NEWPORT,
AND THE SUBSEQUENTATION ON THE 29TH OF AUGUST 1778 (B).

A MAP OF THE COUNTRY WHICH WAS THE SCENE OF OPERATIONS OF
THE NORTHERN ARMY INCLUDING THE WILDERNESS THROUGH
WHICH GENERAL ARNOLD MARCHED TO ATTACK QUEBEC. (B).

S-09774
Workman, Benjamin. <u>Elements of Geography</u>. 11th ed. Philadelphia:
John M'Culloch, 1805.

THE WORLD (F).

THE SOLAR SYSTEM (6).

NORTH AMERICA (32).

THE UNITED STATES OF AMERICA (96).

SOUTH AMERICA (122).

EUROPE (126).

ASIA (152).

AFRICA (158).

S-09967
<u>Bible</u>. Philadelphia: Mathew Carey, 1806.

THE JOURNEYINGS OF THE CHILDREN OF ISRAEL FROM EGYPT THROUGH
THE RED SEA AND WILDERNESS TO THE LAND OF CANAAN (F).

CANAAN OR THE LAND OF PROMISE TO ABRAHAM AND HIS POSTERITY
(8).

ANCIENT EGYPT (34).

THE EASTERN COUNTRIES AS MENTIONED BY MOSES (42).

THE PLACES RECORDED IN THE FIVE BOOKS OF MOSES (42).

THE PURVEYORSHIPS IN THE REIGN OF SOLOMON (268).

THE DOMINIONS OF SOLOMON AND HIS ALLIES (340).

SHEBA WITH THE VOYAGE TO TARSHISH AND OPHIR (340).

MAP OF THE ASSYRIAN, BABYLONIAN, MEDIAN AND PERSIAN EMPIRES
(382).

THE LAND OF MORIAH OR JERUSALEM AND THE ADJACENT COUNTRY
(834).

MAP OF THE COUNTRY TRAVELLED BY THE APOSTLES WITH THE VOYAGE
OF SAINT PAUL TO ROME (930).

S-09974
Bible. Philadelphia: Samuel Bradford, 1806.

    A MAP OF THE JOURNEYINGS OF OUR SAVIOR JESUS CHRIST, AND OF
        THE PLACES MENTIONED OR REFERRED TO IN THE FOUR GOSPELS
        (F).

    A MAP OF THE TRAVELS & VOYAGES OF ST. PAUL, AND OF THE OTHER
        PLACES THAT ARE MENTIONED OR REFERRED TO IN THE BOOKS
        OF THE NEW TESTAMENT THAT FOLLOWS THE GOSPELS (B).

S-10038
Brookes, Richard. <u>Brookes's General Gazetteer Improved</u>.
    Philadelphia: John Bioren, for Jacob Johnson, 1806.

    THE WORLD (F).

    AFRICA (UP).

    NORTH AMERICA (UP).

    SOUTH AMERICA (UP).

    ASIA (UP).

    EUROPE (UP).

    WEST INDIES (UP).

    A MAP OF THE UNITED STATES AND PART OF LOUISIANA (UP).

S-10154
A MAP OF LEWIS & CLARK'S TRACK ACROSS THE WESTERN PORTION OF
    NORTH AMERICA FROM THE MISSISSIPPI TO THE PACIFIC OCEAN.
    William Clark. Philadelphia: Samuel Harrison, 1806.

S-10160
Clavijero, Francisco Javier. <u>The History of Mexico</u>. 3 volumes.
    Richmond, WV: William Pritchard, 1806.

    ANAHUAC, OR THE EMPIRE OF MEXIXO, & THE KINGDOMS OF
        ACOLHUACAN & MICHUACAN &C AS THEY WERE IN THE YEAR
        1521. Volume 1 (F).

    LAKES OF MEXICO. Volume 2 (F).

S-10224
Cramer, Zadok. <u>The Navigator</u>. 5th ed. Pittsburgh: Zadok Cramer, 1806.

MAP OF PITTSBURGH (1).

[MISSISSIPPI RIVER] (13 sheets) (49-77).

S-10342
Edwards, Bryan. <u>A New Atlas of the British West Indies</u>. Philadelphia: James Humphreys, 1806.

A NEW MAP OF THE WEST INDIES (1).

JAMAICA, DIVIDED INTO COUNTIES & PARISHES (2).

BARBADOES (3).

GRENADA (4).

ST. VINCENT (5).

MAP OF THE ISLAND OF DOMINICA FOR THE HISTORY OF THE WEST INDIES (6).

ISLAND OF ST. CHRISTOPHERS (7).

ISLAND OF ANTIGUA (8).

VIRGIN ISLANDS (9).

ISLAND OF TOBAGO (10).

ST. DOMINGO (11).

S-10405
Ferguson, James. <u>Astronomy Explained</u>. Philadelphia: Mathew Carey, 1806.

THE SOLAR SYSTEM (plate I).

A MAP OF THE EARTH UPON WHICH ARE MARKED THE HOURS AND THE MINUTES OF TRUE TIMES OF THE ENTRANCE & EXIT OF VENUS IN ITS PASSAGE OVER THE SON'S DISC JUNE 6TH 1761 (plate XVII).

S-10462
Furlong, Lawrence. <u>The American Coast Pilot</u>. 5th ed. Newburyport, MA: Edmund Blunt, 1806.

THE EASTERN END OF THE ISLE OF SABLE (16).

PLAN OF PORTLAND (144).

PORTSMOUTH (148).

NEWBURYPORT (150).

HARBOUR OF ANNIS SQUAM IN IPSWICH BAY (154).

BOSTON BAY (160).

CAPE POGE AND ADJACENT SHOALS (176).

PLAN OF NEWPORT HARBOUR (178).

CHART OF LONG ISLAND SOUND (186).

NEW YORK (188).

THE BAY AND RIVER OF DELAWARE (192).

THE BAY OF CHESAPEAKE FROM ITS ENTRANCE TO BALTIMORE (196).

CHARLESTON HARBOUR (206).

S-10570
Hoff's Agricultural and Commercial Almanac. Charleston: John
    Hoff, 1806.

PLAN OF THE CITY OF CHARLESTON SOUTH CAROLINA (F).

S-10638
THE UNITED STATES GEOGRAPHICAL AMUSEMENT. Jacob Johnson.
    Philadelphia: s.n., 1806.

S-10909
Morse, Jedidiah. Geography Made Easy. 10th ed. Boston: Joseph
    Buckingham, for Thomas and Andrews, 1806.

A NEW MAP OF THE WORLD WITH THE LATEST DISCOVERIES (F).

A MAP OF NORTH AMERICA FROM THE LATEST DISCOVERIES (50).

S-11180
Pons, Francois. A Voyage to the Eastern Part of Terra Firma.
    3 volumes. New York: Isaac Riley, 1806.

CARTE DE LA CAPITAINERIE GENERALE DE CARACAS (B).

S-11331
Scott, Joseph. A Geographical Description of Pennsylvania.
     Philadelphia: Robert Cochran, 1806.

     PENNSYLVANIA (F).

S-11392
Snowden, Richard. The History of North and South America.
     2 volumes in 1. Philadelphia: Jacob Johnson, 1806.

     NORTH AMERICA. Volume 1 (F).

     SOUTH AMERICA. Volume 1 (147).

S-11633
Message from the President of the United States, Communicating
     Discoveries Made in Exploring the Missouri. Washington: Way
     and Way, 1806.

     MAP OF THE WASHITA RIVER IN LOUISIANA (B).

S-11994
Anville, Jean d'. Ten Maps for Rollin's Antient History. Boston:
     Etheridge and Bliss, 1807. (Note: These maps accompany
     Rollin's 12th ed. of Ancient History of the Egyptians...,
     entry number S-13515).

     THE EAST (1).

     GRAECIA MAGNA INCLUDING SICILY (2).

     THE CARTHAGINIAN EMPIRE IN AFRICA (3).

     EGYPT WITH LIBYA (4).

     A CHART OF THE EXPEDITION OF CYRUS THE YOUNGER AND THE
          RETURN OF 10000 GREEKS ACCORDING TO XENOPHON (5).

     MAP FOR THE EXPEDITION OF HANNIBAL WHEREIN HIS PASSAGE INTO
          ITALY AND HIS PRINCIPAL MARCHES MARKED (6).

     THE WORLD AS KNOWN TO THE ANTIENTS (7).

     ASIA MINOR AND THE EUXIN SEA (8).

GREECE (9).

GREECE WITH THE NORTHERN PROVINCE (10).

S-12125
Bible. New York: Collins, Benjamin Perkins, 1807.

> CANAAN FROM THE TIME OF JOSHUA TO THE BABYLONISH CAPTIVITY [In Joshua] (UP).

> A MAP OF THE COUNTRY TRAVELLED BY THE APOSTLES WITH THE VOYAGE OF SAINT PAUL TO ROME [In Acts of the Apostles] (UP).

S-12180
The Boston Directory. Boston: Munroe and Francis, for Sampson and Murdock, 1807.

> PLAN OF BOSTON (F).

S-12190
Bowditch, Nathaniel. The American Practical Navigator. 2nd ed. Newburyport, MA: Edmund Blunt, 1807.

> CHART OF THE ATLANTIC OCEAN (F).

S-12208
MAP OF THE CITY OF NEW YORK AND THE ISLAND OF MANHATTAN, AS LAID OUT BY THE COMMISSIONERS APPOINTED BY THE LEGISLATURE. William Brieges. New York: s.n., 1807.

S-12220
Brown, John. A Dictionary of the Holy Bible. 2nd ed. 2 volumes. Pittsburgh: Zadok Cramer, 1807.

> THE HOLY LAND AND ADJACENT COUNTRIES. Volume 1 (96).

> A MAP OF THE COUNTRIES AND PLACES MENTIONED IN THE NEW TESTAMENT. Volume 2 (288).

S-12286
Charnock, John. Biographical Memoirs of Lord Viscount Nelson. New York: M'Farlane and Long, for Evert Duyckinck, 1807.

DISPOSITION OF THE ENGLISH & FRENCH FLEETS AT THE
    COMMENCEMENT OF THE ACTION, AUGUST 1ST, 1798
    [Nile River] (F).

S-12790
Hubbard, John. Rudiments of Geography. 3rd ed. Troy, NY: Wright,
    Goodenow, and Stockwell, 1807.

    MAP OF THE WORLD WITH THE LATEST DISCOVERIES (F).

S-12791
Hubbard, John. Rudiments of Geography. 3rd ed. Walpole, NH:
    Nichols and Hale, for Thomas and Thomas, 1807.

    MAP OF THE WORLD WITH THE LATEST DISCOVERIES (F).

S-12996
Marshall, John. The Life of George Washington. Philadelphia:
    Caleb Wayne, 1807.

    BOSTON WITH ITS ENVIRONS (B).

    A PLAN OF NEW YORK ISLAND, PART OF LONG ISLAND &C SHEWING
        THE POSITION OF AMERICAN AND BRITISH ARMIES, BEFORE,
        AT, AND AFTER THE ENGAGEMENT ON THE HEIGHTS, AUGUST
        27TH, 1776 (B).

    A MAP OF THE COUNTRY FROM RACETON RIVER IN EAST JERSEY TO
        ELK HEAD IN MARYLAND (B).

    A MAP OF THE COUNTRY WHICH WAS THE SCENE OF OPERATIONS OF
        THE NORTHERN ARMY; INCLUDING THE WILDERNESS THROUGH
        WHICH GENERAL ARNOLD MARCHED TO ATTACK QUEBEC (B).

    A MAP OF PART OF RHODE ISLAND SHEWING THE POSITIONS OF THE
        AMERICAN AND BRITISH ARMIES AT THE SIEGE OF NEWPORT AND
        THE SUBSEQUENT ACTION ON THE 29TH OF AUGUST 1778 (B).

    MAP OF NEW PARTS OF VIRGINIA, NORTH CAROLINA, SOUTH CAROLINA
        & GEORGIA (B).

    PLAN OF THE INVESTMENT AND ATTACK OF YORK IN VIRGINIA (B).

    PLAN OF THE SIEGE OF CHARLESTON IN S. CAROLINA (B).

    A PLAN OF THE COUNTRY FROM FRUG'S POINT TO CROTON RIVER
        SHEWING THE POSITIONS OF THE AMERICAN AND BRITISH
        ARMIES FROM THE 12TH OF OCTOBER 1776 UNTIL THE
        ENGAGEMENT ON THE WHITE PLAINS ON THE 28TH (B).

A PLAN OF THE NORTHERN PART OF NEW JERSEY, SHEWING THE
        POSITIONS OF THE AMERICAN AND BRITISH ARMIES AFTER
        CROSSING THE NORTH RIVER IN 1776 (B).

S-13104
Mitchill, Samuel Latham. The Picture of New York. New York: Isaac
    Riley and Brisban and Brannan, 1807.

    PLAN OF THE CITY OF NEW YORK (F).

S-13144
Morse, Jedidiah. Geography Made Easy. 11th ed. Boston: Joseph
    Buckingham, for Thomas and Andrews, 1807.

    A NEW MAP OF THE WORLD WITH THE LATEST DISCOVERIES (F).

    A MAP OF NORTH AMERICA FROM THE LATEST DISCOVERIES (50).

S-13393
Pike, Zebulon. An Account of a Voyage up the Mississippi River,
    from St. Louis to Its Source. Washington: s.n., 1807.

    MAP OF THE MISSISSIPPI RIVER FROM THE SOURCE TO THE MOUTH OF
        THE MISSOURI (B).

S-13515
Rollin, Charles. The Ancient History of the Egyptians.... 12th
    ed. 8 volumes. Boston: Etheridge and Bliss and Charles
    Williams, 1807-1811.

    SEE ENTRY S-11994 FOR MAP LISTINGS.

S-13554
Scott, Joseph. Elements of Geography. Philadelphia: Kimber and
    Conrad, 1807.

    A NEW MAP OF THE WORLD (F).

S-13555
Scott, Joseph. A Geographical Description of the States of
    Maryland and Delaware. Philadelphia: Kimber and Conrad,
    1807.

    MARYLAND (F).

    DELAWARE (155).

S-13740
Lloyd, Thomas. <u>Trial of Thomas O. Selfridge</u>. Boston: Russell and
    Cutler, 1807.

    [BOSTON, NEAR THE OLD STATE HOUSE] (B).

S-14217
A MAP OF THE STATE OF VERMONT. James Whitelaw. s.l.: s.n., 1807.

S-14242
Workman, Benjamin. <u>Elements of Geography</u>. 12th ed. Philadelphia:
    Ebenezer M'Culloch, 1807.

    WORLD (F).

    THE SOLAR SYSTEM (6).

    NORTH AMERICA (82).

    THE UNITED STATES OF AMERICA (96).

    SOUTH AMERICA (122).

    EUROPE (126).

    ASIA (152).

    AFRICA (158).

S-14264
Adams, George. <u>An Essay on the Use of the Celestial and
    Terrestial Globes</u>. 5th ed. Philadelphia: Dickinson, for
    William Woodward, 1808.

    A GLOBE OF THE WORLD (F).

S-14796
Cramer, Zadok. <u>The Navigator</u>. 6th ed. Pittsburgh: Cramer and
    Spear, for Zadok Cramer, 1808.

    MAP OF PITTSBURGH (3).

    [OHIO RIVER] (13 sheets) (42-82).

    FALLS OF OHIO (72).

    [MISSISSIPPI RIVER] (13 sheets) (94-127).

S-15043
Franklin, Benjamin. The Works of Dr. Benjamin Franklin.
    6 Volumes. Philadelphia: William Duane, 1808-1818.

    A CHART OF THE ATLANTIC OCEAN EXHIBITING THE COURSE OF THE
        GULPH STREAM &C. Volume 3 (254).

S-15193
Harris, Hannah. Book of Maps. Providence: s.n., 1808.

    [RHODE ISLAND] (1).

    [NEW ENGLAND] (2).

    [MISSISSIPPI AND ALABAMA] (3).

    [NEW JERSEY] (4).

    [GREAT BRITAIN AND IRELAND] (5).

    [OHIO] (6).

    [TENNESSEE AND KENTUCKY] (7).

    [UNITED STATES] (8).

S-15277
Hubbard, John. The Rudiments of Geography. 4th ed. Troy, NY:
    Wright, Goodenow and Stockwell, 1808.

    MAP OF THE WORLD WITH THE LATEST DISCOVERIES (F).

S-15278
Hubbard, John. The Rudiments of Geography. 4th ed. Walpole, NH:
    Cheever Felch, for Thomas and Thomas, 1808.

    MAP OF THE WORLD WITH THE LATEST DISCOVERIES (F).

S-15336
Josephus, Flavius. The Works of Flavius Josephus. 4 volumes. New
    York: Thomas Simpson, 1808.

    A MAP OF SUCH PLACES MENTIONED IN THE NEW TESTAMENT AS WERE
        IN GREECE, CYPRUS ASIA &C. Volume 3 (F).

    A NEW MAP OF THE SEVERAL COUNTRIES CITIES TOWNS &C MENTIONED
        IN THE NEW TESTAMENT AS WERE IN THE HOLY LAND AND PARTS
        ADJOINING. Volume 3 (F).

A MAP OF THE SEVERAL REGIONS MENTIONED IN THE NEW TESTAMENT
TOGETHER WITH THE CITIES AND TOWNS MOST REMOTE FROM THE
HOLY LAND. Volume 3 (F).

S-15628
Molina, Juan. The Geographical, Natural & Civil History of Chili.
Middletown, CT: Isaac Riley, 1808.

A MAP OF CHILI IN SOUTH AMERICA (F).

S-15654
Morse, Jedidiah. The History of America. 4th ed. Philadelphia:
Bartram and Reynolds, for Thomas and Andrews, 1808.

A GENERAL MAP OF NORTH AMERICA FROM THE BEST AUTHORITIES
(F).

SOUTH AMERICA FROM THE BEST AUTHORITIES (viii).

S-15655
Morse, Jedidiah. A New Gazetteer of the Eastern Continent. 2nd
ed. Boston: Joseph Buckingham, for Thomas and Andrews, 1808.

EUROPE (F).

AFRICA (UP).

ASIA (UP).

S-15803
O'Neill, John. A New and Easy System of Geography and Popular
Astronomy. Baltimore: Dobbin and Murphy, 1808.

WORLD (F).

SOLAR SYSTEM (F).

S-15998
THE FIRST ACTUAL SURVEY OF THE STATE OF N. CAROLINA. Jonathan
Price. Philadelphia: Samuel Harrison, 1808.

S-16129
Saint Pierre, Jacques. Studies of Nature. Philadelphia: Abraham
Small, for Birch and Small, 1808.

THE ATLANTIC HEMISPHERE (104).

S-16307
Thierry, Jean. <u>Examination of the Claim of the United States</u>. New
    Orleans: Jean Thierry, 1808.

    PLANO DE LA CIUDAD DE NUEVA ORLEANS (B).

    PLAN DE LA HABITACION DE DON BERHAN GRAVIER (B).

S-16615
Van Rensselaer, Solomon. <u>Report of the Trials of the Causes of
    Elisha Jenkins vs. Solomon Van Rensselaer</u>. Albany: Croswell
    and Frary, 1808.

    MAP OF THE STATE STREET AREA OF ALBANY N.Y. (F).

S-16734
Whittington, Rev. <u>Travels Through Spain and Part of Portugal</u>.
    Boston: Belcher and Armstrong, for White and Burditt, 1808.

    SPAIN AND PORTUGAL (F).

S-16836
<u>The American Coast Pilot</u>. 6th ed. Newburyport, MA: Edmund Blunt,
    1809.

    THE EASTERN END OF THE ISLE OF SABLE (16).

    PLAN OF PORTLAND HARBOUR (150).

    PLAN OF PORTSMOUTH HARBOUR (154).

    PLAN OF NEWBURYPORT HARBOUR (158).

    HARBOUR OF ANNIS SQUAM IN IPSWICH BAY (160).

    BOSTON BAY (166).

    CAPE POGE AND ADJACENT SHOALS (184).

    CHART OF LONG ISLAND SOUND (190).

    NEW YORK (194).

    THE BAY AND RIVER OF DELAWARE (200).

    CHESAPEAKE BAY FROM ITS ENTRANCE TO BALTIMORE (208).

A CHART OF THE COAST OF NORTH CAROLINA BETWEEN CAPE HATTERAS
    & CAPE FEAR (210).

CHARLESTON HARBOUR (214).

CHART OF THE HARBOUR OF VERA CRUZ (268).

S-16999
Bible. New York: Elliot and Eastburn, 1809.

    A MAP OF PALESTINE DESCRIBING THE TRAVELS OF JESUS CHRIST
        (F).

    PALESTINE OR THE HOLY LAND (54).

S-17003
Bible. Philadelphia: Mathew Carey, 1809.

    THE JOURNEYINGS OF THE CHILDREN OF ISRAEL FROM EGYPT THROUGH
        THE RED SEA AND WILDERNESS TO THE LAND OF CANAAN (F).

    CANAAN OR THE LAND OF PROMISE TO ARRAHAM AND HIS POSTERITY
        (8).

    ANCIENT EGYPT (34).

    THE PLACES RECORDED IN THE FIVE BOOKS OF MOSES (42).

    THE EASTERN COUNTRIES AS MENTIONED BY MOSES (42).

    CANAAN FROM THE TIME OF JOSHUA TO THE BABYLONISH CAPTIVITY
        (172).

    THE PURVEYORSHIPS IN THE REIGN OF SOLOMON (268).

    A MAP OF THE ASSYRIAN, BABYLONIAN, MEDIAN, AND PERSIAN
        EMPIRES (282).

    DOMINIONS OF SOLOMON AND HIS ALLIES (340).

    SHEBA WITH THE VOYAGE TO TARSHISH AND OPHIR (340).

    THE LAND OF MORIAH OR JERUSALEM AND THE ADJACENT COUNTRY
        (833).

    MAP OF THE COUNTRY TRAVELLED BY THE APOSTLES WITH THE VOYAGE
        OF SAINT PAUL TO ROME (930).

S-17067
The Boston Directory. Boston: Munroe, Francis and Parker, for
    Edward Cotton, 1809.

    PLAN OF BOSTON (F).

S-17149
Carey, Mathew. Carey's American Atlas. Philadelphia: Mathew
    Carey, 1809.

    A MAP OF THE UNITED STATES COMPILED CHIEFLY FROM THE STATE
        MAPS AND OTHER AUTHENTIC INFORMATION. Samuel Lewis.
        (1).

    THE BRITISH POSSESSIONS IN NORTH AMERICA. Samuel Lewis (2).

    VERMONT FROM ACTUAL SURVEY (3).

    THE STATE OF NEW HAMPSHIRE COMPILED CHIEFLY FROM ACTUAL
        SURVEYS. Samuel Lewis (4).

    THE PROVINCE OF MAINE FROM THE BEST AUTHORITIES. Samuel
        Lewis (5).

    THE STATE OF MASSACHUSETTS COMPILED FROM THE BEST
        AUTHORITIES. Samuel Lewis (6).

    THE STATE OF RHODE ISLAND COMPILED FROM THE BEST
        AUTHORITIES. Hurley Harris (7).

    CONNECTICUT FROM THE BEST AUTHORITIES (8).

    THE STATE OF NEW YORK COMPILED FROM THE BEST AUTHORITIES.
        Samuel Lewis (9).

    THE STATE OF NEW JERSEY COMPILED FROM THE MOST AUTHENTIC
        INFORMATION (10).

    THE STATE OF PENNSYLVANIA REDUCED WITH PERMISSION FROM
        READING HOWELL'S MAP. Samuel Lewis (11).

    DELAWARE FROM THE BEST AUTHORITIES. Samuel Lewis (12).

    THE STATE OF MARYLAND FROM THE BEST AUTHORITIES. Samuel
        Lewis (13).

    THE STATE OF VIRGINIA FROM THE BEST AUTHORITIES. Samuel
        Lewis (14).

    THE STATE OF NORTH CAROLINA FROM THE BEST AUTHORITIES, &C.
        Samuel Lewis (15).

THE STATE OF SOUTH CAROLINA FROM THE BEST AUTHORITIES.
Samuel Lewis (16).

GEORGIA FROM THE BEST AUTHORITIES (17).

KENTUCKY REDUCED FROM ELIHU BARKER'S LARGE MAP (18).

A MAP OF THE TENNASSEE STATE FORMERLY PART OF NORTH CAROLINA
TAKEN CHIEFLY FROM SURVEYS BY CAPT. S. SMITH & OTHERS
(19).

A MAP OF SOUTH AMERICA ACCORDING TO THE BEST AUTHORITIES
(20).

A CHART OF THE WEST INDIES FROM THE LATEST MARINE JOURNALS
AND SURVEYS (21).

A MAP OF THE DISCOVERIES MADE BY CAPTS. COOK & CLERKE IN THE
YEAR 1778 & 1779 BETWEEN THE EASTERN COAST OF ASIA AND
THE WESTERN COAST OF NORTH AMERICA (22).

PLAT OF THE SEVEN RANGES OF TOWNSHIPS BEING PART OF THE
TERRITORY OF THE UNITED STATES. N.W. OF THE RIVER OHIO
(23).

A MAP OF PART OF THE N.W. TERRITORY OF THE UNITED STATES
COMPILED FROM ACTUAL SURVEYS AND THE BEST INFORMATION.
Samuel Lewis (24).

LOUISIANA (25).

S-17691
Guthrie, William. A New Geographical, Historical, and Commercial
Grammar. 2 volumes. Philadelphia: Brown and Merritt, for
Johnson and Warner, 1809.

THE WORLD. Volume 1 (F).

EUROPE. Volume 1 (54).

SWEDEN, DENMARK, NORWAY AND FINLAND FROM THE BEST
AUTHORITIES. Volume 1 (80).

SOUTHERN PART OF RUSSIA OR MUSCOVY IN EUROPE. Volume 1
(102).

NORTHERN PART OF RUSSIA OR MUSCOVY IN EUROPE. Volume 1
(102).

ENGLAND AND WALES FROM THE BEST AUTHORITIES. Volume 1 (130).

SCOTLAND FROM THE BEST AUTHORITIES. Volume 1 (286).

IRELAND FROM THE BEST AUTHORITIES. Volume 1 (328).

FRANCE. Volume 1 (358).

NETHERLANDS FROM THE BEST AUTHORITIES. Volume 1 (418).

THE SEVEN UNITED PROVINCES FROM THE BEST AUTHORITIES. Volume 1 (424).

GERMANY FROM THE BEST AUTHORITIES. Volume 1 (436).

POLAND FROM THE BEST AUTHORITIES. Volume 1 (478).

SWITZERLAND WITH ITS SUBJECTS & ALLIES. Volume 1 (516).

SPAIN AND PORTUGAL FROM THE BEST AUTHORITIES. Volume 1 (530).

CHART OF THE WORLD. Volume 2 (F).

ITALY FROM THE BEST AUTHORITIES. Volume 2 (12).

TURKEY IN EUROPE AND HUNGARY. Volume 2 (40).

ASIA. Volume 2 (58).

HINDOSTAN, OR INDIA FROM THE BEST AUTHORITIES. Volume 2 (100).

AFRICA. Volume 2 (194).

SOUTH AMERICA. Volume 2 (262).

NORTH AMERICA. Volume 2 (262).

A MAP OF THE UNITED STATES AND PART OF LOUISIANA. Volume 2 (308).

WEST INDIES. Volume 2 (386).

S-18130
Morse, Jedidiah. <u>A Compendious History of New England</u>. 2nd ed. Newburyport, MA: Joseph Cushing, for Thomas and Whipple, 1809.

NEW ENGLAND (F).

S-18131
Morse, Jedidiah. Geography Made Easy. Boston: Joseph Buckingham,
    for Thomas and Andrews, 1809.

    A NEW MAP OF THE WORLD WITH THE LATEST DISCOVERIES (F).

    A MAP OF NORTH AMERICA FROM THE LATEST DISCOVERIES (72).

S-18321
Parish, Elijah. A Compendious History of New England. 2nd ed.
    Newburyport, MA: Thomas and Whipple, 1809.

    A CORRECT MAP OF THE WORLD WITH THE LATEST DISCOVERIES (F).

    NORTH AMERICA (12).

S-18474
Ramsay, David. The History of South Carolina. 2 volumes.
    Charleston, SC: David Longwith, 1809.

    A NEW AND ACCURATE MAP OF THE PROVINCE OF SOUTH CAROLINA IN
        NORTH AMERICA. Volume 1 (F).

    A PLAN OF CHARLESTON FROM A SURVEY OF EDWD. CRISP IN 1704.
        Volume 2 (F).

S-18584
Seaman, Valentine. A Dissertation on the Mineral Waters of
    Saratoga. 2nd ed. New York: Collins and Perkins, 1809.

    A VIEW AND SECTION OF THE ROCK SPRING AT SARATOGA (F).

S-18649
Snowden, Richard. The History of North and South America.
    2 volumes in 1. Philadelphia: Alexander and Phillips, for
    Johnson and Warner, 1809.

    NORTH AMERICA. Volume 1 (F).

    SOUTH AMERICA. Volume 2 (F).

S-18665
Spafford, Horatio. General Geography. Hudson: Croswell and Frary,
    1809.

MAP OF THE WORLD FROM THE LATEST DISCOVERIES (F).

UNITED STATES: OR FREDON (148).

S-18775
The Travels of Capts. Lewis & Clarke. Philadelphia: Hubbard
    Lester, 1809.

    MAP OF THE COUNTRY INHIBITED BY THE WESTERN TRIBES OF
        INDIANS (F).

S-19239
Williams, Samuel. The Natural and Civil History of Vermont. 2nd
    ed. Burlington: Samuel Mills, 1809.

    A MAP OF THE STATE OF VERMONT (F).

S-19277
Workman, Benjamin. Elements of Geography. 13th ed. Philadelphia:
    John M'Culloch, 1809.

    WORLD (F).

    THE SOLAR SYSTEM (6).

    SOUTH AMERICA (120).

    EUROPE (124).

    ASIA (152).

    AFRICA (156).

S-19516
Bible. Philadelphia: Mathew Carey; New York: Donald Frazer, 1810.

    A MAP OF PALESTINE DESCRIBING THE TRAVELS OF JESUS CHRIST
        (832).

S-19522
Macknight, James. A New Literal Translation from the Original
    Greek of All the Apostolical Epistles. Volume 1. Boston:
    Wells and Wait, 1810.

    [MEDITERRANEAN SEA] (F).

S-19598
The Boston Directory. Boston: Munroe and Francis, for Edward
    Cotton, 1810.

    PLAN OF BOSTON (F).

S-19897
A MERCATOR MAP OF THE STARRY HEAVENS, COMPREHENDING THE WHOLE
    EQUINOCTICAL, AND TERMINATED BY THE POLAR CIRCLES. William
    Croswell. Boston: John Eliot, 1810.

S-19988
Carey, Mathew. Carey's Minor Atlas. Philadelphia: Mathew Carey,
    1810.

    THE UNITED STATES OF AMERICA (1).

    VERMONT FROM ACTUAL SURVEYS (2).

    THE STATE OF NEW HAMPSHIRE. Samuel Lewis (3).

    PROVINCE OF MAINE (4).

    MASSACHUSETTS (5).

    RHODE ISLAND (6).

    CONNECTICUT (7).

    NEW YORK (8).

    NEW JERSEY (9).

    PENNSYLVANIA (10).

    DELAWARE (11).

    OHIO AND N.W. TERRITORY (12).

    TENNASSEE: LATELY THE S.W. TERRITORY (13).

    NORTH CAROLINA (14).

    KENTUCKEY (15).

    VIRGINIA (16).

    MARYLAND (17).

    SOUTH CAROLINA (18).

MISSISSIPPI TERRITORY AND GEORGIA (19).

LOUISIANA (20).

S-20025
Eddy, Thomas. <u>Observations on Canal Navigation</u>. New York: s.n.,
     1810.

     [WESTERN NEW YORK] (F).

S-20443
Jamieson, John. <u>An Account of the Empire of Marocco</u>.
     Philadelphia: Fry and Kammerer, for Francis Nichols, 1810.

     MAP OF WEST BARBARY, INCLUDING SUSE & TAFILELT, FORMING THE
          DOMINIONS OF THE PRESENT EMPEROR OF MAROCCO (B).

     MAP OF THE TRACT OF THE CARAVANS, ACROSS SAHARA, FROM FAS TO
          TIMBUCTOO (B).

S-20788
Morse, Jedidiah. <u>The American Gazetteer</u>. 3rd ed. Boston: Joseph
     Buckingham, for Thomas and Andrews, 1810.

     NORTH AMERICA (F).

     SOUTH AMERICA (UP).

S-20844
<u>A New Atlas of the British West Indies</u>. Charleston, SC: Morford
     and Willington, 1810.

     A NEW MAP OF THE WEST INDIES (1).

     JAMAICA, DIVIDED INTO COUNTIES & PARISHES (2).

     BARBADOES (3).

     GRENADA (4).

     MAP OF THE ISLAND OF DOMINICA (5).

     ISLAND OF ST. CHRISTOPHERS (6).

     ST. VINCENT (7).

     ISLAND OF ANTIGUA (8).

131

VIRGIN ISLANDS (9).

ISLAND OF TOBAGO (10).

ST. DOMINGO (11).

S-20991
Parish, Elijah. _A New System of Modern Geography_. Newburyport,
    MA: Thomas and Whipple, 1810.

A CORRECT MAP OF THE WORLD WITH THE LATEST DISCOVERIES (F).

NORTH AMERICA (26).

S-21001
Payne, John. _A New and Complete History of Europe_. New York:
    s.n., 1810.

EUROPE (F).

RUSSIA OR MUSCOVY IN EUROPE FROM THE LATEST AUTHORITIES
    (22).

SWEDEN, DENMARK & NORWAY FROM THE LATEST AUTHORITIES (74).

GERMANY AND THE NETHERLANDS FROM THE LATEST AUTHORITIES
    (148).

SWITZERLAND (224).

ITALY (240).

SPAIN AND PORTUGAL (298).

THE NETHERLANDS WITH THE ROADS FROM THE LATEST AUTHORITIES
    (360).

ENGLAND AND WALES (414).

IRELAND FROM THE LATEST AUTHORITIES (576).

A NEW AND ACCURATE MAP OF FRANCE DIVIDED INTO DEPARTMENTS,
    WITH THE NETHERLANDS &C. (606).

DISPOSITION OF THE ENGLISH & FRENCH FLEETS AT THE
    COMMENCEMENT OF ACTION, AUGUST 1ST 1798 (700).

S-21076
Phillips, Richard. <u>A General View of the Manners, Customs and
    Curiosities of Nations</u>. 2 volumes. Philadelphia: John
    Bouvier, for Johnson and Warner, 1810.

    EUROPE. Volume 1 (xii).

    GREAT BRITAIN AND IRELAND. Volume 1 (xxii).

    A MAP OF THE UNITED STATES AND PART OF LOUISIANA. Volume 1
        (xxxvi).

    SOUTH AMERICA. Volume 1 (xxxviii).

    ASIA. Volume 1 (116).

    AFRICA. Volume 2 (10).

    NORTH AMERICA. Volume 2 (188).

S-21089
Pike, Zebulon. <u>An Account of Expeditions to the Sources of the
    Mississippi</u>. Philadelphia: John Binns, for Cornelius Conrad,
    1810.

    THE FIRST PART OF CAPTN. PIKE'S CHART OF THE INTERNAL PART
        OF LOUISIANA. Anthony Nau (plate I, B).

    A CHART OF THE INTERNAL PART OF LOUISIANA (plate II, B).

    A MAP OF THE INTERNAL PROVINCES OF NEW SPAIN (B).

    A SKETCH OF THE VICE ROYALTY EXHIBITING THE SEVERAL
        PROVINCES AND ITS APPROXIMATION TO THE INTERNAL
        PROVINCES OF NEW SPAIN (B).

    MAP OF THE MISSISSIPPI RIVER FROM THE SOURCE TO THE MOUTH OF
        THE MISSOURI. Nicholas King (B).

    FALLS OF ST. ANTHONY (B).

S-21090
Pinkerton, John. <u>A General Collection of the Best and Most
    Interesting Voyages and Travels</u>. 6 volumes. Philadelphia:
    Kimber and Conrad, 1810-1812.

    AZORES BY CORFINO AND FLEURIEU. Volume 2 (81).

    SCILLEY ISLANDS. Volume 2 (728).

S-21289
Schultz, Christian. Travels on an Inland Voyage. 2 volumes. New
     York: Isaac Riley, 1810.

     A MAP OF THE UNITED STATES INCLUDING LOUISIANA. Volume 1
          (xviii).

     A MAP OF THE HUDSON AND MOHAWK RIVERS. Volume 1 (128).

     A MAP OF THE OHIO RIVER AND PART OF THE MISSISSIPPI. Volume
          2 (F).

     MAP OF THE MISSISSIPPI RIVER CONTAINING THE ROUTE FROM THE
          MOUTH OF THE OHIO TO NEW ORLEANS. Volume 2 (112).

S-22003
Weems, Mason. The Life of George Washington. 10th ed.
     Philadelphia: Mathew Carey, 1810.

     MAP OF THE UNITED STATES (F).

S-22047
A CORRECT MAP OF THE STATE OF VERMONT. 2nd ed. James Whitelaw.
     s.l.: s.n., 1810.

S-22353
Bible. New York: Ezra Sargeant, 1811.

     MAP OF THE JOURNEYINGS OF THE ISRAELITES FROM EGYPT TO THE
          LAND OF CANAAN [In Numbers] (UP).

     A MAP OF ANCIENT ISRAEL DIVIDED INTO THE TWELVE TRIBES OF
          ISRAEL [In Ezekiel] (UP).

     A MAP OF THE DIFFERENT PLACES MENTIONED IN THE NEW TESTAMENT
          WITH ST. PAUL'S YOYAGES FROM PHILIPPI TO OPRE AND FROM
          CAESAREA TO ROME [In Acts of the Apostles] (UP).

S-22355
Bible. Philadelphia: Mathew Carey, 1811.

     THE JOURNEYINGS OF THE CHILDREN OF DAVID FROM EGYPT THROUGH
          THE RED SEA AND WILDERNESS TO THE LAND OF CANAAN (F).

     CANAAN OR THE LAND OF PROMISE TO ABRAHAM AND HIS POSTERITY
          (6).

     ANCIENT EGYPT (34).

134

THE PLACES RECORDED IN THE FIVE BOOKS OF MOSES (42).

THE EASTERN COUNTRIES AS MENTIONED BY MOSES (42).

CANAAN FROM THE TIME OF JOSHUA TO THE BABYLONIAN CAPTIVITY (172).

THE PURVEYORSHIPS IN THE REIGN OF SOLOMON (268).

MAP OF THE ASSYRIAN, BABYLONIAN, MEDIAN AND PERSIAN EMPIRES (282).

DOMINIONS OF SOLOMON AND HIS ALLIES (340).

SHEBA WITH THE VOYAGE TO TARSHISH AND OPHIR (340).

THE LAND OF MORIAH OR JERUSALEM AND THE ADJACENT COUNTRY (834).

MAP OF THE COUNTRY TRAVELLED BY THE APOSTLES WITH THE VOYAGE OF SAINT PAUL TO ROME (930).

S-22409
Brown, John. A Dictionary of the Holy Bible. 2nd Pittsburgh ed. Pittsburgh: Cramer, Spear and Eichbaum, 1811.

THE HOLY LAND AND ADJACENT COUNTRIES (96).

A MAP OF THE COUNTRIES & PLACES MENTIONED IN THE NEW TESTAMENT WHERE THE GOSPEL WAS PLANTED BY THE APOSTLES (289).

S-22445
Bowditch, Nathaniel. The New American Practical Navigator. 3rd ed. Newburyport, MA: Edward Little, 1811.

CHART OF THE ATLANTIC OCEAN (F).

THE CIRCLES, ZONES, &C. OF THE ARTIFICIAL GLOBE OR SPHERE (48).

S-22446
Bowditch, Nathaniel. The New American Practical Navigator. 3rd ed. New York: Edmund Blunt, 1811.

CHART OF THE ATLANTIC OCEAN (F).

THE CIRCLES, ZONES, &C. OF THE ARTIFICIAL GLOBE OR SPHERE (60).

S-22479
Carey, Mathew. <u>Carey's General Atlas</u>. Philadelphia: Mathew Carey,
  1811.

  A MAP OF THE WORLD FROM THE BEST AUTHORITIES (1).

  A CHART OF THE WORLD ACCORDING TO MERCATORS PROJECTION
    SHEWING THE LATEST DISCOVERIES OF CAPT. COOK (2).

  AN ACCURATE MAP OF EUROPE FROM THE BEST AUTHORITIES (3).

  SWEDEN, DENMARK, NORWAY AND FINLAND FROM THE BEST
    AUTHORITIES (4).

  THE RUSSIAN EMPIRE IN EUROPE AND ASIA (5).

  SCOTLAND WITH THE PRINCIPAL ROADS FROM THE BEST AUTHORITIES
    (6).

  AN ACCURATE MAP OF ENGLAND AND WALES WITH THE PRINCIPAL
    ROADS FROM THE BEST AUTHORITIES (7).

  A MAP OF IRELAND ACCORDING TO THE BEST AUTHORITIES (8).

  THE SEVEN UNITED PROVINCES OF HOLLAND, FRIESLAND, GRONINGEN,
    OVERYSSEL, GELDER, UTRECHT AND ZEALAND (9).

  THE AUSTRIAN, FRENCH AND DUTCH NETHERLANDS FROM THE BEST
    AUTHORITIES (10).

  THE EMPIRE OF GERMANY WITH THE 13 CANTONS OF SWITZERLAND
    FROM THE BEST AUTHORITIES (11).

  FRANCE DIVIDED INTO CIRCLES AND DEPARTMENTS (12).

  A MAP OF THE SEAT OF WAR IN FRANCE WITH THE COUNTRY DIVIDED
    INTO ITS SEVERAL DEPARTMENTS (13).

  TURKEY IN EUROPE AND HUNGARY, FROM THE BEST AUTHORITIES
    (14).

  SPAIN AND PORTUGAL FROM THE BEST AUTHORITIES (15).

  ITALY AND SARDINIA FROM THE BEST AUTHORITIES (16).

  SWITZERLAND ACCORDING TO THE BEST AUTHORITIES (17).

  POLAND SHEWING THE CLAIMS OF RUSSIA, PRUSSIA & AUSTRIA UNTIL
    THE LATE DEPREDATIONS (18).

  ASIA ACCORDING TO THE BEST AUTHORITIES (19).

CHINA DIVIDED INTO ITS GREAT PROVINCES ACCORDING TO THE BEST AUTHORITIES (20).

AN ACCURATE MAP OF HINDOSTAN OR INDIA FROM THE BEST AUTHORITIES (21).

AFRICA ACCORDING TO THE BEST AUTHORITIES (22).

THE BRITISH POSSESSIONS IN NORTH AMERICA FROM THE BEST AUTHORITIES (23).

A MAP OF THE UNITED STATES, COMPILED FROM THE STATE MAPS AND OTHER AUTHENTIC INFORMATION. Samuel Lewis (24).

VERMONT FROM ACTUAL SURVEY (25).

THE STATE OF NEW HAMPSHIRE COMPILED CHIEFLY FROM THE BEST AUTHORITIES. Samuel Lewis (26).

THE PROVINCE OF MAINE, FROM THE BEST AUTHORITIES. Samuel Lewis (27).

THE STATE OF MASSACHUSETTS COMPILED FROM THE BEST AUTHORITIES. Samuel Lewis (28).

THE STATE OF RHODE ISLAND COMPILED FROM THE SURVEYS AND OBSERVATIONS OF CALEB HARRIS. Harding Harris (29).

CONNECTICUT FROM THE BEST AUTHORITIES (30).

THE STATE OF NEW YORK COMPILED FROM THE BEST AUTHORITIES (31).

THE STATE OF NEW JERSEY COMPILED FROM THE BEST AUTHORITIES (32).

THE STATE OF PENNSYLVANIA REDUCED WITH PERMISSION FROM READING HOWELL'S MAP. Samuel Lewis (33).

DELAWARE FROM THE BEST AUTHORITIES (34).

THE STATE OF MARYLAND. Samuel Lewis (35).

THE STATE OF VIRGINIA FROM THE BEST AUTHORITIES. Samuel Lewis (36).

THE STATE OF NORTH CAROLINA FROM THE BEST AUTHORITIES &C. Samuel Lewis (37).

THE STATE OF SOUTH CAROLINA FROM THE BEST AUTHORITIES.
Samuel Lewis (38).

GEORGIA FROM THE BEST AUTHORITIES (39).

KENTUCKY, REDUCED FROM ELIHU BARKER'S LARGE MAP. Elihu
Barker (40).

A MAP OF THE TENNASSEE STATE FORMERLY PART OF NORTH CAROLINA
TAKEN FROM SURVEYS (41).

A MAP OF SOUTH AMERICA ACCORDING TO THE BEST AUTHORITIES
(42).

A CHART OF THE WEST INDIES FROM THE LATEST MARINE JOURNALS
AND SURVEYS (43).

A MAP OF THE COUNTRIES SITUATED ABOUT THE NORTH POLE (44).

A MAP OF THE DISCOVERIES MADE BY CAPTS. COOK & CLERKE IN THE
YEARS 1778 & 1779 BETWEEN THE EASTERN COAST OF ASIA AND
THE WESTERN COAST OF NORTH AMERICA (45).

PLAT OF THE SEVEN RANGES OF TOWNSHIPS BEING PART OF THE
TERRITORY OF THE UNITED STATES N.W. OF THE RIVER OHIO
(46).

A MAP OF PART OF THE N.W. TERRITORY OF THE UNITED STATES
COMPILED FROM ACTUAL SURVEYS AND THE BEST INFORMATION.
Samuel Lewis (47).

A MAP OF THE FRENCH PART OF ST. DOMINGO (48).

A MAP OF THOSE COUNTRIES IN WHICH THE APOSTLES TRAVELLED IN
PROPAGATING CHRISTIANITY (49).

LOUISIANA (50).

S-22481
Carpenter, Lant. An Introduction to the Geography of the New
Testament. Cambridge, MA: Hilliard and Metcalf, for William
Hilliard, 1811.

THE COUNTRIES SPOKEN OF IN THE NEW TESTAMENT (1).

GREECE, ASIA MINOR, &C. (5).

PALESTINE (27).

JERUSALEM (44).

S-22541
Clarke, Edward. <u>Travels in Various Countries of Europe, Asia, and Africa</u>. Philadelphia: Enos Bronson, for Anthony Finley, 1811.

> PLAN OF THE ISLAND AND TOWN OF TSCHERCHASKOY THE CAPITAL OF DON COSSACKS (216).

S-22636
Cramer, Zadok. <u>The Navigator</u>. 7th ed. Pittsburgh: Cramer, Spear and Eichbaum, 1811.

> MAP OF PITTSBURGH (11).

> [OHIO RIVER] (13 sheets) (76-142).

> FALLS OF OHIO (124).

> [MISSISSIPPI RIVER] (13 sheets) (179-223).

S-22741
MAP OF THE WESTERN PART OF THE STATE OF NEW YORK SHEWING THE ROUTE OF A PROPOSED CANAL FROM LAKE ERIE TO HUDSON'S RIVER. John Eddy. Newark: Peter Maverick, 1811.

S-23206
Lendrum, John. <u>A Concise and Impartial History of the American Revolution</u>. 2 volumes. Trenton: James Oram, 1811.

> UNITED STATES. Volume 1 (F).

> NEW JERSEY. Volume 2 (F).

S-23287
Martin, John. <u>The Conquest of Canaan</u>. Frankford, PA: Coale and Gilbert, 1811.

> THE LAND OF CANAAN AS DIVIDED AMONG THE TWELVE TRIBES (F).

> THE JOURNEYINGS OF THE ISRAELITES THRU THE WILDERNESS (F).

S-23288
Martin, John. <u>The Conquest of Canaan</u>. Frankford, PA: Coale and Gilbert, 1811.

THE LAND OF CANAAN AS DIVIDED AMONG THE TWELVE TRIBES (F).

THE JOURNEYINGS OF THE ISRAELITES THRU THE WILDERNESS (F).

S-23439
Morse, Jedidiah. Geography Made Easy. 14th ed. Boston: Joseph
    Buckingham, for Thomas and Andrews, 1811.

    A NEW MAP OF THE WORLD WITH THE LATEST DISCOVERIES (F).

    A MAP OF NORTH AMERICA FROM THE LATEST DISCOVERIES (56).

S-23641
Paxton, John. The Stranger's Guide. Philadelphia: s.n., 1811.

    TO THE CITIZENS OF PHILADELPHIA, THIS NEW PLAN OF THE CITY
        AND ITS ENVIRONS TAKEN FROM ACTUAL SURVEY (F).

S-23642
TO THE CITIZENS OF PHILADELPHIA, THIS NEW PLAN OF THE CITY AND
    ITS ENVIRONS TAKEN FROM ACTUAL SURVEY IS RESPECTFULLY
    DEDICATED. John Paxton. Philadelphia: s.n., 1811.

S-23956
Snowden, Richard. The History of North and South America.
    2 volumes in 1. Philadelphia: Alexander and Phillips, for
    Johnson and Warner, 1811.

    NORTH AMERICA. Volume 1 (F).

    SOUTH AMERICA. Volume 2 (F).

S-24414
Weems, Mason. The Life of George Washington. 11th ed.
    Philadelphia: Mathew Carey, 1811.

    [UNITED STATES] (F).

S-24501
Workman, Benjamin. Elements of Geography. 14th ed. Philadelphia:
    William M'Culloch, 1811.

    THE SOLAR SYSTEM (F).

    NORTH AMERICA (80).

SOUTH AMERICA (122).

EUROPE (128).

ASIA (156).

AFRICA (168).

S-24632
Arrowsmith, Aaron. <u>A New and Elegent General Atlas</u>. Boston:
    Thomas and Andrews, 1812. (Note: This is identical to
    S-26144).

THE WORLD (1).

THE WORLD ON MERCATORS PROJECTION (2).

EUROPE (3).

UNITED KINGDOMS OF GREAT BRITAIN AND IRELAND (4).

SCOTLAND (5).

FRANCE (6).

NETHERLANDS (7).

RUSSIA IN EUROPE (8).

AUSTRIAN DOMINIONS (9).

PRUSSIAN STATES (10).

SPAIN AND PORTUGAL (11).

TURKEY IN EUROPE (12).

HOLLAND (13).

DENMARK (14).

SWEDEN AND NORWAY (15).

SWITZERLAND (16).

GERMANY NORTH OF THE MAYN (17).

GERMANY SOUTH OF THE MAYN (18).

ITALY (19).

ASIA (20).

ASIA MINOR (21).

CHINA (22).

JAPAN (23).

HINDOOSTAN (24).

CHART OF THE EAST INDIA ISLANDS EXHIBITING THE SEVERAL
    PASSAGES BETWEEN THE INDIAN AND PACIFIC OCEANS (25).

PERSIA (26).

AUSTRALASIA (27).

POLYNESIA (28).

NORTH AMERICA (29).

NEW HAMPSHIRE (30).

MASSACHUSETTS (31).

MAINE (32).

VERMONT (33).

RHODE ISLAND (34).

CONNECTICUT (36).

NEW YORK (37).

NEW JERSEY (38).

PENNSYLVANIA (39).

DELAWARE (40).

MARYLAND (41).

VIRGINIA (42).

NORTH CAROLINA (43).

SOUTH CAROLINA (44).

GEORGIA (45).

KENTUCKY (46).

142

TENNESSEE (47).

OHIO (48).

MISSISSIPPI TERRITORY (49).

LOUISIANA (50).

BRITISH POSSESSIONS IN NORTH AMERICA (51).

SPANISH DOMINIONS IN NORTH AMERICA (52).

VICEROYALTY OF NEW GRANADA (53).

GOVERNMENT OF CARACAS WITH GUIANA (54).

VICEROYALY OF PERU (55).

CHILI (56).

VICEROYALTY OF LAPLATA (57).

WEST INDIES (58).

SOUTH AMERICA (59).

AFRICA (60).

EGYPT (61).

WEST AFRICA (62).

COLONY OF THE CAPE OF GOOD HOPE (63).

S-24633
Arrowsmith, Aaron. <u>A New and Elegent General Atlas</u>. Philadelphia:
    s.n., 1812.

THE WORLD (1).

THE WORLD ON MERCATORS PROJECTION (2).

EUROPE (3).

UNITED KINGDOMS OF GREAT BRITAIN AND IRELAND (4).

SCOTLAND (5).

FRANCE (6).

NETHERLANDS (7).

RUSSIA IN EUROPE (8).

AUSTRIAN DOMINIONS (9).

PRUSSIAN STATES (10).

SPAIN AND PORTUGAL (11).

TURKEY IN EUROPE (12).

HOLLAND (13).

DENMARK (14).

SWEDEN AND NORWAY (15).

SWITZERLAND (16).

GERMANY NORTH OF THE MAYN (17).

GERMANY SOUTH OF THE MAYN (18).

ITALY (19).

ASIA (20).

ASIA MINOR (21).

CHINA (22).

JAPAN (23).

HINDOOSTAN (24).

CHART OF THE EAST INDIA ISLANDS EXHIBITING THE SEVERAL
     PASSAGES BETWEEN THE INDIAN AND PACIFIC OCEANS (25).

PERSIA (26).

AUSTRALASIA (27).

POLYNESIA (28).

NORTH AMERICA (29).

NEW HAMPSHIRE (30).

MASSACHUSETTS (31).

MAINE (32).

VERMONT (33).

RHODE ISLAND (34).

CONNECTICUT (36).

NEW YORK (37).

NEW JERSEY (38).

PENNSYLVANIA (39).

DELAWARE (40).

MARYLAND (41).

VIRGINIA (42).

NORTH CAROLINA (43).

SOUTH CAROLINA (44).

GEORGIA (45).

KENTUCKY (46).

TENNESSEE (47).

OHIO (48).

MISSISSIPPI TERRITORY (49).

LOUISIANA (50).

BRITISH POSSESSIONS IN NORTH AMERICA (51).

SPANISH DOMINIONS IN NORTH AMERICA (52).

VICEROYALTY OF NEW GRANADA (53).

GOVERNMENT OF CARACAS WITH GUIANA (54).

VICEROYALY OF PERU (55).

CHILI (56).

VICEROYALTY OF LAPLATA (57).

WEST INDIES (58).

SOUTH AMERICA (59).

AFRICA (60).

EGYPT (61).

WEST AFRICA (62).

COLONY OF THE CAPE OF GOOD HOPE (63).

S-24634
MAP OF AMERICA (4 sheets). Aaron Arrowsmith. Philadelphia: s.n., 1812.

S-24826
Bible. Philadelphia: Mathew Carey, 1812. (Note: Includes an extra illustrated edition).

A MAP OF PALESTINE DESCRIBING THE TRAVELS OF JESUS CHRIST (681).

CANAAN OR THE LAND OF PROMISE TO ABRAHAM AND HIS POSTERITY. ill. ed. (8).

ANCIENT EGYPT. ill. ed. (34).

THE JOURNEYINGS OF THE CHILDREN OF ISRAEL FROM EGYPT THROUGH THE RED SEA AND WILDERNESS TO THE LAND OF CANAAN. ill. ed. (42).

THE PLACES RECORDED IN THE FIVE BOOKS OF MOSES. ill. ed. (42).

THE EASTERN COUNTRIES AS MENTIONED BY MOSES. ill. ed. (42).

CANAAN FROM THE TIME OF JOSHUA TO THE BABYLONISH CAPTIVITY ill. ed. (172).

THE PURVEYORSHIPS IN THE REIGN OF SOLOMON. ill. ed. (260).

MAP OF THE ASSYRIAN, BABYLONIAN, MEDIAN AND PERSIAN EMPIRES ill. ed. (292).

THE DOMINIONS OF SOLOMON AND HIS ALLIES. ill. ed. (340).

SHEBA WITH THE VOYAGE TO TARSHISH AND OPHIR. ill. ed. (340).

THE LAND OF MORIAH OR JERUSALEM AND THE ADJACENT COUNTRY ill. ed. (834).

A MAP OF THE COUNTRY TRAVELLED BY THE APOSTLES WITH THE VOYAGE OF SAINT PAUL TO ROME. ill. ed. (930).

S-24834
Bible. Philadelphia: Mathew Carey, 1812.

    THE LAND OF MORIAH OR JERUSALEM AND THE ADJACENT COUNTRY
        (F).

    MAP OF THE COUNTRY TRAVELLED BY THE APOSTLES WITH THE VOYAGE
        OF SAINT PAUL TO ROME (930).

S-24929
Brewster, David. The American Edition of the Edinburgh
    Encyclopedia. 18 volumes. Philadelphia: Parker and
    Delaplaine, 1812-1831.

    AFRICA. Volume 1 (400).

    N. AMERICA. Volume 1 (B).

    S. AMERICA. Volume 1 (B).

    AUSTRIA. Volume 4 (402).

    ENGLAND. Volume 8 (859).

    FRANCE. Volume 9 (B).

    MAP OF THE WESTERN AND EASTERN HEMISPHERES. Volume 9 (B).

    CHART OF THE WORLD ON MERCATORS PROJECTION. Volume 9 (B).

    CHINA. Volume 10 (B).

    IRELAND. Volume 11 (B).

    ITALY. Volume 12 (407).

    BATTLE OF KOLLIN. Volume 14 (plate CCCLXXXIV).

    BATTLE OF ROSBACH. Volume 14 (plate CCCLXXXV).

    BATTLE OF LISSA OR LEUTHEN. Volume 14 (plate CCCLXXXVI).

    SCOTLAND. Volume 17 (400).

    ASIA. Volume 18 (B).

    MOON. Volume 18 (plate CCCC).

S-24939
Brookes, Richard. Brookes's General Gazetteer Improved. 2nd
    American ed. Philadelphia: Johnson and Warner, 1812.

    THE WORLD (F).

    AFRICA (UP).

    NORTH AMERICA (UP).

    SOUTH AMERICA (UP).

    ASIA (UP).

    EUROPE (UP).

    WEST INDIES (UP).

    THE NORTH WESTERN TERRITORIES OF THE UNITED STATES (UP).

    THE EASTERN STATES WITH PART OF CANADA (UP).

    THE SOUTHERN STATES AND MISSISSIPPI TERRITORY (UP).

    THE MIDDLE STATES AND WESTERN TERRITORIES OF THE UNITED
        STATES INCLUDING THE SEAT OF THE WESTERN WAR (UP).

S-25014
Calmet, Augustin. Great Dictionary of the Holy Bible. 5 volumes.
    Charlestown, MA: Samuel Etheridge, 1812-1817.

    PLAN OF THE JOURNEY FROM EGYPT TO THE RED SEA. Volume 3
        (UP).

    JERUSALEM AND PLACES ADJACENT. Volume 3 (UP).

    GEOGRAPHY AND SUPPOSED ASTRONOMY OF JOSHUA'S MIRA. Volume 3
        (UP).

    A MAP OF THE WORLD AS KNOWN TO THE ANCIENTS, SHEWING THE
        SETTLEMENTS OF THE SONS OF NOAH. Volume 3 (UP).

    A MAP OF THE JOURNEYINGS OF THE CHILDREN OF ISRAEL FROM
        EGYPT THROUGH THE WILDERNESS TO CANAAN. Volume 3 (UP).

    A MAP OF THE LAND OF CANAAN, SHEWING THE SITUATION OF THE
        PRINCIPAL PLACES MENTIONED IN THE HISTORIES OF JOSHUA &
        THE JUDGES. Volume 3 (UP).

A MAP SHEWING THE SITUATION OF THE PRINCIPAL PLACES
MENTIONED IN THE HISTORY OF THE KINGS OF JUDAH &
ISRAEL. Volume 3 (UP).

A MAP OF THE LAND OF ISRAEL, SHEWING THE SITUATION OF THESE
PLACES WHAT ARE MENTIONED BY THE FOUR EVANGELISTS.
Volume 3 (UP).

THE TERRAQUEOUS GLOBE. Volume 3 (UP).

SUPPOSED SITUATION IN PARADISE. Volume 4 (UP).

GEOGRAPHICAL ILLUSTRATIONS OF SCRIPTURE HISTORIES,
PARTICULARLY JOURNEYS. Volume 4 (UP).

JERUSALEM AT DIFFERENT PERIODS. (4 maps). Volume 4. (UP).

ORIGIN OF THE RIVER GANGES. Volume 5 (UP).

MAP OF MEMPHIS. Volume 5 (UP).

MAP OF ASIA SHEWING THE SUPPOSED SITUATIONS OF PARADISE.
Volume 5 (UP).

MAP OF ASIA. Volume 5 (UP).

MAP OF EUROPE SHEWING THE SUPPOSED SETTLEMENTS OF JAPHET.
Volume 5 (UP).

TRAVELS OF ISRAEL IN THE WILDERNESS. Volume 5 (UP).

A MAP OF CANAAN FOR GENERAL PURPOSES. Volume 5 (UP).

A MAP OF CANAAN, ADAPTED TO THE BOOK OF GENESIS. Volume 5
(UP).

A MAP OF CANAAN, ADAPTED TO THE BOOK OF JUDGES. Volume 5
(UP).

A MAP OF CANAAN, ADAPTED TO THE BOOK OF SAMUEL. Volume 5
(UP).

MAP OF EUROPE. Volume 5 (UP).

MAP OF AFRICA SHEWING THE SUPPOSED SETTLEMENTS OF HORN.
Volume 5 (UP).

MAP OF AFRICA. Volume 5 (UP).

A MAP OF CANAAN, SHEWING THE CAPTICITES OF ISRAEL AND JUDAE.
Volume 5 (UP).

149

S-25316
MAP OF THE COUNTRY THIRTY MILES ROUND THE CITY OF NEW YORK. John
    Eddy. New York: s.n., 1812.

S-25498
Gass, Patrick. <u>Journal of the Voyages and Travels of a Corps of
    Discovery, under the Command of Capt. Lewis and Capt. Clarke
    of the Army of the United States</u>. 4th ed. Philadelphia:
    Mathew Carey, 1812.

    LOUISIANA (F).

S-25742
Jefferson, Thomas. <u>The Proceedings of the Government of the
    United States, in Maintaining the Public Right to the Beach
    of the Mississippi Adjacent to New Orleans</u>. New York: Ezra
    Sargeant, 1812.

    [GRAVIER'S PLANTATION AND ENVIRONS] (F).

S-25778
TO THE OFFICERS OF THE ARMY AND THE CITIZENS OF THE UNITED STATES
    THIS MAP OF UPPER AND LOWER CANADA AND UNITED STATES. Thomas
    Kensett. New Haven: s.n., 1812.

S-25838
MAP OF THE NORTHERN PART OF THE STATE OF NEW YORK. Amos Lay.
    Newark: s.n., 1812.

S-25932
Malham, John. <u>The Naval Gazetteer</u>. 2 volumes. Baltimore: Edward
    Coale, 1812.

        A GENERAL CHART OF THE WORLD ON MERCATORS PROJECTION
            EXHIBITING ALL NEW DISCOVERIES AND THE TRACKS OF THE
            DIFFERENT CIRCUM-NAVIGATIONS. Volume 1 (F).

        A CORRECT CHART OF THE WEST COAST OF AFRICA. Volume 1 (14).

        A CORRECT CHART OF THE SOUTHERN COASTS OF AFRICA FROM THE
            EQUATOR TO THE CAPE OF GOOD HOPE. Volume 1 (14).

        A CORRECT CHART OF THE EAST COAST OF NORTH AMERICA. Volume 1
            (30).

        A CORRECT CHART OF THE COASTS OF SOUTH AMERICA FROM THE
            EQUATOR TO CAPE HORN. Volume 1 (30).

A CORRECT CHART OF THE WEST COAST OF NORTH AMERICA FROM
     BHERING'S STRAITS TO NOOTKA SOUND. Volume 1 (30).

A CORRECT CHART OF THE BALTIC SEA. Volume 1 (70).

A CORRECT CHART OF THE ENGLISH CHANNEL. Volume 1 (192).

A CORRECT CHART OF THE IRISH SEA, WITH ST. GEORGE'S CHANNEL.
     Volume 1 (526).

A CORRECT CHART OF THE COAST OF PORTUGAL. Volume 2 (49).

A CORRECT CHART OF THE COASTS OF HINDOSTAN. Volume 2 (92).

A CORRECT CHART OF THE MEDITERRANEAN SEA. Volume 2 (132).

A CORRECT CHART OF THE NORTH SEA. Volume 2 (202).

A CORRECT CHART OF THE INDIAN OCEAN. Volume 2 (205).

A CORRECT CHART OF THE GERMAN SEA. Volume 2 488).

S-26061
Melish, John. A Description of the British Possessions in North
     America. Philadelphia: Palmer and Palmer, 1812.

MAP OF THE SEAT OF WAR IN NORTH AMERICA (F).

S-26062
Melish, John. Travels in the United States in the Years 1806 and
     1807, and 1809, 1810, and 1811. 2 volumes. Philadelphia:
     Palmer and Palmer, 1812.

MAP OF THE UNITED STATES OF AMERICA. Volume 1 (F).

CHART OF THE ATLANTIC OCEAN. Volume 1 (vii).

VIEW OF THE COUNTRY ROUND PITTSBURG. Volume 2 (54).

FALLS OF OHIO. Volume 2 (149).

KENTUCKY. Volume 2 (176).

OHIO. Volume 2 (208).

VIEW OF THE COUNTRY ROUND ZANESVILLE. Volume 2 (231).

VIEW OF THE COUNTRY ROUND THE FALLS OF NIAGARA. Volume 2
     (318).

S-26142
Morse, Jedidiah. The American Universal Geography. 6th ed. 2
    volumes. Boston: Thomas and Andrews, 1812.

    THE WORLD. Volume 1 (F).

    NORTH AMERICA. Volume 1 (136).

    SOUTH AMERICA. Volume 1 (712).

    EUROPE. Volume 2 (F).

    ASIA. Volume 2 (434).

    AFRICA. Volume 2 (762).

S-26143
Morse, Jedidiah. Geography Made Easy. 15th ed. Boston: Thomas and
    Andrews, 1812.

    A NEW MAP OF THE WORLD WITH THE LATEST DISCOVERIES (F).

    A MAP OF NORTH AMERICA FROM THE LATEST DISCOVERIES (62).

S-26144
Morse, Jedidiah. A New...General Atlas. Boston: Thomas and
    Andrews, 1812. (Note: See S-24632 for maps).

S-26346
O'Neill, John. A New and Easy System of Geography and Popular
    Astronomy. Baltimore: Fry and Kammerer, for Lucas and Coale,
    1812.

    WORLD (F).

    UNITED STATES (44).

    SOLAR SYSTEM (B).

S- 26379
Parish, Elijah. A New System of Modern Geography. 2nd ed.
    Newburyport, MA: Charles Norris, for Edward Little, 1812.

    A CORRECT MAP OF THE WORLD WITH THE LATEST DISCOVERIES (F).

    NORTH AMERICA (24).

S-26440
Ordinances of the Corporation of the City of Philadelphia.
    Philadelphia: Moses Thomas, 1812.

    A PORTRATURE OF THE CITY OF PHILADELPHIA IN THE PROVINCE OF
        PENNSYLVANIA IN AMERICA (282).

S-26635
Robertson, William. An Historical Disquition Concerning the
    Knowledge Which the Ancients Had of India. Volume 2.
    Philadelphia: Augustine Fagan, for Johnson and Warner, 1812.

    MAP OF THE SOUTH EAST PART OF ASIA, FOR ILLUSTRATING DR.
        ROBERTSON'S HISTORICAL DISQUITION (384).

    MAP OF THE SOUTH EAST PART OF ASIA, ACCORDING TO PTOLEMY,
        FOR ILLUSTRATING DR. ROBERTSON'S HISTORICAL DISQUITION
        (384).

S-26651
Rollin, Charles. The Ancient History of the Egyptians. 8 volumes.
    New York: Evert Duyckinck and Ward and Ward, 1812.

    A MAP OF THE RETREAT OF THE TEN THOUSAND. Volume 3 (336).

    A VIEW OF THE CITY AND PORT OF ALEXANDRIA AND ISLE OF
        PHAROS. Volume 4 (F).

    A MAP OF THE PLACES ADJACENT TO ISSUS. Volume 5 (F).

    THE FORTIFICATIONS OF THE ATHENIANS AND SYRACUSANS. Volume 7
        (F).

S-27202
MAP OF THE BOUNTY LANDS IN THE ILLINOIS TERRITORY. John Gardiner.
    Washington: U.S. General Land Office, 1812.

S-27508
Weems, Mason. The Life of George Washington. 12th ed.
    Philadelphia: Mathew Carey, 1812.

    THE UNITED STATES OF AMERICA (F).

S-27566
Williamson, Hugh. <u>The History of North Carolina</u>. 2 volumes.
    Philadelphia: Fry and Kammerer, for Thomas Dobson, 1812.

    NORTH CAROLINA. Volume 1 (F).

S-27886
<u>Bible</u>. New York: George Long, for Evert Duyckinck, John Tiebout,
    Waite and Waite, 1813.

    THE JOURNEYINGS OF THE CHILDREN OF ISRAEL FROM EGYPT THROUGH
        THE RED SEA AND WILDERNESS TO THE LAND OF CANAAN
        [In Numbers] (UP).

    MAP OF THE COUNTRY TRAVELLED BY THE APOSTLES WITH THE VOYAGE
        OF SAINT PAUL TO ROME [In Acts of the Apostles] (UP).

S-27893
<u>Bible</u>. Philadelphia: Mathew Carey, 1813.

    THE JOURNEYINGS OF THE CHILDREN OF ISRAEL FROM EGYPT THROUGH
        THE RED SEA AND WILDERNESS TO THE LAND OF CANAAN (F).

    CANAAN OR THE LAND OF PROMISE TO ABRAHAM AND HIS POSTERITY
        (8).

    ANCIENT EGYPT (34).

    THE PLACES RECORDED IN THE FIVE BOOKS OF MOSES (42).

    THE EASTERN COUNTRIES AS MENTIONED BY MOSES (42).

    CANAAN FROM THE TIME OF JOSHUA TO THE BABYLONISH CAPTIVITY
        (172).

    THE PURVEYORSHIPS IN THE REIGN OF SOLOMON (268).

    MAP OF THE ASSYRYIAN, BABYLONIAN, MEDIAN AND PERSIAN EMPIRES
        (282).

    THE DOMINIONS OF SOLOMON AND HIS ALLIES (340).

    SHEBA WITH THE VOYAGE TO TARSHISH AND OPHIR (340).

    THE LAND OF MORIAH OR JERUSALEM AND THE ADJACENT COUNTRY
        (834).

    MAP OF THE COUNTRY TRAVELLED BY THE APOSTLES WITH THE VOYAGE
        OF SAINT PAUL TO ROME (929).

S-28004
Bradford, Alden. <u>Evangelical History</u>. Boston: Bradford and Read, 1813.

   PALESTINE (31).

   [MEDITERRANEAN SEA] (412).

S-28063
Caesar, Caius Julius. <u>C. Julii Caesaris, Quae Extant</u>. Philadelphia: Mathew Carey, 1813.

   GALLIA VETIUS (vii).

   ITALIAE ANTIQUAE (192).

   CONSPECTUS LOCORUM BELLI AFRICANI (330).

S-28152
Clarke, Edward. <u>Travels in Various Countries of Europe, Asia, and Africa</u>. 2nd American ed. New York: Thomas Fay, 1813.

   PLAN OF THE ISLAND AND TOWN OF TSCHERCHASKOY, THE CAPITAL OF THE DON COSSACKS (172).

   PART OF THE PROVINCE OF RASTOF IN THE GOVERNMENT OF NOVOGOROD SEVERSKI (200).

S-28282
Davies, Benjamin. <u>A New System of Modern Geography</u>. 3rd ed. Philadelphia: Jordan Downing, for Johnson and Warner, 1813.

   MAP OF THE WORLD WITH THE MOST RECENT DISCOVERIES (F).

   EUROPE (24).

   ASIA (146).

   NORTH AMERICA (260).

   SOUTH AMERICA (406).

   AFRICA (420).

S-28315
Melish, John. <u>A Description of the British Possessions in North America</u>. 3rd ed. Philadelphia: John Melish, 1813.

A MAP OF THE SEAT OF WAR IN NORTH AMERICA (F).

VIEW OF THE COUNTRY ROUND THE FALLS OF NIAGARA (18).

S-28327
Dickinson, Rodolphus. <u>Elements of Geography</u>. Boston: Bradford and
    Read, 1813.

    THE WORLD (F).

    MAP OF THE UNITED STATES INCLUDING LOUISIANA (106).

S-28606
Smith, David. <u>A Gazetteer of the Province of Upper Canada</u>. New
    York: Pelsue and Gould, for Prior and Dunning, 1813.

    MAP OF THE STRAIGHTS OF NIAGARA FROM LAKE ERIE TO LAKE
        ONTARIO (UP).

    PLAN OF THE CITY OF QUEBEC (UP).

S-28641
Gimbrede, Thomas. <u>A Collection of Plates</u>. Charlestown, MA: Samuel
    Etheridge, 1813.

    A MAP OF THE WORLD AS KNOWN TO THE ANCIENTS, SHEWING THE
        SETTLEMENTS OF THE SONS OF NOAH (B).

S-28653
Gordon, James. <u>The History of the Irish Rebellion</u>. Philadelphia:
    Griggs and Dickinson, for John Clarke, 1813.

    A NEW MAP OF IRELAND (F).

S-28756
<u>The History of the Irish Rebellion, in the Year 1798</u>.
    Philadelphia: Griggs and Dickinson, for John Clarke, 1813.

    A NEW MAP OF IRELAND (F).

S-28851
Josephus, Flavius. <u>The Works of Flavius Josephus</u>. 4 Volumes.
    Philadelphia: Thomas Simpson, 1813.

    PLAN OF JERUSALEM FROM THE MOST APPROVED AUTHORITIES. Vol. 2
        (F).

A MAP OF SUCH PLACES MENTIONED IN THE NEW TESTAMENT AS WERE
    IN GREECE, CYPRUS, ASIA, &C. Vol. 3 (F).

A NEW MAP OF THE SEVERAL COUNTRIES, CITIES, TOWNS &C
    MENTIONED IN THE NEW TESTAMENT AS WERE IN THE HOLY LAND
    AND PARTS ADJOINING. Vol. 3? (F).

S-28965
Livingston, Edward. An Answer to Mr. Jefferson's Justification
    of His Conduct in the Case of the New Orleans Batture.
    Philadelphia: William Fry, 1813.

    PLAN SHEWING ALLUVIAL LANDS OR BATTURES ON THE MISSISSIPPI
        (F).

    PLAN SHEWING THE DISTRIBUTION OF THE JESUITS PLANTATION (F).

S-29010
M'Culloch, John. A Concise History of the United States. 4th ed.
    Philadelphia: M'Culloch and M'Culloch, 1813.

    UNITED STATES OF AMERICA (F).

S-29045
MAP OF NEW LONDON AND ITS VICINITY. New Haven, CT: Amos
    Doolittle, 1813.

S-29139
Melish, John. A Description of East and West Florida and the
    Bahama Islands, &c.. Philadelphia: Palmer and Palmer, 1813.

    MAP OF THE SOUTHERN SECTION AND BAHAMA ISLANDS, SHEWING THE
        SEAT OF WAR IN THAT DEPARTMENT (3).

S-29140
Melish, John. A Description of the British Possessions in North
    America. 3rd ed. Philadelphia: Palmer and Palmer, 1813.

    MAP OF THE SEAT OF WAR IN NORTH AMERICA (3).

S-29141
Melish, John. Description of the Seat of War. Philadelphia: s.n.,
    1813.

    VIEW OF THE COUNTRY ROUND THE FALLS OF NIAGARA (10).

EAST END OF LAKE ONTARIO (18).

PLAN OF MONTREAL, WITH A MAP OF THE ISLANDS AND ADJOINING
COUNTRY (20).

S-29143
Melsih, John. A Military and Topographical Atlas of the United
States. Philadelphia: Palmer and Palmer, 1813.

MAP OF THE SEAT OF WAR IN NORTH AMERICA (6).

VIEW OF THE COUNTRY ROUND THE FALLS OF NIAGARA (10).

EAST END OF LAKE ONTARIO (18).

PLAN OF MONTREAL, WITH A MAP OF THE ISLANDS AND ADJOINING
COUNTRY (20).

A MAP OF THE SOUTHERN SECTION OF THE UNITED STATES INCLUDING
THE FLORIDA AND BAHAMA ISLANDS SHEWING THE SEAT OF WAR
IN THAT DEPARTMENT (34).

MAP OF THE AMERICAN COAST FROM LYNHAVEN BAY TO NARRAGANSET
BAY (18).

MAP OF THE DETROIT RIVER AND ADJACENT COUNTRY FROM THE
ORIGINAL DRAWING BY A BRITISH SOLDIER (18).

PLAN OF QUEBEC AND ADJACENT COUNTRY SHEWING THE PRINCIPAL
ENCAMPMENTS AND WORKS OF THE BRITISH AND FRENCH ARMIES
DURING THE SIEGE BY GENERAL WOLFE IN 1759 (18).

S-29223
Morse, Jedidiah. Geography Made Easy. 16th ed. Boston: Joseph
Buckingham, for Thomas and Andrews, 1813.

A NEW MAP OF THE WORLD WITH THE LATEST DISCOVERIES (F).

A MAP OF NORTH AMERICA FROM THE LATEST DISCOVERIES (62).

S-29277
New Edinburgh Encyclopaedia. 2nd ed. 18 volumes. New York:
Whiting, 1813-1831.

S. AMERICA. Volume 1 (B).

[SOLAR SYSTEM]. Volume 3 (plate XXXIII).

AUSTRIA. Volume 4 (100).

ENGLAND. Volume 8 (859).

FRANCE. Volume 9 (846).

EASTERN HEMISPHERE. Volume 9 (846).

WESTERN HEMISPHERE. Volume 9 (846).

CHART OF THE WORLD ON MERCATORS PROJECTION. Volume 9 (846).

IRELAND. Volume 11 (B).

ITALY. Volume 12 (400).

BATTLE OF KOLLIN. Volume 14 (424).

BATTLE OF ROSBACH. Volume 14 (424).

BATTLE OF LISSA AND LEUTHEN. Volume 14 (424).

SCOTLAND. Volume 17 (400).

ASIA. Volume 18 (B).

S-29374
Nichols, Francis. An Elementary Treatise of Geography.
    Philadelphia: William Fry, for Francis Nichols, 1813.

    EXPLANATORY MAP (B).

S-29394
Official Documents Relative to the Operation of the British Army.
    Philadelphia: George Palmer, 1813.

    PLAN OF QUEBEC AND ADJACENT COUNTRY SHEWING THE PRINCIPAL
        ENCAMPMENTS AND WORKS OF THE BRITISH AND FRENCH ARMIES
        DURING THE SIEGE BT GENERAL WOLFE IN 1759. John Melish
        (F).

S-29440
Parish, Elijah. Sacred Geography. Boston: Samuel Armstrong, 1813.

    THE PRINCIPAL COUNTRIES MENTIONED IN THE SACRED SCRIPTURES
        (F).

S-29441
Park, Mungo. <u>Travels in the Interior Districts of Africa</u>. New
      York: James Oram, for Evert Duyckinck, 1813.

      THE ROUTE OF MR. MUNGO PARK FROM PISANIA TO THE RIVER GAMBIA
          TO SILLA ON THE RIVER JOLIBA OR NIGER (F).

S-29816
MAP OF UPPER CANADA DESCRIBING ALL THE NEW SETTLEMENTS,
      TOWNSHIPS, &C. WITH THE COUNTRIES ADJACENT FROM QUEBEC TO
      LAKE HURON. David Smyth. New York: Prior and Dunning, 1813.

S-29819
Snowden, Richard. <u>The History of North and South America</u>.
      2 volumes in 1. Philadelphia: Lydia Bailey, for Johnson and
      Warner, 1813.

      NORTH AMERICA. Volume 1 (F).

      SOUTH AMERICA. Volume 2 (F).

S-29836
Spafford, Horatio. <u>A Gazetteer of the States of New York</u>. Albany:
      Henry Southwick, 1813.

      STATE OF NEW YORK (F).

S-29910
Tacitus, Cornelius. <u>The Works of Cornelius Tacitus</u>. 6 volumes.
      Philadelphia: William Fry, for Edward Earle, 1813.

      THE ANCIENT WORLD AS KNOWN TO THE ROMANS DESIGNED FOR THE
          WORK OF TACITUS. Volume 1 (F).

      ASIA DESIGNED FOR THE WORKS OF TACITUS. Robert de Vaugondy.
          Volume 1 (B).

      ITALY DESIGNED FOR THE WORKS OF TACITUS. Robert de Vaugondy.
          Volume 3 (B).

      PLAN OF JERUSALEM ACCORDING TO D'ANVILLE. Volume 4 (B).

      GERMANY DESIGNED FOR THE WORKS OF TACITUS. Robert de
          Vaugondy. Volume 5 (293).

S-30530
MAP OF THE NORTHERN PART OF THE UNITED STATES AND THE SOUTHERN
    PART OF THE CANADAS. James Whitelaw. Bradford, VT: James
    Wilson, 1813.

S-30564
Wood, James. <u>A Dictionary of the Holy Bible</u>. 2 volumes. New York:
    Griffin and Rudd, 1813.

    A MAP OF THE PROMISED LAND AND SYRIA (226).

S-30567
Woodhouselee, Alexander. <u>Elements of General History</u>. 2nd
    American ed. Philadelphia: Francis Nichols, 1813.

    ORBIS TERRARUM VETERIBUS NOTUS (B).

    ITALIA, GRAECIA, ASIA, &C. (B).

S-30570
Worcester, Joseph. <u>Worcester's Ancient Atlas</u>. Boston: Cummings
    and Hilliard, 1813.

    ROMAN EMPIRE (1).

    ANCIENT ITALY (2).

    ANCIENT GREECE (3).

    ASIA MINOR (4).

    PALESTINE OR HOLY LAND (5).

S-30622
Adams, Daniel. <u>Atlas to Adams' Geography</u>. Boston: West and Blake,
    1814.

    THE WORLD (1).

    NORTH AMERICA (2).

    UNITED STATES (3).

    NEW ENGLAND STATES (4).

    SOUTH AMERICA (5).

    EUROPE (6).

ASIA (7).

AFRICA (8).

S-30694
Anville, Jean d'. <u>Atlas to the Ancient Geography</u>. New York:
    M'Dermut and Arden, 1814.

ORBIS VETERIBUS NOTUS (1).

GRAECIA ANTIQUA (2).

ORBIS ROMANI PARS OCCIDENTALIS (3).

ORBIS ROMANI PARS ORIENTALIS (4).

ITALIA ANTIQUA (5).

GALLIA ANTIQUA (6).

ASIA QUEVULGO MINOR DICITOR ET SYRIA (7).

PALESTINA (8).

AEGYPTUS ANTIQUA (9).

BRITANNIA ANTIQUA (10).

S-30714
<u>An Atlas of Ten Select Maps of Ancient Geography, Both Sacred and
    Profane</u>. Philadelphia: John Watson, 1814.

TERRA VETERIBUS NOTA (1).

ROMANUM IMPERIUM (2).

ORIENTIS TABULA (3).

GRAECIA ANTIQUA (4).

ITALIA ANTIQUA (5).

THE PLACES RECORDED IN THE FIVE BOOKS OF MOSES (6).

THE EASTERN COUNTRIES AS MENTIONED BY MOSES (7).

CANAAN, ARAM, &C. (8).

THE LAND OF MORIAH OR JERUSALEM AND THE ADJACENT COUNTRY
    (9).

162

STATE OF NATIONS AT THE CHRISTIAN AERA (10).

ROMANI IMPERII &C TYPUS (11).

S-30865
Bible. 3rd ed. New York: Thomas Collins, 1814.

PALESTINE [In Exodus] (UP).

A MAP OF THE JOURNEYINGS OF THE CHILDREN OF ISRAEL FROM
        EGYPT THROUGH THE WILDERNESS TO CANAAN [In Numbers]
        (UP).

MAP OF THE PLACES MENTIONED IN THE NEW TESTAMENT
        ILLUSTRATING PAUL'S TRAVELS AND ALSO HIS VOYAGE FROM
        CAESAREA TO ROME [In Acts of the Apostles] (UP).

S-30878
Bible. New York: Eastburn and Kirk, 1814.

A MAP OF THE DIFFERENT PLACES MENTIONED IN THE NEW TESTAMENT
        WITH ST. PAUL'S VOYAGES FROM PHILIPPI TO TYRE AND FROM
        CAESAREA TO ROME [In Acts of the Apostles] (UP).

S-31086
Carey, Mathew. Carey's American Pocket Atlas. 4th ed.
        Philadelphia: Mathew Carey, 1814.

UNITED STATES (F).

VERMONT FROM ACTUAL SURVEY (20).

THE STATE OF NEW HAMPSHIRE. Samuel Lewis (28).

MAINE (32).

MASSACHUSETTS (38).

RHODE ISLAND (52).

CONNECTICUT (60).

NEW JERSEY (84).

PENNSYLVANIA (92).

DELAWARE (102).

OHIO (106).

UPPER TERRITORIES OF THE UNITED STATES (110).

MARYLAND (116).

VIRGINIA (124).

KENTUCKY (130).

NORTH CAROLINA (138).

TENNASSEE (144).

SOUTH CAROLINA (148).

MISSISSIPPI TERRITORY (160).

LOUISIANA (164).

MISSOURI TERRITORY, FORMERLY LOUISIANA (166).

S-31087
Carey, Mathew. Carey's General Atlas. Philadelphia: Mathew Carey, 1814.

A MAP OF THE WORLD FROM THE BEST AUTHORITIES (1).

A CHART OF THE WORLD ACCORDING TO MERCATORS PROJECTION SHEWING THE LATEST DISCOVERIES OF CAPTAIN COOK (2).

A NEW AND ACCURATE MAP OF NORTH AMERICA FROM THE BEST AUTHORITIES (3).

THE BRITISH POSSESSIONS IN NORTH AMERICA FROM THE LATEST AUTHORITIES (4).

MAP OF THE UNITED STATES OF AMERICA (5).

VERMONT FROM ACTUAL SURVEY (6).

THE STATE OF NEW HAMPSHIRE COMPILED CHIEFLY FROM ACTUAL SURVEYS. Samuel Lewis (7).

THE DISTRICT OF MAINE (8).

THE STATE OF MASSACHUSETTS (9).

THE STATE OF RHODE ISLAND COMPILED CHIEFLY FROM ACTUAL SURVEYS. Samuel Lewis (10).

CONNECTICUT FROM THE BEST AUTHORITIES (11).

THE STATE OF NEW YORK (12).

THE STATE OF NEW JERSEY COMPILED FROM THE MOST AUTHENTIC
INFORMATION (13).

PENNSYLVANIA (14).

DELAWARE FROM THE BEST AUTHORITIES (15).

MARYLAND (16).

A CORRECT MAP OF VIRGINIA (17).

NORTH CAROLINA FROM THE LATEST SURVEYS. Samuel Lewis (18).

THE STATE OF SOUTH CAROLINA FROM THE BEST AUTHORITIES.
Samuel Lewis (19).

THE STATE OF GEORGIA (20).

KENTUCKY (21).

THE STATE OF TENNESSEE (22).

MISSISSIPPI (23).

THE STATE OF OHIO WITH PART OF UPPER CANADA (24).

THE UPPER TERRITORIES OF THE UNITED STATES (25).

LOUISIANA (26).

MISSOURI TERRITORY FORMERLY LOUISIANA (27).

PLAT OF THE SEVEN RANGES OF TOWNSHIPS BEING PART OF THE
TERRITORY OF THE UNITED STATES NORTH WEST OF THE RIVER
OHIO (28).

MEXICO OR NEW SPAIN (29).

A CHART OF THE WEST INDIES FROM THE LATEST MARINE JOURNALS
AND SURVEYS (30).

A MAP OF THE FRENCH PART OF ST. DOMINGO (31).

A NEW MAP OF SOUTH AMERICA FROM THE LATEST AUTHORITIES (32).

A MAP OF CARACAS (33).

PERU (34).

CHILI AND PART OF THE VICEROYALTY OF LA PLATA (35).

A MAP OF BRAZIL NOW CALLED NEW PORTUGAL (36).

EUROPE (37).

SWEDEN, DENMARK, NORWAY AND FINLAND FROM THE BEST
AUTHORITIES (38).

RUSSIAN EMPIRE (39).

SCOTLAND WITH THE PRINCIPAL ROADS FROM THE BEST AUTHORITIES
(40).

AN ACCURATE MAP OF ENGLAND AND WALES WITH THE PRINCIPAL
ROADS FROM THE BEST AUTHORITIES (41).

A MAP OF IRELAND ACCORDING TO THE BEST AUTHORITIES (42).

HOLLAND OR THE SEVEN UNITED PROVINCES AND THE NETHERLANDS
(43).

GERMANY (44).

FRANCE DIVIDED INTO CIRCLES AND DEPARTMENTS (45).

TURKEY IN EUROPE AND HUNGARY FROM THE BEST AUTHORITIES (46).

SPAIN AND PORTUGAL (47).

ITALY AND SARDINIA FROM THE BEST AUTHORITIES (48).

SWITZERLAND ACCORDING TO THE BEST AUTHORITIES (49).

POLAND (50).

ASIA ACCORDING TO THE BEST AUTHORITIES (51).

CHINA DIVIDED INTO ITS GREAT PROVINCES ACCORDING TO THE BEST
AUTHORITIES (52).

AN ACCURATE MAP OF HINDOSTAN OR INDIA FROM THE BEST
AUTHORITIES (53).

THE ISLANDS OF THE EAST INDIES WITH THE CHANNELS BETWEEN
INDIA, CHINA AND NEW HOLLAND (54).

A NEW AND ACCURATE MAP OF NEW SOUTH WALES WITH NORFOLK AND
LORD HOWE'S ISLANDS PORT JACKSON &C FROM ACTUAL SURVEYS
(55).

AFRICA ACCORDING TO THE BEST AUTHORITIES (56).

A MAP OF THE COUNTRIES SITUATED ABOUT THE NORTH POLE (57).

A MAP OF THE DISCOVERIES MADE BY CAPTAIN COOK AND CLERKE IN
    THE YEARS 1778 AND 1779 BETWEEN THE EASTERN COAST OF
    ASIA AND THE WESTERN COAST OF NORTH AMERICA (58).

S-31136
Chateaubriand, Francois. Travels in Greece, Palestine, Egypt, and
    Barbary, during the Years 1806 and 1807. New York: Van
    Winkle and Wiley, 1814.

    A MAP AS ADAPTED TO THESE TRAVELS (51).

    A NEW PLAN OF JERUSALEM (276).

S-31260
Cramer, Zadok. The Navigator. 8th ed. Pittsburgh: Robert
    Ferguson, for Cramer, Spear and Eichbaum, 1814.

    MAP OF PITTSBURGH (11).

    [OHIO RIVER] (13 sheets) (75-138).

    FALLS OF OHIO (117).

    [MISSISSIPPI RIVER] (13 sheets) (175-224).

S-31304
PLAN OF THOSE PARTS OF BOSTON. Benjamin Dearborn. Boston: s.n.,
    1814.

S-31400
Ellicott, Andrew. The Journal of Andrew Ellicott. Philadelphia:
    William Fry, 1814.

    [OHIO RIVER] (18).

    [MISSISSIPPI RIVER] (26).

    [GULF COAST BETWEEN NEW ORLEANS AND MOBILE BAY] (202).

    [COAST OF EAST FLORIDA] (299).

    [OKEFENOKEE SWAMP] (142).

S-31583
Gillies, Charles. <u>The History of Ancient Greece</u>. 4 volumes. New
    York: M'Dermut and Arden, 1814.

    THE WESTERN DIVISION OF THE GRECIAN COLONIES AND CONQUESTS.
        Volume 1 (xii).

    THE EASTERN DIVISION OF THE GRECIAN COLONIES AND CONQUESTS.
        Volume 2 (viii).

S-31589
Gleason, Benjamin. <u>Remembrancer, Geography on a New and Improved
    Plan</u>. 2nd ed. Boston: Munroe and Francis, 1814.

    THE WORLD (F).

S-31699
Herodotus. <u>Herodotus</u>. 4 volumes. Philadelphia: William Fry, for
    Edward Earle, 1814.

    ANCIENT EGYPT. Volume 1 (F).

    THE WORLD ACCORDING TO THE IDEA OF HERODOTUS. Volume 2 (F).

    AFRICA ANTIQUA. Volume 3 (F).

S-31751
Homerus. <u>Homeri Ilias</u>. 2 volumes. New York: George Long, for
    Duyckinck, Mesier, Ronalds, and Burtus, 1814.

    GRAECIAE ANTIQUAE ET INSULARUM CONSPECTUS. Volume 1 (F).

    ASIA MINOR. Volume 2 (F).

S-31902
A NEW AND CORRECT MAP OF THE SEAT OF WAR IN LOWER CANADA. Amos
    Lay. Philadelphia: s.n., 1814.

S-31924
Lewis, Meriwether. <u>History of the Expedition Under the Command of
    Captains Lewis and Clark</u>. 2 volumes. Philadelphia: James
    Maxwell, for Bradford and Inskeep, 1814.

    [MISSOURI RIVER NEAR BON HOMME ISLAND, SOUTH DAKOTA].
        Volume 1 (F).

[MISSOURI RIVER BETWEEN THE PORTAGE AND MEDICINE RIVERS].
    Volume 1 (260).

A MAP OF LEWIS AND CLARK'S TRACK ACROSS THE WESTERN PORTION
    OF NORTH AMERICA FROM THE MISSISSIPPI TO THE PACIFIC
    OCEAN. Volume 2 (F).

[COLUMBIA RIVER NEAR STRAWBERRY ISLAND]. Volume 2 (52).

[COLUMBIA RIVER NEAR CAPE DISAPPOINTMENT]. Volume 2 (70).

S-32098
Melish, John. Military Documents. Philadelphia: George Palmer,
    1814.

VIEW OF THE COUNTRY ROUND THE FALLS OF NIAGARA (10).

EAST END OF LAKE ONTARIO (18).

PLAN OF MONTREAL WITH A MAP OF THE ISLANDS AND ADJOINING
    COUNTRY (20).

S-32175
Morse, Jedidiah. A Compendious and Complete System of Modern
    Geography. Boston: Joseph Buckingham, for Thomas and
    Andrews, 1814.

CHART OF THE WORLD (F).

THE SOLAR SYSTEM (16).

A GENERAL MAP OF NORTH AMERICA FROM THE BEST AUTHORITIES
    (72).

SOUTH AMERICA FROM THE BEST AUTHORITIES (314).

ASIA (516).

AFRICA (624).

S-32176
Morse, Jedidiah. Geography Made Easy. 17th ed. Boston: Joseph
    Buckingham, for Thomas and Andrews, 1814.

MAP OF THE WORLD (F).

A MAP OF NORTH AMERICA FROM THE LATEST DISCOVERIES (62).

169

S-32177
Morse, Jedidiah. <u>Geography Made Easy</u>. From 16th Boston ed. Troy:
    Parker and Bliss, 1814.

    MAP OF THE WORLD (F).

    A MAP OF NORTH AMERICA FROM THE LATEST DISCOVERIES (62).

S-32408
O'Neill, John. <u>A New and Easy System of Geography and Popular</u>
    <u>Astronomy</u>. 3rd ed. Baltimore: Joseph Robinson, for Fielding
    Lucas, 1814.

    WORLD (F).

    SOLAR SYSTEM (6).

    UNITED STATES (44).

S-32432
Parish, Elijah. <u>A New System of Modern Geography</u>. Newburyport,
    MA: Horatio Allen, for William Allen, 1814.

    A CORRECT MAP OF THE WORLD WITH THE LATEST DISCOVERIES (F).

    NORTH AMERICA (24).

S-32490
Philadelphia Society for Promoting Agriculture. <u>Memoirs of the</u>
    <u>Philadelphia Society for Promoting Agriculture</u>. Volume 3.
    Philadelphia: Lydia Bailey, for Johnson and Warner, 1814.

    A PLAN SHEWING THE RELATIONAL SITUATION OF THE SENECA AND
        CAYUGA LAKES (28).

S-32546
Porter, Robert. <u>A Narrative of the Campaign in Russia During the</u>
    <u>Year 1812</u>. Baltimore: William Fry, for Edward Coale, 1814.

    RETREAT OF THE FRENCH ARMY FROM MOSCOW TO THE BANKS OF THE
        NEIMEN (F).

    ADVANCE OF THE FRENCH ARMY TO MOSCOW (F).

S-32547
Porter, Robert. <u>A Narrative of the Campaign in Russia During the Year 1812</u>. Hartford: Loomis and Richards, for Andrus and Starr, 1814.

ADVANCE OF THE FRENCH ARMY TO MOSCOW (F).

RETREAT OF THE FRENCH ARMY FROM MOSCOW TO THE BANKS OF THE NEIMEN (F).

S-32549
Porter, Robert. <u>A Narrative of the Campaign in Russia During the Year 1812</u>. Hartford, CT: Loomis and Richards, for George Sheldon, 1814

RETREAT OF THE FRENCH ARMY FROM MOSCOW TO THE BANKS OF THE NEIMEN (F).

ADVANCE OF THE FRENCH ARMY TO MOSCOW (F).

PLAN OF THE FIELD OF BATTLE OF THE MOSKWA, SEPTEMBER 7, 1812 (B).

PLAN OF THE FIELD OF BATTLE OF MALO-JAROSLAVETZ, 24 OCTOBER 1812 (B).

S-32556
Potter, Paraclete. <u>Maps of the World, North America, United States of America, South America, Europe, Asia, Africa</u>. Poughkeepsie, NY: s.n., 1814.

THE WORLD (1).

NORTH AMERICA (2).

UNITED STATES (3).

SOUTH AMERICA (4).

EUROPE (5).

ASIA (6).

AFRICA (7).

S-33638
Weems, Mason. The Life of George Washington. 10th ed.
    Philadelphia: Mathew Carey, 1814.

    THE UNITED STATES OF AMERICA (F).

S-33639
Weems, Mason. The Life of George Washington. 12th ed.
    Philadelphia: Mathew Carey, 1814.

    THE UNITED STATES OF AMERICA (F).

S-33733
Workman, Benjamin. Elements of Geography. 15th ed. Philadelphia:
    Griggs and Dickinson, for William M'Culloch, 1814.

    THE WORLD (F).

    THE SOLAR SYSTEM (6).

    NORTH AMERICA (83).

    SOUTH AMERICA (134).

    EUROPE (152).

    ASIA (180).

    AFRICA (194).

S-33842
Blunt, Edmund. The American Coast Pilot. 8th ed. New York: Edmund
    Blunt, 1815.

    [ISLE OF SABLE] (xvi).

    PLAN OF PORTLAND HARBOUR (120).

    PLAN OF PORTSMOUTH HARBOUR (122).

    PLAN OF NEWBURYPORT HARBOUR (126).

    HARBOUR OF ANNIS SQUAM IPSWICH BAY (128).

    BOSTON BAY (134).

    CAPE POGE AND ADJACENT SHOALS (152).

    PLAN OF NEWPORT HARBOUR (154).

CHART OF LONG ISLAND SOUND (160).

NEW YORK (162).

THE BAY AND RIVER OF DELAWARE (164).

THE BAY OF CHESAPEAKE FROM ITS ENTRANCE TO BALTIMORE (168).

A CHART OF THE COAST OF NORTH CAROLINA BETWEEN CAPE HATTERAS
    AND CAPE FEAR (176).

OCRACOCK BAR INCLUDING SHELL CASTLE (176).

CHARLESTON HARBOUR (180).

CHART OF THE HARBOUR OF VERACRUZ (275).

S-33891
An Atlas of Ten Select Maps of Ancient Geography. Philadelphia:
    John Melish, 1815.

TERRA VETERIBUS NOTA (1).

ROMANUM IMPERIUM (2).

ORIENTIS TABULA (3).

GRAECIA ANTIQUA (4).

ITALIA ANTIQUA (5).

THE PLACES RECORDED IN THE FIVE BOOKS OF MOSES (6).

THE EASTERN COUNTRIES AS MENTIONED BY MOSES (7).

THE LAND OF MORIAH OR JERUSALEM AND THE ADJACENT COUNTRY
    (8).

STATE OF NATIONS AT THE CHRISTIAN AERA (9).

ROMANI IMPERII &C TYPUS (10).

S-33909
A PLAN OF BALDWIN [MAINE] COPIED AND REDUCED FROM THE ORIGINAL IN
    THE LAND OFFICE. Boston: Wells and Lilly, 1815.

S-34072
Bible. Philadelphia: Mathew Carey, 1815.

THE JOURNEYINGS OF THE CHILDREN OF ISRAEL FROM EGYPT THROUGH
THE RED SEA AND WILLDNERNESS TO THE LAND OF CANAAN (F).

A MAP SHEWING THE SITUATION OF THE GARDEN OF EDEN, MOUNT
ARARAT WITH OTHER COUNTRIES AND PLACES MENTIONED IN THE
SCRIPTURES (2).

MAP OF THE COUNTRIES PEOPLED BY THE DESCENDANTS OF CAIN (6).

CANAAN OR THE LAND OF PROMISE TO ABRAHAM AND HIS POSTERITY
(8).

ANCIENT EGYPT (34).

THE CITY OF JERUSALEM (372).

SYRIA AND ASSYRIA (282).

THE PURVEYORSHIPS IN THE REIGN OF SOLOMON (340).

THE LAND OF MORIAH OR JERUSALEM AND THE ADJACENT COUNTRY
(334).

THE COUNTRIES TRAVELLED BY THE APOSTLES (930).

S-34217
Brookes, Richard. Brookes' General Gazetteer Improved. Baltimore:
    Joseph Robinson, for Joseph Cushing, 1815.

NORTH AMERICA (F).

AFRICA (5).

SOUTH AMERICA (16).

ASIA (25).

EUROPE (146).

S-34483
Cummings, Jacob. A School Atlas, Accompanying Ancient and Modern
    Geography. Boston: Cummings and Hilliard, 1815.

THE WORLD (1).

NORTH AMERICA (2).

THE UNITED STATES OF AMERICA (3).

SOUTH AMERICA (4).

EUROPE (5).

BRITAIN OR THE UNITED KINGDOM OF ENGLAND, SCOTLAND AND
        IRELAND (6).

ASIA (7).

AFRICA (8).

S-34534
Davies, Benjamin. New System of Modern Geography. 4th ed.
    Philadelphia: Jacob Johnson, 1815.

THE WORLD (F).

EUROPE (xxiv).

ASIA (146).

NORTH AMERICA (240).

SOUTH AMERICA (408).

AFRICA (420).

S-34595
Drake, Daniel. Natural and Statistical View, or Picture of
    Cincinnati and the Miami Country. Cincinnati: Looker and
    Wallace, 1815.

PLAN OF CINCINNATI, INCLUDING ALL THE ADDITIONS AND
        SUBDIVISIONS (F).

MAP OF THE MIAMI COUNTRY (34).

S-34811
MAP OF THE DISTRICT OF MAINE FROM THE LATEST AND BEST
    AUTHORITIES. Moses Greenleaf. Boston: Jacob Cummings, 1815.

S-34959
A MAP OF THE STATE OF OHIO FROM ACTUAL SURVEY. Benjamin Hough.
    Chillicothe: Hough, Bourne and Meiser, 1815.

S-35027
Jones, Calvin. _A Description of Wier's Cave in Augusta County,_
    Virginia. Albany: Henry Southwick, 1815.

    [WIER'S CAVE] (F).

S-35030
Josephus, Flavius. _The Genuine Works of Flavius Josephus._
    7 volumes. New York: Fanshaw and Clayton, for David
    Huntington, 1815.

    JERUSALEM. Volume 2 (F).

S-35069
Labaume, Eugene. _A Circumstantial Narrative of the Campaign in_
    Russia. Philadelphia: James Maxwell, for John Conrad, 1815.

    PLAN OF THE FIELD OF BATTLE OF MALO-JAROSLAVETZ, 24 OCTOBER
        1812 (185).

S-35100
Lewis, Samuel. _Epitomised System of Geography_. Philadelphia:
    Edward Parker, 1815.

    UNITED STATES (i).

    NORTH AMERICA (20).

    SOUTH AMERICA (64).

    EUROPE (70).

    ASIA (86).

    AFRICA (94).

S-35247
Melish, John. _A Military and Topographical Atlas of the United_
    States. Philadelphia: John Melish, 1815.

    MAP OF THE SEAT OF WAR IN NORTH AMERICA. Part 1 (4).

    VIEW OF THE COUNTRY ROUND THE FALLS OF NIAGARA. Part 1 (10).

    EAST END OF LAKE ONTARIO. Part 1 (18).

    PLAN OF MONTREAL WITH A MAP OF THE ISLANDS AND ADJOINING
        COUNTRY. Part 1 (20).

A MAP OF THE SOUTHERN SECTION OF THE UNITED STATES INCLUDING
THE FLORIDAS AND BAHAMA ISLANDS SHEWING THE SEAT OF WAR
IN THAT DEPARTMENT. Part 2 (F).

AMERICA COAST FROM LYNHAVEN TO NARRAGANSET BAY. Part 2 (21).

PLAN OF QUEBEC AND ADJACENT COUNTRY SHEWING THE PRINCIPAL
ENCAMPMENTS AND WORKS OF THE BRITISH AND FRENCH ARMIES
DURING THE SIEGE BY GENERAL WOLFE IN 1759. Part 3 (F).

MAP OF THE RIVER ST. LAWRENCE AND ADJACENT COUNTRY FROM
WILLIAMSBURG TO MONTREAL. Part 3 (11).

EAST END OF LAKE ONTARIO AND RIVER ST. LAWRENCE FROM
KINGSTON TO FRENCH MILLS. Part 3 (B).

MAP OF THE SEAT OF WAR AMONG THE CREEK INDIANS. Part 3 (B).

MAP OF NEW ORLEANS AND ADJACENT COUNTRY. Part 3 (B).

MAP OF DETROIT RIVER AND ADJACENT COUNTRY. Part 3 (B).

S-35248
Melish, John. <u>The Traveller's Directory Through the United
States</u>. Philadelphia: George Palmer, for John Melish, 1815.

MAP OF THE UNITED STATES OF AMERICA (F).

BOSTON AND ADJACENT COUNTRY (4).

NEW YORK AND ADJACENT COUNTRY (8).

PHILADELPHIA AND ADJACENT COUNTRY (10).

BALTIMORE ANNAPOLIS AND ADJACENT COUNTRY (14).

S-35249
Melish, John. <u>Travels Through the United States</u>. 2 volumes.
Philadelphia: George Palmer, for John Melish, 1815.

MAP OF THE UNITED STATES OF AMERICA. Volume 1 (F).

CHART OF THE ATLANTIC OCEAN. Volume 1 (vii).

VIEW OF THE COUNTRY ROUND PITTSBURGH. Volume 2 (54).

FALLS OF OHIO. Volume 2 (149).

KENTUCKY. Volume 2 (184).

OHIO. Volume 2 (208).

VIEW OF THE COUNTRY ROUND ZANESVILLE. Volume 2 (230).

VIEW OF THE COUNTRY ROUND THE FALLS OF NIAGARA. Volume 2 (318).

S-35565
Park, Mungo. The Journal of a Mission to the Interior of Africa, in the Year 1805. Philadelphia: William Fry, for Edward Earle, 1815.

MAP TO ILLUSTRATE THE JOURNAL OF MUNGO PARK'S LAST MISSION INTO AFRICA (F).

[NIGER RIVER] (256).

S-35680
Porter, Robert. A Narrative of a Campaign in Russia, During the Year 1812. Hartford: David Huntington, Mercein and Mercein, 1815.

ADVANCE OF THE FRENCH ARMY TO MOSCOW (6).

RETREAT OF THE FRENCH ARMY FROM MOSCOW TO THE BANKS OF THE NEIMEN (23).

S-35681
Porter, Robert. A Narrative of a Campaign in Russia, During the Year 1812. Philadelphia: David Robinson, for William M'Carty, 1815.

RETREAT OF THE FRENCH ARMY FROM MOSCOW TO THE BANKS OF THE NEIMEN (vii).

S-35706
Prideaux, Humphrey. The Old and New Testaments Connected in the History of the Jews. 4 volumes. Charlestown, MA: John M'Kown, for the Middlesex Bookstore, 1815-1816.

PALAESTINA SEU TERRA SANITA. Volume 1 (112).

THE LAND OF MORIAH OR JERUSALEM AND THE ADJACENT COUNTRY. Volume 1 (287).

GRAECIA ANTIQUA. Volume 1 (406).

AEGYPTUS ANTIQUA. Volume 2 (10).

ASIA MINOR ANTIQUA. Volume 3 (19).

IMPERIUM PERSICUM ANTIQUUM. Volume 3 (128).

SYRIA ET ASSYRIA. Volume 4 (7).

S-35806
Rollin, Charles. <u>The Ancient History of the Egyptians....</u>
    4 volumes. Hartford: Hart and Lincoln, for Silas Andrus,
    1815.

    TERRA VETERIBUS NOTA. Volume 1 (12).

    AEGYPTUS ANTIQUA. Volume 1 (197).

    ITALIA ANTIQUA. Volume 2 (8).

    GRAECIA ANTIQUA. Volume 2 (13).

    AFRICA ANTIQUA. Volume 3 (3).

    SYRIA ET ASSYRIA. Volume 3 (8).

    ASIA MINOR ANTIQUA. Volume 4 (7).

    IMPERIUM PERSICUM ANTIQUUM. Volume 4 (8).

S-35807
Rollin, Charles. <u>The Ancient History of the Egyptians....</u>
    10 volumes. New York: Van Winkle and Wiley, for David
    Huntington, 1815.

    MAP EXHIBITING THE MARCHES OF ALEXANDER, HANNIBAL &C JULIUS
        CAESAR. Volume 1. William Darby (F).

S-35967
Snowden, Richard. <u>The History of North and South America</u>.
    2 volumes in 1. Philadelphia: William Greer, for Johnson and
    Warner, 1815.

    NORTH AMERICA. Volume 1 (F).

    SOUTH AMERICA. Volume 2 (F).

S-36453
<u>The Virginia Intelligence for 1815</u>. Richmond: A. Works, 1815.

    VIRGINIA (F).

S-36534
Weems, Mason. The Life of George Washington. 14th ed.
    Philadelphia: Mathew Carey, 1815.

    UNITED STATES (F).

S-36647
The World, A School Atlas. Boston: Cummings and Hilliard, 1815.

    THE WORLD (1).

    NORTH AMERICA (2).

    THE UNITED STATES OF AMERICA (3).

    SOUTH AMERICA (4).

    EUROPE (5).

    BRITAIN OR THE UNITED KINGDOM OF ENGLAND, SCOTLAND AND
        IRELAND (6).

    ASIA (7).

    AFRICA (8).

S-36782
Badia y Leblich, Domingo. The Travels of Ali Bey. 2 volumes.
    Philadelphia: Mathew Carey, 1816.

    MAP OF NORTHERN AFRICA. Volume 1 (237).

S-36783
Badia y Leblich, Domingo. The Travels of Ali Bey. 2nd American
    ed. 2 volumes. Philadelphia: James Maxwell, for John Conrad,
    1816.

    MAP OF NORTHERN AFRICA. Volume 1 (F).

S-36955
Bible. Philadelphia: Mathew Carey, 1816.

    A MAP SHEWING THE SITUATION OF THE GARDEN OF EDEN WITH THE
        COUNTRIES AND PLACES MENTIONED IN THE SCRIPTURE (2).

    A MAP OF THE COUNTRIES PEOPLED BY THE DESCENDANTS OF HAM
        (6).

A MAP OF THE COUNTRIES PEOPLED BY THE DESCENDANTS OF SHEM
(6).

CANAAN OR THE LAND OF PROMISE TO ABRAHAM AND HIS POSTERITY
(8).

ANCIENT EGYPT (34).

THE PLACES RECORDED IN THE FIVE BOOKS OF MOSES (43).

THE EASTERN COUNTRIES AS MENTIONED BY MOSES (43).

THE JOURNEYINGS OF THE CHILDREN OF ISRAEL FROM EGYPT THROUGH
THE RED SEA AND WILDERNESS TO THE LAND OF CANAAN (52).

THE PURVEYORSHIPS IN THE REIGN OF SOLOMON (268).

THE CITY OF JERUSALEM (278).

MAP OF THE ASSYRIAN, BABYLONIAN, MEDIAN AND PERSIAN EMPIRES
(282).

DOMINIONS OF SOLOMON AND HIS ALLIES (340).

SHEBA WITH THE VOYAGE TO TARSHISH AND OPHIR (340).

THE LAND OF MORIAH OR JERUSALEM AND THE ADJACENT COUNTRY
(834).

MAP OF THE COUNTRY TRAVELLED BY THE APOSTLES WITH THE VOYAGE
OF SAINT PAUL TO ROME (930).

S-37035
Boerstler, Charles. <u>Battle of the Beaver Dams</u>. Baltimore: s.n.,
1816.

DIAGRAM TO SHEW THE RELATIVE POSITIONS, DISTANCES, &C
ATTACHED BY THE COURT TO THE PROCEEDINGS IN THE CASE OF
COLONEL BOERSTLER (3).

S-37092
Brookes, Richard, revised by Jedidiah Morse. <u>The General
Gazetteer</u>. Boston: Thomas White, for Melvin Lord, 1816.

THE WESTERN HEMISPHERE OR NEW WORLD (F).

THE EASTERN HEMISPHERE OR OLD WORLD (F).

S-37101
Brown, John. _Dictionary of the Holy Bible_. Albany: Henry
    Southwick, 1816.

    EGYPT (220).

S-37104
Brown, William. _The History of Missions_. 2 volumes. Philadelphia:
    Benjamin Coles, 1816.

    MAP OF THE WORLD FROM THE BEST AUTHORITIES (F).

S-37161
Campbell, John. _Travels in South Africa_. Andover, MA: Flagg and
    Gould, 1816.

    SOUTH AFRICA (16).

    JUNCTION OF THE YELLOW AND GRADOCK RIVERS AND JUNCTION OF
        THE YELLOW AND ALEXANDER RIVERS (231).

S-37178
Carey, Mathew. _Carey's General Atlas_. Philadelphia: Mathew Carey,
    1816.

    A MAP OF THE WORLD FROM THE BEST AUTHORITIES (1).

    A CHART OF THE WORLD ACCORDING TO MERCATORS PROJECTION (2).

    A NEW AND ACCURATE MAP OF NORTH AMERICA FROM THE BEST
        AUTHORITIES (3).

    THE BRITISH POSSESSIONS IN NORTH AMERICA FROM THE LATEST
        AUTHORITIES (4).

    MAP OF THE UNITED STATES OF AMERICA (5).

    VERMONT FROM ACTUAL SURVEY (6).

    THE STATE OF NEW HAMPSHIRE COMPILED CHIEFLY FROM ACTUAL
        SURVEYS (7).

    THE DISTRICT OF MAINE (8).

    THE STATE OF MASSACHUSETTS (9).

    THE STATE OF RHODE ISLAND COMPILED FROM THE SURVEYS AND
        OBSERVATIONS OF CALEB HARRIS. Harding Harris (10).

CONNECTICUT FROM THE BEST AUTHORITIES (11).

THE STATE OF NEW YORK (12).

THE STATE OF NEW JERSEY COMPILED FROM THE MOST AUTHENTIC
INFORMATION (13).

PENNSYLVANIA (14).

DELAWARE FROM THE BEST AUTHORITIES (15).

MARYLAND (16).

A CORRECT MAP OF VIRGINIA (17).

NORTH CAROLINA FROM THE LATEST AUTHORITIES (18).

THE STATE OF SOUTH CAROLINA FROM THE BEST AUTHORITIES (19).

THE STATE OF GEORGIA (20).

KENTUCKY (21).

THE STATE OF TENNESSEE (22).

MISSISSIPPI TERRITORY (23).

THE STATE OF OHIO WITH PART OF UPPER CANADA (24).

THE UPPER TERRITORIES OF THE UNITED STATES (25).

LOUISIANA (26).

MISSOURI TERRITORY (27).

PLAT OF THE SEVEN RANGES OR TOWNSHIPS BEING PART OF THE
TERRITORY OF THE UNITED STATES NW OF THE RIVER OHIO
(28).

MEXICO OR NEW SPAIN (29).

WEST INDIES (30).

A MAP OF THE FRENCH PART OF ST. DOMINGO (31).

A NEW MAP OF SOUTH AMERICA FROM THE LATEST AUTHORITIES (32).

A MAP OF CARACAS (33).

PERU (34).

CHILI AND PART OF THE VICEROYALTY OF LA PLATA (35).

A MAP OF BRAZIL NOW CALLED NEW PORTUGAL (36).

EUROPE (37).

SWEDEN, DENMARK, NORWAY AND FINLAND FROM THE BEST
AUTHORITIES (38).

PRUSSIAN EMPIRE (39).

SCOTLAND WITH THE PRINCIPAL ROADS FROM THE BEST AUTHORITIES
(40).

AN ACCURATE MAP OF ENGLAND AND WALES WITH THE PRINCIPAL
ROADS FROM THE BEST AUTHORITIES (41).

A MAP OF IRELAND ACCORDING TO THE BEST AUTHORITIES (42).

HOLLAND OR THE SEVEN UNITED PROVINCES AND THE NETHERLANDS
(43).

GERMANY (44).

FRANCE DIVIDED INTO CIRCLES AND DEPARTMENTS (45).

TURKEY IN EUROPE AND HUNGARY FROM THE BEST AUTHORITIES (46).

SPAIN AND PORTUGAL (47).

ITALY AND SARDINIA FROM THE BEST AUTHORITIES (48).

SWITZERLAND ACCORDING TO THE BEST AUTHORITIES (49).

POLAND (50).

ASIA ACCORDING TO THE BEST AUTHORITIES (51).

CHINA DIVIDED INTO ITS GREAT PROVINCES ACCORDING TO BEST
AUTHORITIES (52).

AN ACCURATE MAP OF HINDOSTAN IN INDIA FROM THE BEST
AUTHORITIES (53).

THE ISLANDS OF THE EAST INDIES WITH THE CHANNELS BETWEEN
INDIA, CHINA AND NEW HOLLAND (54).

A NEW AND ACCURATE MAP OF NEW SOUTH WALES WITH NORFOLK AND
LORD HOWE'S ISLANDS, PORT JACKSON &C FROM ACTUAL SURVEY
(55).

AFRICA ACCORDING TO THE BEST AUTHORITIES (56).

A MAP OF THE COUNTRIES SITUATED ABOUT THE NORTH POLE (57).

A MAP OF THE DISCOVERIES MADE BY CAPTAINS COOK AND CLERKE IN
THE YEARS 1778 AND 1779 BETWEEN THE EASTERN COAST OF
ASIA AND WESTERN COAST OF NORTH AMERICA (58).

S-37265
Clay, Henry. Speech of Henry Clay. New York: Sherman and Pudney,
1816.

THE UNITED STATES OF AMERICA (B).

S-37388
Darby, William. A Geographical Description of the State of
Louisiana. Philadelphia: John Bioren, for John Melish, 1816.

MAP OF PART OF LOUISIANA COPIED FROM HOMANS MAP (F).

S-37399
Davies, Benjamin. A New System of Modern Geography. 3rd ed.
Philadelphia: Johnson and Warner, 1816.

EUROPE (24).

ASIA (146).

NORTH AMERICA (260).

SOUTH AMERICA (408).

AFRICA (420).

S-37402
Davies, John. A Brief Statement of Facts Showing the Importance
of a Bridge over the River Susquehanna, at Connowingo Creek.
Baltimore: John Wane, 1816.

PLAT SHOWING THE NEW TURNPIKE ROAD FROM BALTIMORE TO
PHILADELPHIA ALSO THE BRANCHES TO MCCALLS FERRY AND
ROCK RUN BRIDGE (F).

S-37704
Gibbon, Edward. The History of the Decline and Fall of the Roman
Empire. 2nd American ed. 8 Volumes. Philadelphia: Abraham
Small, for Nicklin and Riley, 1816.

EASTERN PART OF THE ROMAN EMPIRE. Volume 2 (vii).

THE PARTS OF EUROPE AND ASIA ADJACENT TO CONSTANTINOPLE.
Volume 2 (220).

WESTERN PART OF THE ROMAN EMPIRE. Volume 3 (vii).

S-37964
A MAP AND CHART OF THE BAYS, HARBOURS, POST ROADS, AND
SETTLEMENTS IN PASSAMAQUODDY AND MACHIAS WITH THE LARGE
ISLAND OF GRAND MANAN. B.R. Jones. Washington: s.n., 1816.

S-38025
Labaume, Eugene. A Circumstanstantial Narrative of the Campaign
in Russia. 2nd American ed. Hartford: Russell and Russell,
for Sheldon and Goodrich, 1816.

PLAN OF THE FIELD OF BATTLE OF THE MOSKWA, SEPTEMBER 7, 1812
(B).

PLAN OF THE FIELD OF BATTLE OF MALO-JAROSLAVETZ, 24 OCTOBER
1812 (B).

S-38026
Labaume, Eugene. A Circumstanstantial Narrative of the Campaign
in Russia. 2nd American ed. Hartford: Russell and Russell,
for Silas Andrus, 1816.

PLAN OF THE FIELD OF BATTLE OF THE MOSKWA, SEPTEMBER 7, 1812
(B).

PLAN OF THE FIELD OF BATTLE OF MALO-JAROSLAVETZ, 24 OCTOBER
1812 (B).

S-38031
La Rochejaquelein, Marie. Memoirs of the Marchioness de Laroche
Jaquelein. Philadelphia: Mathew Carey, 1816.

A MAP OF THE VENDEE SOUTH OF THE LOIRE (F).

S-38034
Latour, Arsene. Atlas to the Historical Memoir of the War in West
Florida and Louisiana. Philadelphia: John Conrad, 1816.

A GENERAL MAP OF THE SEAT OF WAR IN LOUISIANA AND WEST
FLORIDA (1).

PLAN SHEWING THE ATTACK MADE BY A BRITISH SQUADRON ON FORT
BOWYER AT MOBILEPOINT ON THE 15 SEPTEMBER 1815 (2).

PLAN OF THE ATTACK MADE BY THE BRITISH BARGES ON FIVE
AMERICAN GUNBOATS ON THE 14TH DECEMBER 1814 (3).

MAP SHEWING THE LANDING OF THE BRITISH ARMY ITS SEVERAL
ENCAMPMENTS AND FORTIFICATION ON THE MISSISSIPPI (4).

PLAN OF THE ATTACK MADE BY MAJOR GENERAL JACKSON ON A
DIVISION OF THE BRITISH ARMY COMMANDED BY MAJOR GENERAL
J. KEANE ON THE 23RD DECEMBER 1814 (5).

PLAN OF THE ATTACK AND DEFENCE OF THE AMERICAN LINES BELOW
NEW ORLEANS ON THE 5TH JANUARY 1815 (6).

PLAN OF FORT ST. PHILIP AT PLAQUEMINES SHEWING THE POSITION
OF THE BRITISH VESSELS WHEN BOMBARDING THE FORT (7).

MAP OF MOBILE POINT AND PARTS OF THE BAY AND DAUPHINE ISLAND
(8).

S-38201
Maverick, Peter. General Atlas. New York: Maverick and Duane,
1816.

THE WORLD (1).

NORTH AMERICA (2).

SOUTH AMERICA (3).

EUROPE (4).

ASIA (5).

AFRICA (6).

S-38219
Melish, John. A Geographical Description of the United States.
Philadelphia: John Melish, 1816.

BOSTON AND ADJACENT COUNTRY (60).

NEW YORK AND ADJACENT COUNTRY (72).

PHILADELPHIA AND ADJACENT COUNTRY (82).

BALTIMORE ANNAPOLIS AND ADJACENT COUNTRY (90).

SPECIMEN OF THE COUNTY MAPS TO BE CONSTRUCTED BY VIRTURE OF
AN ACT OF THE LEGISLATURE DIRECTING THE FORMATION OF A
MAP OF PENNSYLVANIA (178).

S-38220
Melish, John. <u>Geographical Description of the United States</u>. 2nd
ed. Philadelphia: Thomas Palmer, for John Melish, 1816.

BOSTON AND VICINITY (62).

NEW YORK AND ADJACENT COUNTRY (72).

PHILADELPHIA AND ADJACENT COUNTRY (80).

BALTIMORE ANNAPOLIS AND ADJACENT COUNTRY (86).

SPECIMEN OF THE COUNTY MAPS TO BE CONSTRUCTED BY VIRTURE OF
AN ACT OF ACT OF THE LEGISLATURE DIRECTING THE
FORMATION OF A MAP OF PENNSYLVANIA (181).

S-38221
MAP OF THE UNITED STATES WITH THE CONTIGUOUS BRITISH & SPANISH
POSSESSIONS COMPILED FROM THE LATEST & BEST AUTHORITIES.
John Melish. Philadelphia: Vallance and Tanner, for John
Melish, 1816.

S-38222
Melish, John. <u>The Traveller's Directory Through the United
States</u>. 3rd ed. Philadelphia: Palmer and Palmer, 1816.

MAP OF THE UNITED STATES OF AMERICA (F).

BOSTON AND ADJACENT COUNTRY (6).

NEW YORK AND ADJACENT COUNTRY (10).

PHILADELPHIA AND ADJACENT COUNTRY (14).

BALTIMORE ANNAPOLIS AND ADJACENT COUNTRY (16).

S-38223
Melish, John. <u>Melish's Universal School Atlas</u>. Philadelphia: John
Melish, 1816.

ELEMENTARY MAP [EUROPE] (1).

MAP OF THE WORLD (2).

THE WORLD ON MERCATOR'S PROJECTION WITH ALL THE LATEST
DISCOVERIES (3).

AMERICA (4).

EUROPE (5).

ASIA &C (6).

AFRICA (7).

UNITED STATES (8).

S-38291
Morier, James. <u>A Journey Through Persia, Armenia, and Asia Minor,
      to Constantinople, in the Years 1808 and 1809</u>. Philadelphia:
      George Palmer, for Mathew Carey and Wells and Lilly, 1816.

   SKETCH OF THE COUNTRIES SITUATED BETWEEN SHIRTZ AND
         CONSTANTINOPLE SHEWING THE ROUTE OF HIS MAJESTY'S
         MISSION (xii).

S-38293
Morse, Jedidiah. <u>Geography Made Easy</u>. 18th ed. Boston: Thomas and
      Andrews, 1816.

   A NEW MAP OF THE WORLD WITH THE LATEST DISCOVERIES (F).

   A MAP OF NORTH AMERICA FROM THE LATEST DISCOVERIES (62).

S-38294
Morse, Jedidiah. <u>Geography Made Easy</u>. 2nd Troy ed. Troy, NY:
      Parker and Bliss, 1816.

   A NEW MAP OF THE WORLD WITH THE LATEST DISCOVERIES (F).

   A MAP OF NORTH AMERICA FROM THE LATEST DISCOVERIES (62).

S-38529
O'Neill, John. <u>A New and Easy System of Geography and Popular
      Astronomy</u>. 4th ed. Baltimore: Joseph Robinson, for Fielding
      Lucas, 1816.

   WORLD (F).

   UNITED STATES (54).

   SOLAR SYSTEM (306).

189

S-38617
Philippart, John. <u>Memoirs, &c. &c. of General Moreau</u>.
     Philadelphia: Mathew Carey; Boston: Wells and Lilly, 1816.

     MAP OF THE COURSE OF THE RHINE IN THE ENVIRONS OF STRASBOURG
     (F).

S-38633
Picket, Albert. <u>Geographical Grammar</u>. New York: Smith and Forman,
     1816.

     THE WORLD (B).

     UNITED STATES (B).

     NORTH AMERICA (B).

     SOUTH AMERICA (B).

     EUROPE (B).

     ASIA (B).

     AFRICA (B).

S-38644
Pinkerton, John. <u>An Atlas for the Use of Schools</u>. Boston: Thomas
     and Andrews, 1816.

     THE WORLD (1).

     EUROPE (2).

     ASIA (3).

     AFRICA (4).

     UNITED KINGDOMS OF GREAT BRITAIN AND IRELAND (5).

     UNITED STATES (6).

     NORTH AMERICA (7).

S-38645
Pinkerton, John. <u>A Modern Atlas</u>. Philadelphia: Thomas Dobson,
     1816.

     WESTERN HEMISPHERE (1).

EASTERN HEMISPHERE (2).

NORTHERN HEMISPHERE (3).

SOUTHERN HEMISPHERE (4).

EUROPE (5).

BRITISH ISLES (6).

ENGLAND SOUTHERN PART (7).

ENGLAND NORTHERN PART (8).

SCOTLAND SOUTHERN PART (9).

SCOTLAND NORTHERN PART (10).

IRELAND (11).

REMOTE BRITISH ISLES (12).

FRANCE (13).

RUSSIA IN EUROPE (14).

AUSTRIAN DOMINIONS (15).

RUSSIAN DOMINIONS (16).

SPAIN AND PORTUGAL (17).

TURKEY IN EUROPE (18).

POLAND (19).

HOLLAND (20).

THE NETHERLANDS (21).

SCANDINAVIA (22).

DENMARK (23).

PORTUGAL (24).

SWITZERLAND (25).

GERMANY NORTH OF THE MAYN (26).

GERMANY SOUTH OF THE MAYN (27).

NORTHERN ITALY (28).

SOUTHERN ITALY (29).

ASIA (30).

TURKEY IN ASIA (31).

CHINA (32).

JAPAN (33).

HINDOSTAN (34).

PERSIA (35).

ARABIA (36).

EAST INDIA ISLES (37).

AUSTRALASIA (38).

POLYNESIA (39).

NORTH AMERICA (40).

UNITED STATES OF AMERICA NORTHERN PART (41).

UNITED STATES OF AMERICA SOUTHERN PART (42).

SPANISH DOMINIONS IN NORTH AMERICA NORTHERN PART (43).

SPANISH DOMINIONS IN NORTH AMERICA MIDDLE PART (44).

SPANISH DOMINIONS IN NORTH AMERICA SOUTHERN PART (45).

BRITISH POSSESSIONS IN NORTH AMERICA (46).

WEST INDIES (47).

SOUTH AMERICA (48).

LA PLATA (49).

PERU (50).

NEW GRANADA (51).

THE CARACAS (52).

CHILI (53).

AFRICA (54).

EGYPT (55).

ABYSSINIA AND NUBIA (56).

NORTHERN AFRICA (57).

WESTERN AFRICA (58).

SOUTHERN AFRICA (59).

THE WORLD ON MERCATOR'S PROJECTION WESTERN PART (60).

THE WORLD ON MERCATOR'S PROJECTION EASTERN PART (61).

S-38655
Plates and Maps of the Travels of Ali Bey. Philadelphia: James
    Maxwell, for John Conrad, 1816.

    AFRICA (B).

S-38864
Salt, Henry. A Voyage to Abyssinia. Philadelphia: Lydia Bailey,
    for Mathew Carey, 1816.

    MAP OF PART OF ABYSSINIA (F).

S-38934
Simpson, James. A Visit to Flanders in July, 1815. New York:
    Jonathan Seymour, for Samuel Campbell, 1816.

    PLAN OF THE BATTLE OF WATERLOO (F).

S-39079
Thomson, John. Historical Sketches of the Late War between the
    United States and Great Britain. Philadelphia: John Bioren,
    for Thomas Desilver, 1816.

    SIEGE AND DEFENSE OF FORT ERIE (F).

    A PLAN OF FORT SANDUSKY (154).

S-39080
Thomson, John. Historical Sketches of the Late War between the
    United States and Great Britain. Richmond, VA: George
    Cottom, 1816.

193

SIEGE AND DEFENSE OF FORT ERIE (F).

A PLAN OF FORT SANDUSKY (154).

S-39081
Thomson, John. Historical Sketches of the Late War between the
    United States and Great Britain. 2nd ed. Philadelphia: John
    Bioren, for Thomas Desilver, 1816.

A PLAN OF FORT SANDUSKY (158).

SIEGE AND DEFENSE OF FORT ERIE (302).

S-39082
Thomson, John. Historical Sketches of the Late War between the
    United States and Great Britain. 3rd ed. Philadelphia: John
    Bioren, for Thomas Desilver, 1816.

A PLAN OF FORT SANDUSKY (158).

SIEGE AND DEFENSE OF FORT ERIE (302).

S-39823
Wilkinson, James. Diagrams and Plans. Philadelphia: Abraham
    Small, 1816.

SKETCH OF THE RIVER ST. LAWRENCE (1).

SKETCH OF TRENTON (2).

PART OF NEW JERSEY (3).

AFFAIR OF PRINCETON (6).

PART OF THE RIVER ST. LAWRENCE (7).

SKETCH OF THE ST. LAWRENCE (8).

DISPOSITION OF THE AMERICAN TROOPS ON THE 30TH MARCH 1811
    (9).

SACKETS HARBOUR (10).

NIAGARA RIVER (11).

BATTLE OF BRIDGEWATER. 4 MAPS (12-14).

MAP OF THE STRAIGHTS OF NIAGARA (15).

MAP OF MAJOR GENERAL ROSA'S ROUTE WITH THE BRITISH COLUMN
    FROM BENEDUT TO THE PATUXENT TO THE CITY OF WASHINGTON
    (16).

THE AFFAIR OF BLODENSBURG (17).

[PHILADELPHIA AND ENVIRONS] (18).

PLAN OF ROUSES POINT AT THE FOOT OF LAKE CHAMPLAIN (19).

PART OF VERMONT (20).

S-39842
Winder, Rider. <u>Remarks on a Pamphlet entitled "An Inquiry
    Respecting the Capture of Washington by the British on the
    24th of August, 1814, with &c., &c. by Spectator."</u>.
    Baltimore: Joseph Robinson, 1816.

    [WASHINGTON AND ENVIRONS] (F).

S-39877
Workman, Benjamin. <u>Elements of Geography</u>. 16th ed. Philadelphia:
    William M'Carty, 1816.

    THE WORLD (F).

    THE SOLAR SYSTEM (iv).

    UNITED STATES OF AMERICA (96).

    SOUTH AMERICA (134).

    EUROPE (152).

    ASIA (180).

    AFRICA (194).

S-39925
Adams, Robert. <u>The Narrative of Robert Adams</u>. Boston: Wells and
    Lilly, 1817.

    MAP TO ILLUSTRATE THE NARRATIVE OF ROBERT ADAMS' ROUTE IN
        AFRICA (F).

S-39926
Adams, Daniel. <u>School Atlas to Adam's Geography</u>. Boston: Lincoln and Edmands, 1817.

THE WORLD (1).

NORTH AMERICA (2).

UNITED STATES (3).

NEW ENGLAND STATES (4).

SOUTH AMERICA (5).

EUROPE (6).

ASIA (7).

AFRICA (8).

S-40198
<u>Bible</u>. Brattleborough, VT: John Holbrook, 1817.

THE JOURNIES OF THE CHILDREN OF ISRAEL FROM EGYPT THROUGH THE WILDERNESS TO CANAAN (146).

THE PLACES RECORDED IN THE FIVE BOOKS OF MOSES (148).

THE EASTERN COUNTRIES AS MENTIONED BY MOSES (148).

A MAP OF CANAAN, PALESTINE, JUDEA, OR THE HOLY LAND AS DIVIDED AMONG THE 12 TRIBES (180).

A MAP OF THE DIFFERENT PLACES MENTIONED IN THE NEW TESTAMENT WITH ST. PAUL'S JOURNEY FROM PHILIPPI TO TYRE AND FROM CAESAREA TO ROME (808).

S-40203
<u>Bible</u>. 2nd American ed. New York: Abraham Paul, for Hitt and Paul, 1817.

A MAP OF THE PROMISED LAND AND SYRIA [In Numbers] (UP).

S-40204
<u>Bible</u>. New York: Thomas Collins, 1817.

A MAP OF CANAAN, PALESTINE, JUDEA OR THE HOLY LAND (50).

A MAP OF THE JOURNEYINGS OF THE CHILDREN OF ISRAEL FROM
    EGYPT THROUGH THE WILDERNESS TO CANAAN (146).

JERUSALEM, WITH THE NEIGHBORING COUNTRY (739).

MAP OF THE PLACES MENTIONED IN THE NEW TESTAMENT
    ILLUSTRATING ST. PAUL'S TRAVELS AND ALSO HIS VOYAGE
    FROM CAESAREA TO ROME (810).

S-40206
Bible. Trenton: Fenton and Fenton, 1817.

CANAAN OR THE LAND OF PROMISE TO ABRAHAM AND HIS POSTERITY
    (8).

THE JOURNEYINGS OF THE CHILDREN OF ISRAEL FROM EGYPT THROUGH
    THE RED SEA AND WILDERNESS TO THE LAND OF CANAAN (16).

ANCIENT EGYPT (34).

THE PLACES RECORDED IN THE FIVE BOOKS OF MOSES (42).

EASTERN COUNTRIES AS MENTIONED BY MOSES (42).

THE CITY OF JERUSALEM (272).

MAP OF THE ASSYRIAN, BABYLONIAN, MEDIAN AND PERSIAN EMPIRES
    (282).

THE DOMINIONS OF SOLOMON AND HIS ALLIES (340).

SHEBA WITH THE VOYAGE TO TARSHISH AND OPHIR (340).

THE LAND OF MORIAH OR JERUSALEM AND THE ADJACENT COUNTRY
    (838).

MAP OF THE COUNTRY TRAVELLED BY THE APOSTLES WITH THE VOYAGE
    OF SAINT PAUL TO ROME (930).

S-40217
Bible. 2 volumes. New York: Paul and Hitt, 1817-1818.

A MAP OF THE DIFFERENT PLACES MENTIONED IN THE NEW TESTAMENT
    WITH ST. PAUL'S VOYAGES FROM PHILIPPI TO TYRE AND FROM
    CAESAREA TO ROME. Volume 1 [In Acts of the Apostles]
    (UP).

S-40244
Bickersteth, Edward. <u>A Scripture Help</u>. Boston: Munroe and
    Francis, for Samuel Parker, 1817.

JERUSALEM AND ITS ENVIRONS (F).

PALESTINE, OR THE HOLY LAND (28).

TRAVELS OF THE APOSTLES THROUGH GREECE, ASIA MINOR, &C.
    (62).

COUNTRIES SPOKEN OF IN THE NEW TESTAMENT (80).

S-40276
Blunt, Edmund. <u>The American Coast Pilot</u>. 9th ed. New York: Edmund
    Blunt, 1817.

THE EASTERN END OF THE ISLE OF SABLE (1).

PLAN OF PORTLAND HARBOUR (120).

PLAN OF PORTSMOUTH HARBOUR (122).

PLAN OF NEWBURYPORT HARBOUR (126).

HARBOUR OF ANNIS SQUAM IN IPSWICH BAY (128).

BOSTON BAY (134).

CAPE POGE AND ADJACENT SHOALS (152).

PLAN OF NEWPORT HARBOUR (154).

CHART OF LONG ISLAND SOUND (160).

NEW YORK HARBOUR (162).

LITTLE EGG HARBOUR (166).

THE BAY AND RIVER OF DELAWARE (166).

BAY OF CHESAPEAKE FROM ITS ENTRANCE TO BALTIMORE (168).

A CHART OF THE COAST OF NORTH CAROLINA BETWEEN CAPE HATTERAS
    AND CAPE FEAR (176).

OCRACOCK BAR INCLUDING SHELL CASTLE (176).

CHARLESTON HARBOUR (182).

SAVANNAH RIVER (184).

CHART OF THE HARBOUR OF VERA CRUZ (242).

S-40278
Blunt, Edmund. <u>Blunt's Stranger's Guide to the City of New York</u>.
    New York: Edmund Blunt, 1817.

    PLAN OF THE CITY OF NEW YORK. William Hooker (F).

S-40296
Bowditch, Nathaniel. <u>The New American Practical Navigator</u>. 4th
    ed. New York: Edmund Blunt, 1817.

    CHART OF THE ATLANTIC OCEAN (F).

S-40325
Broughton, John. <u>A Journey Through Albania</u>. 3 volumes.
    Philadelphia: Mathew Carey, 1817.

    MAP OF ALBANIA. Volume 3 (F).

S-40378
Caesar, Caius Julius. <u>C. Julii Caesaris</u>. 2nd ed. Philadelphia:
    Anthony Griggs, for Mathew Carey, 1817.

    GALLIA VETUS (7).

    ITALIAE ANTIQUAE (B).

S-40386
Campbell, Archibald. <u>Voyage Round the World from 1806-1812</u>. New
    York: Van Winkle and Wiley, 1817.

    TRACK OF THE ECLIPSE'S LONG BOAT FROM SANNACK TO KODIAK (F).

S-40486
Clarke, Edward. <u>Travels in Various Countries of Europe, Asia,
    and Africa</u>. 5th American ed. 2 volumes. Hartford: Barzillai
    Hudson, for John Robbins, 1817.

    PLAN OF THE ISLAND AND TOWN OF TSCHERCHASKOY THE CAPITAL OF
    THE DON COSSACKS (180).

S-40488
Clavijero, Francisco. The History of Mexico. 3 volumes.
    Philadelphia: Thomas Dobson, 1817.

    ANAHUAC, OR THE EMPIRE OF MEXICO, THE KINGDOMS OF ACOLHUACAN
        AND MICHUACAN &C AS THEY WERE IN THE YEAR 1521. Volume
        1 (F).

    LAKES OF MEXICO. Volume 2 (F).

S-40589
Cramer, Zadok. The Navigator. 9th ed. Pittsburgh: Robert
    Ferguson, for Cramer, Spear and Eichbaum, 1817.

    MAP OF PITTSBURGH (10).

    [OHIO RIVER] (13 sheets) (72-126).

    FALLS OF OHIO (107).

    [MISSISSIPPI RIVER] (20 sheets) (159-200).

S-40599
Cummings, Jacob. Questions on the Historical Parts of the New
    Testament. Boston: Cummings and Hilliard, 1817.

    JERUSALEM AND ITS ENVIRONS (F).

    COUNTRIES SPOKEN OF IN THE NEW TESTAMENT (B).

    TRAVELS OF THE APOSTLES THROUGH GREECE, ASIA MINOR, &C. (B).

    PALESTINE OR THE HOLY LAND (B).

S-40600
Cummings, Jacob. Questions on the Historical Parts of the New
    Testament. 2nd ed. Boston: Cummings and Hilliard, 1817.

    JERUSALEM AND ITS ENVIRONS (F).

    COUNTRIES SPOKEN OF IN THE NEW TESTAMENT (B).

    TRAVELS OF THE APOSTLES THROUGH GREECE, ASIA MINOR, &C. (B).

    PALESTINE OR THE HOLY LAND (B).

S-40601
Cummings, Jacob. School Atlas to Cummings Ancient and Modern
    Geography. 4th ed. Boston: Cummings and Hilliard, 1817.

    THE WORLD (1).

    NORTH AMERICA (2).

    THE UNITED STATES OF AMERICA (3).

    SOUTH AMERICA (4).

    EUROPE (5).

    BRITAIN OR THE UNITED KINGDOM OF ENGLAND, SCOTLAND AND
        IRELAND (6).

    ASIA (7).

    AFRICA (8).

S-40617
Darby, William. Geographical Description of the State of
    Louisiana. 2nd ed. New York: Jonathan Seymour, for James
    Olmstead, 1817.

    [MISSISSIPPI AND ALABAMA TERRITORY] (F).

    MAP OF PART OF LOUISIANA COPIED FROM HOMANS MAP (12).

    CHART OF MOBILE, PERDIDE AND PENSACOLA BAYS (316).

S-40635
Delano, Amasa. A Narrative of Voyages and Travels in the Northern
    and Southern Hemispheres. Boston: Eleazer House, for Amasa
    Delano, 1817.

    A CHART AND VIEWS OF PITCAIRNS ISLAND. (135).

S-40705
Dwight, Nathaniel. A System of Universal Geography for Common
    Schools. Albany: Websters and Skinners, 1817.

    THE WORLD (F).

    EUROPE (12).

    ASIA (76).

AFRICA (128).

NORTH AMERICA (148).

UNITED STATES OF AMERICA (156).

SOUTH AMERICA (192).

S-40723
Eaton, John. The Life of Andrew Jackson. Philadelphia: Lydia
    Bailey, for Mathew Carey, 1817,

    A SKETCH OF THE BATTLE OF TALLEDEGA (98).

    THE BATTLE OF HORSE SHOE, 27TH MARCH 1814 (176).

    SKETCH OF AN ATTACK MADE BY MAJOR GENERAL JACKSON ON AN
        INVASION OF THE BRITISH ON THE EVENING OF THE 23RD
        DECEMBER 1814 (324).

S-40975
Hall, John. Tracts on the Constitutional Law of the United
    States. Philadelphia: James Maxwell, for Harrison Hall,
    1817.

    PLAN SHEWING ALLUVIAL LANDS OR BATTURES ON THE MISSISSIPPI
        (F).

    PLAN SHEWING THE DISTRIBUTION OF THE JESUITS PLANTATION (F).

S-41201
Kilbourn, John. The Ohio Gazetteer. 3rd ed. Columbus: Philo
    Olmsted, for John Kilbourn, 1817.

    PLAN EXHIBITING THE GENERAL SHAPE AND RELATIVE POSITION OF
        THE SEVERAL COUNTIES IN THE STATE OF OHIO (8).

    PLAT OF THE TOWN OF COLUMBUS (20).

S-41216
LaBaume, Eugene. Circumstantial Narrative of the Campaign in
    Russia. Hartford: Hamlen and Newton, for Silas Andrus, 1817.

    PLAN OF THE FIELD OF BATTLE OF THE MOSKWA, SEPTEMBER 7, 1812
        (F).

    PLAN OF THE FIELD OF BATTLE OF MALO-JAROSLAVETZ (B).

S-41237
Legh, Thomas. <u>Narrative of a Journey in Egypt</u>. Philadelphia:
    James Maxwell, for Moses Thomas, 1817.

    MAP OF THE NILE FROM THE CATARACTS TO IBRIM (F).

S-41325
Maclure, William. <u>Observations on the Geology of the United
    States of America</u>. Philadelphia: Abraham Small, for William
    Maclure, 1817.

    A MAP OF THE UNITED STATES OF AMERICA (10).

S-41401
MAP OF INDIANA. John Melish. Philadelphia: Melish and Harrison,
    1817.

S-41564
<u>A New and Elegant General Atlas Containing Maps of Each of the
    United States</u>. Baltimore: Fielding Lucas, 1817.

    EASTERN HEMISPHERE (1).

    WESTERN HEMISPHERE (2).

    MERCATOR'S CHART (3).

    EUROPE (4).

    ENGLAND AND WALES (5).

    SCOTLAND (6).

    IRELAND (7).

    SWEDEN AND NORWAY (8).

    DENMARK (9).

    RUSSIAN EMPIRE (10).

    POLAND (11).

    PRUSSIA (12).

    GERMANY (13).

    HUNGARY AND TRANSYLVANIA (14).

HOLLAND (15).

FRANCE (16).

SPAIN AND PORTUGAL (17).

SWITZERLAND (18).

ITALY (19).

TURKEY IN EUROPE (20).

ASIA (21).

TURKEY IN ASIA (22).

HINDOOSTAN (23).

CHINA (24).

TARTARY (25).

PERSIA (26).

AFRICA (27).

EGYPT (28).

AMERICA (29).

SOUTH AMERICA (30).

WEST INDIES (31).

CANADA (32).

UNITED STATES (33).

NEW HAMPSHIRE (34).

MASSACHUSETTS (35).

MAINE (36).

VERMONT (37).

RHODE ISLAND (38).

CONNECTICUT (39).

NEW YORK (40).

NEW JERSEY (41).

PENNSYLVANIA (42).

DELAWARE (43).

MARYLAND (44).

VIRGINIA (45).

NORTH CAROLINA (46).

SOUTH CAROLINA (47).

GEORGIA (48).

KENTUCKY (49).

TENNESSEE (50).

OHIO (51).

LOUISIANA (52).

MISSISSIPPI TERRITORY (53).

UPPER TERRITORIES OF THE UNITED STATES (54).

S-41628
Official Reports of the Canal Commissioners of the State of New
    York. New York: Mercein and Mercein, 1817.

    MAP AND PROFILE OF THE PROPOSED CANAL FROM LAKE ERIE TO
        HUDSON RIVER IN THE STATE OF NEW YORK (B).

S-41629
Official Reports of the Canal Commissioners of the State of New
    York. Newburgh, NY: Benjamin Lewis and Shelton and Kensett,
    1817.

    A PROFILE OF THE EXTENT OF THE LEVELS AND THE PLACES AND
        LIFTS OF THE LOCKS BETWEEN LAKE ERIE AND THE HUDSON
        (F).

S-41805
Phillips, Richard. The Universal Preceptor. Philadelphia: Parker
    and Parker, 1817.

    THE EARTH (106).

S-41806
Phillips, Richard. The Universal Preceptor. 2nd American ed.
    Philadelphia: Joseph Skerrett, for Parker and Parker, 1817.

    THE EARTH (106).

S-41814
Picket, Albert. Geographical Grammar. 2nd ed. New York: Daniel
    Smith, 1817.

    THE WORLD (B).

    UNITED STATES (B).

    NORTH AMERICA (B).

    SOUTH AMERICA (B).

    ASIA (B).

    EUROPE (B).

    AFRICA (B).

S-41988
Riley, James. An Authentic Narrative of the Loss of the American
    Brig Commerce. Hartford, CT: James Riley, 1817.

    A MAP OF PART OF AFRICA DRAWN FROM THE LATEST AUTHORITIES TO
        ILLUSTRATE THE NARRATIVE OF CAPTAIN JAMES RILEY. (F).

S-41989
Riley, James. An Authentic Narrative of the Loss of the American
    Brig Commerce. New York: Mercein and Mercein, 1817.

    A MAP OF PART OF AFRICA DRAWN FROM THE LATEST AUTHORITIES TO
        ILLUSTRATE THE NARRATIVE OF CAPTAIN JAMES RILEY (534).

S-41992
Robbins, Archibald. A Journal Comprising an Account of the Loss
    of the Brig Commerce. Hartford, CT: Frederick Bolles, 1817.

    A MAP OF PART OF AFRICA DRAWN FROM THE LATEST AUTHORITIES TO
        ILLUSTRATE THE NARRATIVE OF CAPTAIN JAMES RILEY (F).

S-42152
Snowden, Richard. The History of North and South America. 2
    volumes in 1. Philadelphia: William Geer, for Benjamin
    Warner, 1817.

    NORTH AMERICA. Volume 1 (F).

    SOUTH AMERICA. Volume 2 (F).

S-42284
Thomson, John. Historical Sketches of the Late War between the
    United States and Great Britain. 4th ed. Philadelphia:
    Thomas Desilver, 1817.

    A PLAN OF FORT SANDUSKY (138).

    A PLAN OF FORT ERIE (302).

S-42863
Weems, Mason. Das Leben Des Georg Waschington. Baltimore:
    Schaffer and Maund; Philadelphia: Mathew Carey, 1817.

    UNITED STATES (F).

S-42929
Wilson, Robert. A Sketch of the Military and Political Power of
    Russia. New York: Kirk and Mercein, 1817.

    SKETCH OF THE MILITARY AND POLITICAL POWER OF RUSSIA IN THE
        YEAR 1817 (F).

S-42945
Woodhouselee, Alexander. Elements of General History. New York:
    Francis Nichols, 1817.

    ORBIS TERRARUM VETERIBUS NOTUS (B).

    ITALIA, GRAECIA, ASIA, &C. (B).

    PALESTINE (B).

S-43109
Atlas Classica. Philadelphia: William Fry, for Anthony Finley,
    1818.

    TERRA VETERIBUS NOTA (1).

GRAECIA ANTIQUA (2).

ORIENTIS TABULA (3).

ROMANUM IMPERIUM (4).

ITALIA ANTIQUA (5).

THE PLACES RECORDED IN THE FIVE BOOKS OF MOSES (6).

CANAAN, ARAM, &C. (7).

THE EASTERN COUNTRIES AS MENTIONED BY MOSES (8).

THE LAND OF MORIAH OR JERUSALEM AND THE ADJACENT COUNTRY (9).

STATE OF NATIONS AT THE CHRISTIAN AERA (10).

S-43240
Barrington, Daines. <u>The Possibility of Approaching the North Pole Asserted</u>. New York, Abraham Paul, for James Eastburn, 1818.

MAP OF THE COUNTRIES AROUND THE NORTH POLE ACCORDING TO THE LATEST DISCOVERIES (F).

S-43297
<u>Bible</u>. Brattleborough, VT: s.n., 1818.

A MAP OF CANAAN, PALESTINE, JUDEA, OR THE HOLY LAND AS DIVIDED AMONG THE 12 TRIBES (F).

S-43306
<u>Bible</u>. Philadelphia: Mathew Carey, 1818.

THE JOURNEYINGS OF THE CHILDREN OF ISRAEL FROM EGYPT THROUGH THE RED SEA AND WILDERNESS TO THE LAND OF CANAAN (F).

MAP OF THE COUNTRY TRAVELLED BY THE APOSTLES WITH THE VOYAGE OF ST. PAUL TO ROME (930).

S-43307
<u>Bible</u>. Philadelphia: Mathew Carey, 1818.

THE JOURNEYINGS OF THE CHILDREN OF ISRAEL FROM EGYPT THROUGH THE RED SEA AND WILDERNESS TO THE LAND OF CANAAN (F).

THE CITY OF JERUSALEM (272).

THE LAND OF MORIAH OR JERUSALEM AND THE ADJACENT COUNTRY (834).

THE COUNTRIES TRAVELLED BY THE APOSTLES (930).

S-43373
Birkbeck, Morris. <u>Letters from Illinois</u>. Philadelphia: Mathew Carey, 1818.

UNITED STATES (27).

S-43417
<u>The Boston Directory</u>. Boston: John Frost, for Edward Cotton, 1818.

PLAN OF BOSTON (F).

S-43442
Breck, Samuel. <u>Sketch of the Internal Improvements Already Made by Pennsylvania</u>. Philadelphia: James Maxwell, 1818.

[HEADWATERS OF THE ALLEGANY, SUSQUEHANNA AND SCHUYKILL RIVERS OF PENNSYLVANIA] (3 sheets) (B).

S-43443
Breck, Samuel. <u>Sketch of the Internal Improvements Already Made by Pennsylvania</u>. 2nd ed. Philadelphia: Moses Thomas, 1818.

THE STATE OF PENNSYLVANIA REDUCED WITH PERMISSION FROM READING HOWELL'S MAP (F).

S-43456
Brown, John. <u>Dictionary of the Holy Bible</u>. 2 volumes. Philadelphia: Benjamin Warner, 1818.

MAP OF THE JOURNEYINGS OF THE ISRAELITES FROM EGYPT TO THE LAND OF CANAAN. Volume 1 (F).

A MAP OF THE PROMISED LAND AND SYRIA. Volume 2 (F).

S-43533
Carey, Mathew. <u>Carey's General Atlas</u>. Philadelphia: Mathew Carey, 1818.

MAP OF THE WORLD FROM THE BEST AUTHORITIES (1).

A CHART OF THE WORLD ACCORDING TO MERCATORS PROJECTION
    SHEWING THE LATEST DISCOVERIES OF CAPTAIN COOK (2).

A NEW AND ACCURATE MAP OF NEW SOUTH WALES WITH NORFOLK AND
    LORD HOWE'S ISLANDS PORT JACKSON &C. FROM ACTUAL
    SURVEYS (3).

AFRICA ACCORDING TO THE BEST AUTHORITIES (4).

MAP OF THE COUNTRIES SITUATED ABOUT THE NORTH POLE (5).

A MAP OF THE DISCOVERIES MADE BY CAPTAINS COOK AND CLERKE IN
    THE YEARS 1778 AND 1779 BETWEEN THE EASTERN COAST OF
    ASIA AND THE WESTERN COAST OF NORTH AMERICA (6).

A NEW AND ACCURATE MAP OF NORTH AMERICA FROM THE BEST
    AUTHORITIES (7).

THE BRITISH POSSESSIONS IN NORTH AMERICA FROM THE LATEST
    AUTHORITIES (8).

MAP OF THE UNITED STATES OF AMERICA (9).

VERMONT FROM ACTUAL SURVEY (10).

THE STATE OF NEW HAMPSHIRE COMPILED CHIEFLY FROM ACTUAL
    SURVEYS. Samuel Lewis (11).

THE DISTRICT OF MAINE (12).

THE STATE OF MASSACHUSETTS (13).

THE STATE OF RHODE ISLAND COMPILED FROM THE SURVEYS AND
    OBSERVATIONS OF CALEB HARRIS (14).

CONNECTICUT FROM THE BEST AUTHORITIES (15).

THE STATE OF NEW YORK (16).

THE STATE OF NEW JERSEY COMPILED FROM THE MOST AUTHENTIC
    INFORMATION (17).

PENNSYLVANIA (18).

DELAWARE FROM THE BEST AUTHORITIES (19).

MARYLAND (20).

A CORRECT MAP OF VIRGINIA (21).

NORTH CAROLINA FROM THE LATEST SURVEYS (22).

THE STATE OF SOUTH CAROLINA FROM THE BEST AUTHORITIES (23).

THE STATE OF GEORGIA (24).

KENTUCKY (25).

THE STATE OF TENNESSEE (26).

THE STATE OF MISSISSIPPI AND ALABAMA TERRITORY (27).

THE STATE OF OHIO AND PART OF UPPER CANADA (28).

THE UPPER TERRITORIES OF THE UNITED STATES (29).

LOUISIANA (30).

MISSOURI TERRITORY FORMERLY LOUISIANA (31).

PLAT OF THE SEVEN RANGES OF TOWNSHIPS BEING PART OF THE TERRITORY OF THE UNITED STATES NORTHWEST OF THE RIVER OHIO (32).

MEXICO OR NEW SPAIN (33).

WEST INDIA (34).

A MAP OF THE FRENCH PART OF ST. DOMINGO (35).

A NEW MAP OF SOUTH AMERICA FROM THE LATEST AUTHORITIES (36).

A MAP OF CARACAS (37).

PERU (38).

CHILI AND PART OF THE VICEROYALTY OF LA PLATA (39).

A MAP OF BRAZIL NOW CALLED NEW PORTUGAL (40).

EUROPE (41).

SWEDEN, DENMARK, NORWAY AND FINLAND FROM THE BEST AUTHORITIES (42).

RUSSIAN EMPIRE (43).

SCOTLAND (44).

AN ACCURATE MAP OF ENGLAND AND WALES WITH PRINCIPAL ROADS FROM THE BEST AUTHORITIES (45).

IRELAND AS REPRESENTED IN THE IMPERIAL PARLIAMENT (46).

HOLLAND OR THE SEVEN UNITED PROVINCES AND THE NETHERLANDS (47).

GERMANY (48).

FRANCE DIVIDED INTO CIRCLES AND DEPARTMENTS (49).

TURKEY IN EUROPE AND HUNGARY FROM THE BEST AUTHORITIES (50).

SPAIN AND PORTUGAL (51).

ITALY AND SARDINIA FROM THE BEST AUTHORITIES (52).

SWITZERLAND ACCORDING TO THE BEST AUTHORITIES (53).

POLAND (54).

ASIA ACCORDING TO THE BEST AUTHORITIES (55).

CHINA DIVIDED INTO ITS GREAT PROVINCES ACCORDING TO THE BEST AUTHORITIES (56).

AN ACCURATE MAP OF HINDOSTAN OR INDIA FROM THE BEST AUTHORITIES (57).

THE ISLANDS OF THE EAST INDIES WITH THE CHANNELS BETWEEN INDIA, CHINA AND NEW HOLLAND (58).

S-43766
Cramer, Zadok. The Navigator. 10th ed. Pittsburgh: Cramer and Spear, 1818.

MAP OF PITTSBURGH (11).

[OHIO RIVER] (13 sheets) (69-123).

FALLS OF OHIO (104).

[MISSISSIPPI RIVER] (13 sheets) (156-197).

S-43782
Cummings, Jacob. First Lessons in Geography and Astronomy. Boston: Cummings and Hilliard, 1818.

MAP OF THE WORLD (F).

NORTH AMERICA (20).

SOUTH AMERICA (26).

EUROPE (38).

ASIA (46).

AFRICA (54).

S-43785
Cummings, Jacob. <u>Questions on the Historical Parts of the New Testament</u>. 3rd ed. Boston: Cummings and Hilliard, 1818.

JERUSALEM AND ITS ENVIRONS (B).

COUNTRIES SPOKEN IN THE NEW TESTAMENT (B).

TRAVELS OF THE APOSTLES THROUGH GREECE, ASIA MINOR, &C. (B).

PALESTINE OR THE HOLY LAND (B).

S-43805
Dana, James. <u>Outlines of the Minerology and Geology of Boston and Its Vicinity</u>. Boston: Cummings and Hilliard, 1818.

A GEOLOGICAL MAP OF BOSTON AND ITS VICINITY (F).

S-43809
Darby, William. <u>The Emigrant's Guide to the Western and Southwestern States and Territories</u>. New York: Kirk and Mercein, 1818.

A MAP OF THE UNITED STATES INCLUDING LOUISIANA (F).

S-43820
Dearborn, Henry. <u>An Account of the Battle of Bunker Hill</u>. Philadelphia: James Maxwell, for Harrison Hall, 1818.

SKETCH OF THE ACTION ON THE HEIGHTS OF CHARLESTOWN 17 JUNE 1775 BETWEEN HIS MAJESTY'S TROOPS UNDER THE COMMAND OF MAJOR GENERAL HOWE AND A LARGE BODY OF AMERICAN REBELS (F).

S-43828
Delano, Amasa. <u>A Narrative of Voyages and Travels, in the Northern and Southern Hemispheres</u>. 2nd ed. Boston: Eleazer House, for Amasa Delano, 1818.

A CHART AND VIEWS OF PITCAIRNS ISLAND (134).

S-43906
Eaton, Amos. <u>An Index to the Geology of the Northern States</u>.
    Leicester, MA: Hori Brown, 1818.

    A GEOLOGICAL TRANSVERSE SECTION EXTENDING FROM CATSKILL
        MOUNTAIN TO THE ATLANTIC (F).

S-43934
Ellis, Henry. <u>Journal of the Proceedings of the Late Embassy to</u>
    <u>China</u>. Philadelphia: Abraham Small, 1818.

    MAP OF THE ROUTE OF THE BRITISH EMBASSY FROM THE MOUTH OF
        THE PEIHO RIVER TO PEKIN AND FROM THENCE TO CANTON IN
        THE YEAR 1816 (F).

S-44209
Grouchy, Emmanuel. <u>Observations Sur la Relation de la Campagne de</u>
    <u>1815</u>. Philadelphia: John Hurtel, 1818.

    THEATRE DE LA CAMPAGNE DE 1815 EN BELGIQUE (67).

    CARTE PARTICULIERE DE LA BATAILLE DE WATERLOO ET DU COMBAT
        DE WAVRES LE 18 JUIN 1815 (67).

S-44221
Halkett, John. <u>Statement Respecting the Earl of Selkirk's</u>
    <u>Settlement upon the Red River</u>. New York: James Eastburn,
    1818.

    SKETCH OF PART OF THE HUDSONS BAY COMPANYS TERRITORY (F).

S-44222
Hall, Basil. <u>Account of a Voyage of Discovery to the West Coast</u>
    <u>of Corea</u>. Philadelphia: Abraham Small, 1818.

    TRACK OF THE ENGLISH SHIP ALCESTE LYRA ALONG THE WESTERN
        COAST OF THE PENINSULA OF COREA. Basil Hall (F).

    CHART OF GREAT LOO CHOO ISLAND. Basil Hall (F).

S-44362
Hollins, William. <u>Remarks on the Intercourse of Baltimore with</u>
    <u>the Western Country</u>. Baltimore: Joseph Robinson, 1818.

    [BALTIMORE AND ENVIRONS] (F).

S-44515
Kilbourn, John. The Ohio Gazetteer. 5th ed. Columbus: John
     Kilbourn, 1818.

     MAP OF OHIO (F).

     PLAT OF THE TOWN OF COLUMBUS (44).

S-44771
Mayo, Robert. Atlas Classica. Philadelphia: Anthony Finley, 1818.
     (Note: SEE S-43109 FOR MAPS).

S-44774
Mayo, Robert. Epitome of Profane Geography. 2nd ed. Philadelphia:
     Robert Mayo, 1818.

     TERRA VETERIBUS NOTA (F).

S-44791
Melish, John. A Geographical Description of the United States.
     3rd ed. Philadelphia: John Melish, 1818.

     BOSTON AND ADJACENT COUNTRY (66).

     NEW YORK AND ADJACENT COUNTRY (76).

     PHILADELPHIA (86).

     BALTIMORE ANNAPOLIS AND ADJACENT COUNTRY (96).

S-44792
Melish, John. A Geographical Description of the World.
     Philadelphia: Melish and Harrison, 1818.

     MAP OF THE WORLD FROM THE LATEST DISCOVERIES (F).

     VIEW OF THE ISTHMUS OF DARIEN ILLUSTRATING THE
          PRACTICABILITY OF A CANAL BETWEEN THE ATLANTIC AND
          PACIFIC OCEANS (240).

     VIEW OF THE ISTHMUS OF SUEZ AND DELTA ILLUSTRATING THE
          CONNECTION BETWEEN THE MEDITERRANEAN AND THE RED SEA
          (252).

S-44794
MAP OF THE UNITED STATES OF AMERICA. John Melish. Philadelphia:
     John Melish, 1818-1822.

S-44910
Morse, Jedidiah. Geography Made Easy. 19th ed. Boston: Ezra
    Lincoln, for Thomas and Andrews, 1818.

    A NEW MAP OF THE WORLD WITH THE LATEST DISCOVERIES (F).

    A NEW MAP OF NORTH AMERICA FROM THE LATEST DISCOVERIES (88).

S-44975
A New Atlas of the West India Islands. Philadelphia: Isaac Riley,
    1818.

    A NEW MAP OF THE WEST INDIES (1).

    ST. DOMINGO (2).

    JAMAICA (3).

    MAP OF THE ISLAND OF DOMINICA. Bryan Edwards (4).

    ST. VINCENT (5).

    VIRGIN ISLANDS (6).

    BARBADOES (7).

    ISLAND OF ANTIGUA (8).

    ISLAND OF ST. CHRISTOPHERS (9).

    ISLAND OF TOBAGO (10).

    GRENADA (11).

S-45048
Memorial of the Freeholders and the Inhabitants of the County of
    St. Lawrence. Albany: Websters and Skinners, 1818.

    [ST. LAWRENCE COUNTY, NEW YORK] (F).

S-45182
O'Reilly, Bernard. Greenland, the Adjacent Seas, and the
    North-west Passage to the Pacific Ocean. New York: Clayton
    and Kingsland, for James Eastburn, 1818.

    MAP OF THE COUNTRIES AROUND THE NORTH POLE ACCORDING TO THE
        LATEST DISCOVERIES (F).

DRAFT OF DISKO ISLAND AND THE ADJACENT COASTS OF WESTERN
GREENLAND (40).

DRAFT OF ISLANDS NORTH OF FROW ISLANDS IN DAVIESS STRAIT
MADE BY OBSERVATION (72).

S-45335
The Picture of New York and Stranger's Guide Through the
Commercial Emporium of the United States. New York: Andrew
Goodrich, 1818.

PLAN OF THE CITY OF NEW YORK (B).

S-45342
Pinkerton, John. A Modern Atlas. Philadelphia: William Fry, for
Thomas Dobson, 1818.

WESTERN HEMISPHERE (1).

EASTERN HEMISPHERE (2).

NORTHERN POLAR HEMISPHERE (3).

SOUTHERN POLAR HEMISPHERE (4).

EUROPE (5).

BRITISH ISLES (6).

ENGLAND, NORTHERN PART (7).

ENGLAND, SOUTHERN PART (8).

SCOTLAND, SOUTHERN PART (9).

SCOTLAND, NORTHERN PART (10).

IRELAND (11).

REMOTE BRITISH ISLES (12).

FRANCE (13).

RUSSIA IN EUROPE (14).

AUSTRIAN DOMINIONS (15).

PRUSSIAN DOMINIONS (16).

SPAIN AND PORTUGAL (17).

TURKEY IN EUROPE (18).

POLAND (19).

HOLLAND (20).

THE NETHERLANDS AND THE COUNTRIES TO THE LEFT BANK OF THE
RHINE (21).

SCANDINAVIA (22).

DENMARK (23).

PORTUGAL (24).

SWISSERLAND (25).

GERMANY NORTH OF THE MAYN (26).

GERMANY SOUTH OF THE MAYN (27).

NORTHERN ITALY (28).

SOUTHERN ITALY (29).

ASIA (30).

TURKEY IN ASIA (31).

CHINA (32).

JAPAN (33).

HINDOSTAN (34).

PERSIA (35).

ARABIA (36).

EAST INDIA ISLES (37).

AUSTRALASIA (38).

POLYNESIA (39).

NORTH AMERICA (40).

UNITED STATES OF AMERICA NORTHERN PART (41).

UNITED STATES OF AMERICA SOUTHERN PART (42).

SPANISH DOMINIONS IN NORTH AMERICA NORTHERN PART (43).

SPANISH DOMINIONS IN NORTH AMERICA MIDDLE PART (44).

SPANISH DOMINIONS IN NORTH AMERICA SOUTHERN PART (45).

BRITISH POSSESSIONS IN NORTH AMERICA (46).

WEST INDIES (47).

SOUTH AMERICA (48).

LA PLATA (49).

PERU (5).

NEW GRANADA (51).

THE CARACAS (52).

CHILI (53).

AFRICA (54).

EGYPT (55).

ABYSSINIA AND NUBIA (56).

NORTHERN AFRICA (57).

WESTERN AFRICA (58).

SOUTHERN AFRICA (59).

THE WORLD ON MERCATORS PROJECTION, WESTERN PART (60).

THE WORLD ON MERCATORS PROJECTION, EASTERN PART (61).

S-45548
Riley, James. An Authentic Narrative of the Loss of the American
    Brig Commerce. 3rd ed. New York: Sanderson and Sanderson,
    for James Riley, 1818.

    A MAP OF PART OF AFRICA DRAWN FROM THE LATEST AUTHORITIES TO
        ILLUSTRATE THE NARRATIVE OF CAPTAIN JAMES RILEY (2).

S-45551
Robbins, Archibald. <u>A Journal Comprising an Account of the Loss
    of the Brig Commerce of Hartford</u>. Hartford: Andrus and Judd,
    1818.

    A MAP TO ILLUSTRATE THE JOURNAL OF ARCHIBALD ROBBINS' ROUTE
        TO AFRICA (F).

S-45552
Robbins, Archibald. <u>A Journal Comprising an Account of the Loss
    of the Brig Commerce of Hartford</u>. 4th ed. Hartford, CT:
    Charles Starr, for Silas Andrus, 1818.

    A MAP TO ILLUSTRATE THE JOURNAL OF ARCHIBALD ROBBINS' ROUTE
        TO AFRICA (F).

S-45553
Robbins, Archibald. <u>A Journal Comprising an Account of the Loss
    of the Brig Commerce of Hartford</u>. 5th ed. Hartford, CT:
    Charles Starr, for Silas Andrus, 1818.

    A MAP TO ILLUSTRATE THE JOURNAL OF ARCHIBALD ROBBINS' ROUTE
        TO AFRICA (B).

S-45554
Robbins, Archibald. <u>A Journal Comprising an Account of the Loss
    of the Brig Commerce of Hartford</u>. 6th ed. Hartford, CT:
    Silas Andrus, 1818.

    A MAP TO ILLUSTRATE THE JOURNAL OF ARCHIBALD ROBBINS' ROUTE
        TO AFRICA (B).

S-45555
Robbins, Archibald. <u>A Journal Comprising an Account of the Loss
    of the Brig Commerce of Hartford</u>. 7th ed. Hartford, CT:
    Charles Starr, for Silas Andrus, 1818.

    A MAP TO ILLUSTRATE THE JOURNAL OF ARCHIBALD ROBBINS' ROUTE
        TO AFRICA (B).

S-45556
Robbins, Archibald. <u>A Journal Comprising an Account of the Loss
    of the Brig Commerce of Hartford</u>. 8th ed. Hartford, CT:
    Charles Starr, for Silas Andrus, 1818.

    A MAP TO ILLUSTRATE THE JOURNAL OF ARCHIBALD ROBBINS' ROUTE
        TO AFRICA (B).

S-45557
Robbins, Archibald. <u>A Journal Comprising an Account of the Loss of the Brig Commerce of Hartford</u>. Rochester: Charles Starr, for Everard Peck, 1818.

    A MAP TO ILLUSTRATE THE JOURNAL OF ARCHIBALD ROBBINS' ROUTE TO AFRICA (B).

S-45595
Rundall, Mary. <u>An Easy Grammar of Sacred History</u>. 2nd American ed. Philadelphia: Mathew Carey, 1818.

    THE JOURNEYINGS OF THE ISRAELITES FROM NAMESE'S TO THE EAST SIDE OF JORDAN (24).

    LAND OF PROMISE IN THE TIME OF ABRAHAM (28).

    CANAAN DIVIDED AMONGST THE TRIBES (32).

S-45744
Snowden, Richard. <u>The History of North and South America</u>. 2 volumes in 1. Philadelphia: William Greer, for Benjamin Warner, 1818.

    SOUTH AMERICA. Volume 1 (F).

    NORTH AMERICA. Volume 2 (F).

S-45905
Tuckey, James. <u>Narrative of an Expedition to Explore the River Zaire</u>. New York: William Gilley, 1818.

    A GENERAL SKETCH OF THE COAST FROM CAPE LOPEZ (F).

    A CHART OF THE RIVER ZAIRE (F).

S-45906
PLAN OF CHARLESTOWN PENINSULA IN THE STATE OF MASSACHUSETTS. Peter Tufts. Boston: Ammin and Smith, 1818.

S-46632
A GENERAL PLAT OF THE MILITARY LANDS BETWEEN THE MISSISSIPPI AND ILLINOIS RIVERS. Nicholas Van Zandt. Washington: s.n., 1818.

S-46755
Weems, Mason. The Life of George Washington. 20th ed.
    Philadelphia: Mathew Carey, 1818.

    UNITED STATES (F).

S-46756
Weems, Mason. The Life of George Washington. 21st ed.
Philadelphia: Mathew Carey, 1818.

    UNITED STATES (F).

S-47046
Baker, John. A View of the Commerce of the Mediterranean.
    Washington: Davis and Force, 1819.

    VIEW OF THE HARBOUR OF PORT MAHON (104)

S-47175
Battle of Waterloo. New York: John Evans, 1819.

    PLAN OF THE CAMPAIGN (184).

    PLAN OF THE CAMPAIGN (400).

S-47211
Bible. Brattleborough, VT: John Holbrook, 1819.

    JOURNEYINGS OF THE CHILDREN OF ISRAEL FROM EGYPT THROUGH THE
        WILDERNESS TO CANAAN (146).

    THE PLACES RECORDED IN THE FIVE BOOKS OF MOSES (148).

    THE EASTERN COUNTRIES AS MENTIONED BY MOSES (148).

    A MAP OF CANAAN, PALESTINE, JUDEA OR THE HOLY LAND AS
        DIVIDED AMONG THE 12 TRIBES (180).

S-47215
Bible. New York: Thomas Collins, 1819.

    A MAP OF CANAAN, PALESTINE, JUDEA OR THE HOLY LAND (50).

    A MAP OF THE JOURNEYINGS OF THE CHILDREN OF ISRAEL FROM
        EGYPT THROUGH THE WILDERNESS TO CANAAN (146).

    JERUSALEM WITH THE NEIGHBORING COUNTRY (730).

A MAP OF THE PLACES MENTIONED IN THE NEW TESTAMENT
ILLUSTRATING ST. PAUL'S TRAVELS AND ALSO HIS VOYAGE
FROM CAESAREA TO ROME (810).

S-47348
Bible Atlas. New Haven, CT: Jocelyn and Jocelyn, 1819.

MAP OF THE WORLD (1).

MAP OF CANAAN FOR GENESIS (2).

JOURNEYINGS OF ISRAEL IN THE WILDERNESS (3).

CANAAN FOR JUDGES (4).

CANAAN FOR SAMUEL (5).

GENERAL MAP OF CANAAN (6).

JERUSALEM AND PLACES ADJACENT (7).

ISRAEL SHEWING THOSE PLACES WHICH ARE MENTIONED BY THE FOUR
EVANGELISTS (8).

PLACES MENTIONED IN THE NEW TESTAMENT ILLUSTRATING ST.
PAUL'S TRAVELS AND VOYAGE FROM CAESAREA TO ROME (9).

S-47349
Bible Atlas. New Haven, CT: Jocelyn and Jocelyn, 1819.

MAP OF THE WORLD (1).

MAP OF CANAAN FOR GENESIS (2).

JOURNEYINGS OF ISRAEL IN THE WILDERNESS (3).

CANAAN FOR JUDGES (4).

CANAAN FOR SAMUEL (5).

GENERAL MAP OF CANAAN (6).

JERUSALEM AND PLACES ADJACENT (7).

ISRAEL SHEWING THOSE PLACES WHICH ARE MENTIONED BY THE FOUR
EVANGELISTS (8).

PLACES MENTIONED IN THE NEW TESTAMENT ILLUSTRATING ST.
PAUL'S TRAVELS AND VOYAGE FROM CAESAREA TO ROME (9).

S-47387
Bonnycastle, Richard. Spanish America. Philadelphia: Abraham
    Small, 1819.

    AMERICA (F).

    COMPARATIVE ALTITUDES OF THE MOUNTAINS IN SPANISH NORTH AND
        SOUTH AMERICA (viii).

S-47413
Brackenridge, Henry. Voyage to South America. 2 volumes.
    Baltimore: John Toy, for Henry Brackenridge, 1819.

    MAP OF SOUTH AMERICA (F).

S-47490
Caesar, Caius Julius. C. Julii Caesaris. 3rd ed. Philadelphia:
    Mathew Carey, 1819.

    GALLIA VETUS (8).

    ITALIAE ANTIQUAE (187).

    CONSPECTUS LOCURUM BELLI AFRICANI (328).

S-47498
Campbell, Archibald. A Voyage Round the World from 1806 to 1812.
    2nd American ed. New York: Broderick and Ritter, 1819.

    TRACK OF THE ECLIPSE'S LONG BOAT FROM SANNACK TO KODIAK (F).

S-47616
The Cincinnati Directory. Cincinnati: Morgan and Lodge, 1819.

    PLAN OF CINCINNATI INCLUDING ALL THE LATE ADDITIONS AND
        SUBDIVISIONS (F).

S-47759
Cummings, Jacob. First Lessons in Geography and Astronomy.
    Boston: Cummings and Hilliard, 1819.

    MAP OF THE WORLD (F).

    NORTH AMERICA (22).

SOUTH AMERICA (26).

EUROPE (38).

ASIA (46).

AFRICA (54).

S-47786
Darby, William. <u>A Tour from the City of New York to Detroit</u>. New
    York: Erastus Worthington, for Kirk and Mercein, 1819.

    [ROUTE FROM NEW YORK TO DETROIT] (F).

    THE STRAITS OF NIAGARA (154).

    ENVIRONS OF DETROIT (184).

S-47802
Dearborn, Henry. <u>A Memoir on the Commerce and Navigation of the</u>
    <u>Black Sea</u>. 2 volumes. Boston: Wells and Lilly, 1819.

    CHART OF THE BLACK SEA, THE SEA OF AZOF, THE SEA OF MARMORA,
        THE ARCHIPELAGO, AND PART OF THE MEDITARRANEAN (B).

    HILLESPORT, OR THE CHANNEL OF THE DARDANELLES (B).

    BOSPHORUS OR THRACE, OR CHANNEL OF THE BLACK SEA (B).

S-48134
MAP OF BOSTON AND ITS VICINITY. John Hales. Boston: John Hales,
    1819.

S-48378
Johnson, Charles. <u>Letters from the British Settlement in</u>
    <u>Pennsylvania</u>. Philadelphia: Harrison Hall, 1819.

    UNITED STATES (F).

    A MAP OF THE ROUTE LEADING TO THE TOWN OF BRITANIA IN THE
        BRITISH SETTLEMENT, SUSQUEHANNA COUNTY, PENNSYLVANIA
        (F).

S-48423
Kilbourn, John. <u>The Ohio Gazetteer</u>. Columbus: Bailhache and
    Scott, for John Kilbourn, 1819.

MAP OF OHIO (8).

MAP OF ASHTABULA COUNTY (29).

MAP OF BELMONT COUNTY (33).

MAP OF BUTLER COUNTY (39).

CLERMONT COUNTY (49).

MAP OF CLINTON COUNTY (51).

PLAT OF COLUMBUS (54).

MAP OF FAIRFIELD COUNTY (67).

MAP OF FRANKLIN COUNTY (73).

MAP OF GALLIA COUNTY (75).

MAP OF GUERNSEY COUNTY (81).

HARRISON COUNTY (84).

JEFFERSON COUNTY (90).

MONROE COUNTY (107).

MAP OF MONTGOMERY COUNTY (108).

MAP OF MUSKINGUM COUNTY (112).

PERRY COUNTY (122).

MAP OF PICKAWAY COUNTY (126).

MAP OF PIKE COUNTY (126).

MAP OF PORTAGE COUNTY (128).

MAP OF ROSS COUNTY (134).

SCIOTO COUNTY (140).

MAP OF TRUMBULL COUNTY (149).

WASHINGTON COUNTY (156).

MAP OF WAYNE COUNTY (158).

S-48447
Labaume, Eugene. <u>A Circumstantial Narrative of the Campaign in Russia</u>. Hartford, CT: Silas Andrus, 1819.

    PLAN OF THE FIELD OF BATTLE OF THE MOSKWA, SEPTEMBER 7, 1812 (B).

    PLAN OF THE FIELD OF BATTLE OF MALO-JAROSLAVETZ, 24 OCTOBER 1812 (B).

S-48551
McMurtrie, Henry. <u>Sketches of Louisville and Its Environs</u>. Louisville: Shadrach Penn, 1819.

    MAP OF THE FALLS OF THE OHIO AND ITS ADJOINING COUNTRIES (F).

S-48578
A MAP OF MASSACHUSETTS, CONNECTICUT AND RHODE ISLAND. Eden Ruggles. Hartford, CT: M.M. Peabody, for R. Hutchinson, 1819.

S-48606
[MARYLAND WITH AN INSERT OF THE CITY OF BALTIMORE]. Baltimore: Fielding Lucas, 1819.

S-48670
Melish, John. <u>The Traveller's Directory</u>. 5th ed. Philadelphia: George Palmer, 1819.

    UNITED STATES OF AMERICA COMPILED FROM THE LATEST AND BEST AUTHORITIES. John Melish (F).

    BOSTON AND ADJACENT COUNTRY (6).

    NEW YORK AND ADJACENT COUNTRY (10).

    PHILADELPHIA AND ADJACENT COUNTRY (14).

    BALTIMORE, ANNAPOLIS AND ADJACENT COUNTRY (16).

S-48764
Morse, Jedidiah. <u>The America Universal Geography</u>. 7th ed. 2 volumes. Charlestown, MA: George Clarke; Boston: Lincoln and Edmands, 1819.

    MAP OF THE WORLD FROM THE BEST AUTHORITIES. Volume 1 (F).

A NEW MAP OF NORTH AMERICA SHEWING ALL THE NEW DISCOVERIES.
Volume 1 (124).

SOUTH AMERICA WITH THE WEST INDIES. Volume 1 (768).

EUROPE. Volume 2 (F).

MAP OF ASIA. Volume 2 (440).

MAP OF AFRICA. Volume 2 (724).

S-48765
Morse, Jedidiah. Geography Made Easy. 20th ed. Utica, NY: William
Williams, 1819.

THE EASTERN HEMISPHERES OR OLD WORLD (F).

WESTERN HEMISPHERE OR NEW WORLD (F).

UNITED STATES (62).

S-49020
Pascalis-Ouviere, Felix. A Statement of the Occurrences during a
Malignant Yellow Fever in the City of New York. New York:
William Mercein, 1819.

A MAP OF OLD (TOWN) AND INFESTED VICINITY (F).

S-49031
Pazos Kanki, Vincente. Letters on the United Provinces of South
America. New York: Jonathan Seymour, 1819.

THE UNITED PROVINCES OF SOUTH AMERICA (F).

S-49034
Pease, John. A Gazetteer of the States of Connecticut and Rhode
Island. Hartford, CT: William Marsh, 1819.

CONNECTICUT (F).

MAP OF RHODE ISLAND AND PROVIDENCE PLANTATIONS (303).

S-49102
Phillips, Richard. The Universal Preceptor. 3rd ed. Philadelphia:
Edwards and Parker, 1819.

THE EARTH (106).

S-49292
The Richmond Directory. Richmond: John Maddox, 1819.

    [RICHMOND, VIRGINIA] (F).

S-49438
Smith, John. The True Travels, Adventures and Observations of
    Captain John Smith. 2 volumes. Richmond: William Gray, 1819.

    VIRGINIA. Volume 1 (148).

S-49443
Snowden, Richard. The History of North and South America. 2
    volumes. Philadelphia: William Greer, for Benjamin Warner,
    1819.

    SOUTH AMERICA. Volume 1 (F).

    NORTH AMERICA. Volume 1 (F).

S-49503
Steel, John. An Analysis of the Mineral Waters of Saratoga and
    Ballston. 2nd ed. Albany: Packard and Van Benthuysen, for
    Daniel Steele, 1819.

    GEOLOGICAL AND GEOGRAPHICAL MAP OF SARATOGA COUNTY (F).

S-49585
Thomas, David. Travels Through the Western Country in the Summer
    of 1816. Auburn, NY: David Rumsey, 1819.

    VINCENNES DISTRICT (F).

S-50086
Weems, Mason. The Life of George Washington. 22nd ed.
    Philadelphia: Mathew Carey, 1819.

    UNITED STATES (F).

S-50652
The Boston Directory. Boston: Edward Cotton, 1806.

    A PLAN OF BOSTON FROM ACTUAL SURVEY. Osgood Carleton (F).

S-51278
Carey, Mathew. <u>Carey's American Pocket Atlas</u>. Philadelphia:
    Mathew Carey, 1814.

    UNITED STATES (1).

    VERMONT FROM ACTUAL SURVEY (20).

    THE STATE OF NEW HAMPSHIRE. Samuel Lewis (28).

    MAINE (32).

    MASSACHUSETTS (38).

    RHODE ISLAND (52).

    CONNECTICUT (60).

    NEW YORK (68).

    NEW JERSEY (84).

    PENNSYLVANIA (92).

    DELAWARE (102).

    OHIO (106).

    UPPER TERRITORIES OF THE UNITED STATES (110).

    MARYLAND (116).

    VIRGINIA (124).

    KENTUCKEY (130).

    NORTH CAROLINA (138).

    TENNASSEE (144).

    SOUTH CAROLINA (148).

    GEORGIA (154).

    MISSISSIPPI TERRITORY (160).

    LOUISIANA (165).

    MISSOURI TERRITORY FORMERLY LOUISIANA (166).

                         --ooOoo--

PART III:

THE AMERICAN BIBLIOGRAPHY,
1639–1819:

INDEXES

DATE OF PUBLICATION INDEX

NOTE: In the case of book citations, the date of publication
refers to the year in which the book was published, not when the
maps, which are contained in the book, were published.   In the
case of map separates, the date of publication refers to the year
in which the map was published.
All references are to page numbers in Parts I and II.

--ooOoo--

PLACE OF PUBLICATION INDEX

NOTE: In the case of book citations, the place of publication refers to the city where the book was published, not where the maps, which are contained in the book, were published. In the case of map separates, the place of publication refers to the city where the map was published.
All references are to page numbers in Parts I and II.

--ooOoo--

NAME INDEX

NOTE: The Name Index lists all authors, cartographers, engravers, publishers, printers, associations, businesses and governmental units.
All references are to page numbers in Parts I and II.

242

244

264

269

278

--ooOoo--

BOOK TITLE INDEX

Note: Longer titles, in some instances, have been truncated at a logical point in the title.
All references are to page numbers in Parts I and II.

282

284

--ooOoo--

MAP TITLE INDEX

NOTE: Map titles which were supplied by the author, i.e., those
which appear in brackets [] in Parts I and II, are not included
in the Map Title Index. These maps can be located by using the
Geographic Index. Longer titles, in some instances, have been
truncated at a logical point in the title.
All references are to page numbers in Parts I and II.

309

313

342

343

--ooOoo--

GEOGRAPHIC INDEX

NOTE· Present-day spelling and accepted usage of words/terms are used in the Geographic Index. See references to and from variant spellings and obsolete place names are provided, when necessary. All references are to page numbers in Parts I and II.

349

350

354

363

--ooOoo--